white. RAF via Terry Panopalis

A trio of Waddington-based Vulcan B.1s fly in line astern formation.
Key Collection

FOREWORD

Key Publishing's blossoming Combat Machines series now examines one of Britain's most famous military aeroplanes, the mighty Avro Vulcan. This aircraft has been covered by various publications over the years, but the opportunity has been taken here to provide a new reference – and to precede the pending release of the newly tooled (and long awaited) 1/72 B.2 plastic model kit from Airfix.

The text provides a basic history of how this iconic bomber came into existence, there is a section exploring Vulcan testing and some of the later trials programmes, while another gives a full service history and there are breakdowns of the various versions and the weapons they carried.

Production and squadron/unit list listings are also included.

Following the author's sections comes The XH558 Story – the 'Vulcan to the Sky' Project – written by the man that did so much to make it all happen, Dr Robert Pleming. And then a Falklands Vulcan detachment veteran, Alastair Montgomery, provides his perspective on the type's contribution during that conflict. Extensive use has been made of previously unpublished or rarely seen images, including some in colour captured during the Vulcan's early career. As such these will provide a most valuable reference source for modellers and pure enthusiasts alike.

It should never be forgotten that the Vulcan was originally designed to be a nuclear bomber – a weapon of mass destruction. Fortunately, it was never called upon to deliver atomic stores in anger and it went on to provide valuable and reliable service to the RAF across three decades. By the time it dropped conventional bombs over the Falklands, right at the end of its active life, the Vulcan had become one of the most popular and adored British aircraft. Anyone wishing to argue that fact cannot have witnessed the huge queues and crowds that were a feature of any airshow with XH558 attending.

It is hoped this guide will provide a useful introduction to this legendary type and prompt those readers new to the subject to look deeper into the Vulcan's history.

Tony Buttler AMRAeS

This view provides excellent forward fuselage and nose detail for a Vulcan prototype (and for the towbar). It was taken on September 7, 1953. Note the Avro/Hawker Siddeley Group badge on the nose.
Key Collection

Authors: Tony Buttler, Alastair Montgomery, Dr Robert Pleming
Series Editor: Chris Clifford
Acknowledgements: The primary sources accessed to provide materials for this work were Avia and Air files in the National Archives at Kew, plus reports held by the Avro Heritage Museum at Woodford. Unit data was compiled mainly from Air-Britain's The Squadrons of the Royal Air Force & Commonwealth 1918-1988 by James

Halley. Thanks to Phil Butler, Terry Panopalis, Dr Robert Pleming and Alastair Montgomery for their help with photographs.
Colour artwork: Andy Hay – Flying Art
Designer: Tom Bagley
Head of Design: Steve Donovan
Chief Content and Commercial Officer: Mark Elliott
Head of Production: Janet Watkins
Group CEO: Adrian Cox
Publisher: Mark Elliott

Key Publishing Ltd: PO Box 100, Stamford, Lincolnshire, PE9 1XQ, United Kingdom.

Distributed by: Seymour Distribution Ltd, 2 Poultry Avenue, London, EC1A 9PP. Tel: 020 7429 4000. Fax: 020 7429 4001.

Printed by: Precision Colour Print, Telford
Printed in England
ISBN: 9781-913295-509

BABY VULCANS AND WHITE PROTOTYPES

Even today the Vulcan prototypes look impressive. Their appearance in the early 1950s must have been a shock to many, when one considers that conventional piston-powered Avro Lincolns and Lancasters were still in service in large numbers.
Tony Buttler

How the Vulcan might have looked! The three-view drawing of the Avro 698 as it was first proposed against Specification B.35/46 in May 1947.
Tony Buttler

The Avro Vulcan story begins in early 1947 with Specification B.35/46. This new requirement outlined the need for a very advanced medium range strategic bomber – and in doing so brought together several then recent developments in aviation and weaponry.

Firstly, this aircraft would carry Britain's Blue Danube nuclear bomb. The very end of World War Two brought the arrival of nuclear weapons onto the world stage. It soon became clear that the Soviet Union was a likely future enemy and the UK would need a nuclear delivery system that matched anything the Soviets could offer.

Secondly, the new type would have to be powered by jets. The bombs dropped on Japan in August 1945 were delivered by the piston-powered Boeing B-29 Superfortress, but soon most of the world's air forces would be equipped with jet fighters. From then on, piston-powered bombers would be extremely vulnerable and the RAF's Avro Lancasters and Lincolns faced obsolesence.

Thirdly, to help the bomber avoid enemy fighters and other defensive weapons, it would need to fly at very high altitude. To that end, B.35/46 specified a cruise altitude between 35,000ft (10,668m) and 50,000ft (15,240m) and a speed of 500kts.

To achieve these aims the designs proposed by industry included truly advanced wing shapes and in mid-1947 two were chosen for prototype construction – the Avro 698 and Handley Page HP.80.

The former featured a delta (triangular) wing, the latter what was termed a crescent wing, and for the late 1940s both were aerodynamically quite revolutionary. The development of these aircraft would be a risk and, because of the urgent need to rush a nuclear deterrent into service, two further steps were taken to support the decision.

- Flying scale model airframes were ordered to provide data and flight experience for these new shapes
- Prototypes of a third strategic bomber type were requested from Vickers. This company's B.35/46 design had a moderately swept ⏩

▲ Original manufacturer's model of the original Avro 698 design.
Avro Heritage

▼ The first Avro 698 Vulcan prototype, VX770, pictured most likely during a Farnborough display.
Tony Buttler

A beautiful colour view of the Avro 707B XV790 in blue livery. The level of redesign required on this aircraft from the original 707 VX784 was considerable. Note the Hawker Siddeley logo on the nose.
Avro Heritage

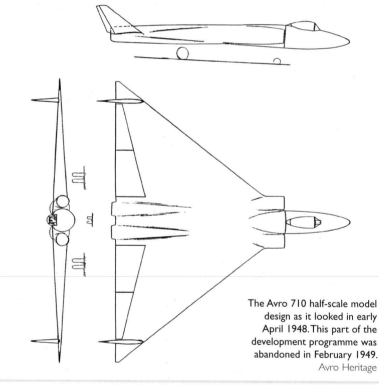

The Avro 710 half-scale model design as it looked in early April 1948. This part of the development programme was abandoned in February 1949.
Avro Heritage

The brand new VX784 possibly before its maiden flight.
Tony Buttler

wing which, aerodynamically, presented less risk than the forms chosen by Avro and Handley Page. No scale model aircraft would be needed, and the type would, in theory, enter service ahead of the other two bombers. As such it would fill the gap in the front line until they arrived

In RAF service the Avro, Handley Page and Vickers designs were named Vulcan, Victor and Valiant respectively, and these three so-called V-Bombers would form the 'V-Force'. For the record, a fourth strategic bomber prototype was produced during this period by Short Brothers. Shorts had been asked to study a bomber back in 1945 but its development was overtaken by events. The resulting Sperrin flew in 1951 but had a near straight wing, which meant, in some respects, it was inferior to its rivals. Consequently, just two prototypes were produced.

A strange beast

As first proposed the 698 looked quite different to the Vulcan we know today. Its four Bristol BE.10 engines were stacked superimposed in two pairs, deep inside the wing. These were fed through two very large circular air intakes and the bomb bay was split into two, one to each side of the engines; wingtip-mounted fins and rudders were another prominent feature. Structurally the delta offered great advantages. The depth of wing section would absorb the various in-flight

The sole two-seat 707C was WZ744. This view provides good rear angle details for this final member of the family.
Tony Buttler

loads, it would provide a low structure weight and ensure plenty of internal space for powerplant, equipment, fuel and bombs.

Detailed design of the 698 began in January 1948 and parts of the layout changed as it progressed. By April, the engines had been re-positioned side-by-side in pairs to either side of the centreline, which made room for

a single central bomb bay. By October, the circular intakes had been replaced by deep slit intakes in the wing root leading edges and the tip fins had also disappeared, with a large central fin now prominent. The final air intake design would allow for larger intakes later, when these were required to supply more powerful engines.

The head of Avro's design team was

Roy Chadwick, but in August 1947 he died in the crash of Avro's Tudor II airliner. His place was taken by chief designer Stuart Davies, while later Roy Ewans (who succeeded Davies as chief engineer) would lead the design of the Vulcan B.2.

Design of the BE.10 (later Olympus) engine was completed in 1949. Over the next decade the power rating was increased to an extraordinary degree. The first official 150-hour type-test was held at a thrust rating of 11,000lb (48.9kN), in 1956 the Olympus was type-tested to 12,000lb (53.3kN), and the ultimate Mk.301 in the Vulcan B.2 produced 20,000lb (88.9kN) of thrust.

Blue Danube was Britain's first operational nuclear weapon, it had a nominal yield of 20 kilotons and was housed inside a casing derived from the wartime Tallboy bomb as carried by the Avro Lancaster. Specification B.35/46 also requested a maximum load of 20,000lb (9,072kg) of conventional stores, of either two 10,000lb (4,536kg) bombs, four 5,000lb (2,268kg) or 20 x 1,000lb (454kg) bombs. With a 10,000lb (4,536kg) load the bomber's still air range had to be 3,350nm (6,208km).

The wing shapes used for the Avro 698 and HP.80 and their nuclear weaponry were not the only ground-breaking elements in this programme. With the Valiant they were the UK's first four-jet bombers, the high altitudes required for long distance missions would demand pressurised cockpits, and they would carry no defensive armament; advanced avionics such as warning devices were to provide a measure of protection instead.

The in-flight wing 'buzz' discovered during WD280's flying programme resulted in the introduction of compound sweep on the Vulcan's wing. It was also test flown on WD280 as shown, the new panels having not yet been painted.
Tony Buttler

The first 707A WD280, again seen as built, was designed for high-speed research as a replacement for the unbuilt Avro 710s.
Tony Buttler

Scale Model Research

The one-third scale Avro 707 research aircraft was to investigate the delta wing's behaviour at low speeds and ➜➜

established, although the delta wing was not at fault.

As a result, VX790 was redesigned and became known as the 707B. There was a new nose and a 12ft-long (3.66m) forward fuselage, which improved the aerodynamic shape and allowed an ejection seat to be fitted. The structure was then light alloy monocoque throughout and there was a 12in (30.5cm) extension to the top of the fin. A Sea Hawk fighter's nose leg was fitted which, in due course was extended by 9in (22.9cm) to give the 707B a better angle of incidence at take-off (this change was also made to the Vulcan's undercarriage).

The aerial debut of VX790 occurred on September 6, 1950, piloted by Wg Cdr Roland Falk who, following Esler's death, had taken over 707 flying. Trials at Boscombe Down confirmed that a tailless aircraft could exhibit entirely satisfactory flying qualities, and in the air VX790 was docile. However, at higher speeds, disturbed airflow from the canopy affected the air intake, partially starving the engine. Modifications made to the intake in February 1951 to counter this resulted in a pronounced 'hump' on VX790's back – but improved the engine airflow in all flight regimes. The irony was that this problem was not relevant to the Vulcan.

One benefit to the bomber discovered by the scale aircraft was tilting the jet exhaust slightly downwards and outwards. Different power settings on the 707s had exposed problems with longitudinal stability and trimming, and the Vulcan's jet nozzles were angled slightly to compensate for their effects. This modification also improved the

What a sight and experience this must have been! Two white Avro 698 Vulcan prototypes and the four surviving Avro 707s in their various colour schemes fly over the crowds at Farnborough in September 1953. Olympus-powered VX777 leads having become airborne for the first time just days earlier, VX770 brings up the rear and the four scale models complete a 'delta formed by deltas'.
Key Collection

low altitudes, and when landing. Any problems would have to be overcome, otherwise it would not matter how well the delta behaved at high speeds. There would also be a half-scale model called the Avro 710 to assess the delta at the high speeds and altitudes required for the bomber. This was to be powered by two Rolls-Royce Avon jet powerplants and the go ahead for two examples of each was given in June 1948, the 707s with serials VX784 and VX790, and the 710s with VX799 and VX808. However, this meant Avro would produce three different aircraft types at once; the workload was too much to handle and so the 710s were cancelled in February 1949.

The 707's structure was all-metal but was kept simple, with a two-spar

wing and a steel tube fuselage covered in light alloy panels. To save time, a standard Meteor F.3 fighter cockpit canopy and nosewheel – and an Athena trainer's main undercarriage – were fitted and a 3,500lb (15.6kN) Rolls-Royce Derwent 5 engine was mounted in the fuselage.

The first 707, VX784, made its maiden flight from Boscombe Down, Wiltshire on September 4, 1949, with Avro test pilot Flt Lt Samuel 'Red' Esler at the controls. It flew well and attended the Society of British Aircraft Constructors (SBAC) Show at Farnborough just a day or two later. Tragically, however, VX784 crashed near Blackbushe airfield on the last day of September, killing Esler. The reasons behind the loss have never been

Rear view of prototype VX770 at the start of its career when it had four Avon engines installed. The photo was taken in August 1952, most likely before its maiden flight.
Tony Buttler

Vulcan VX770 shown during an assessment flight by the Aeroplane & Armament Experimental Establishment at Boscombe Down. The Avro logo appears on the upper portion of the fin.
Tony Buttler

bomber's longitudinal stability. In September 1956 VX790 suffered a landing accident, it never flew again and was subsequently scrapped.

More 707s and dazzling hues

Further 707s followed, with two 'high speed' 707As coming next. These had the 707B's forward fuselage but introduced a new wing with root intakes, much more in line with the Vulcan. A 3,600lb (16.0kN) Derwent 8 was fitted and Roly Falk took the first example, WD280, on its maiden flight from Boscombe Down on June 14, 1951. Over a year later WD280 had powered controls installed, which again did not affect the Vulcan. In truth the 707/Vulcan programmes were growing apart, but WD280 flight trials did bring a very important change to the latter's wing.

As it pulled G when flying at maximum speed and altitude, WD280 suffered from a high-frequency vibration or 'buzz'. This was serious because the Vulcan would easily reach these speeds and heights. As a result, the leading edge was given compound sweep; the sweep angle on the inner part of the outer wing was reduced but on the outer wing further increased. The new kinked mainplane (branded the Phase 2 Wing) was successfully tested by WD280 and was introduced to the production line on the ninth Vulcan. The previous eight had the original 'straight'

The second Avro 707A was WZ736.
Tony Buttler

leading edge but most were updated retrospectively. In 1956 WD280 was taken to Australia to serve as a research aircraft at RAAF Laverton. It flew for the final time in 1963.

A further 707A, WZ736, was ordered in November 1951 for more general research along with a pair of two-seat 707Cs, WZ739 and WZ744, for pilot training at Boscombe Down

(WZ739 was not built). The 707A WZ736 first flew on February 20, 1953 and was Struck Off Charge in May 1962. Avro 707C WZ744 first flew on July 1, 1953 and was employed by the Royal Aircraft Establishment (RAE) Farnborough until June 1966. From 1958 it participated in some of the initial trials with fly-by-wire control systems. ❯❯

The second Vulcan prototype VX777 landing at Farnborough in 1953. At this stage it still sported the original pure delta wing with a fixed angle of sweep along the entire leading edge.
Key Collection

Vulcan VX770 on August 31, 1953, in a view which shows perfectly how well the engines were faired into the wing roots, Sapphire engines being installed.
Tony Buttler

Test pilot Roly Falk brings VX770 in to display at the September 1952 Farnborough show, an event that was by all accounts superb and never to be forgotten. It must have been a cool day because almost everyone in the crowd is wearing an overcoat, so VX770 (at the time still not named Vulcan) would have warmed everyone's heart; XH558 was still doing that just a few years ago.
Key Collection

A big feature of the 707 family was exotic colours: VX784 was never painted but VX790 had a bright gloss blue livery, WD280 was salmon pink to begin with and then bright red, WZ736 was bright orange and WZ744 silver with a matt black anti-glare panel ahead of its cockpit.

In general the five Avro 707s proved to be very useful research aircraft for the aviation industry as a whole, but the loss of the first example and necessary modifications to the others – which were not representative of the Vulcan – caused delays and destroyed much of the potential contribution to the bomber programme. That said, the introduction of the tilted jet exhaust and particularly the compound wing sweep were vital contributions. Three 707s still exist today.

Big bomber arrives

The two full-size prototypes carried the serials VX770 and VX777 (the name Vulcan was revealed in October 1952). Assembly of the first machine began in spring 1951; the Olympus was not yet available and so, to ensure parts of the flight envelope could be explored, VX770 had four 6,500lb (28.9kN) thrust Rolls-Royce Avon R.A.3 engines installed. As built, VX770 was little more than a 'flying shell' and had just a single pilot's seat. Roly Falk took the first prototype on its maiden flight on August 30, 1952

and a week or so later he displayed it at the Farnborough show. Display was probably an understatement though; VX770 had a fighter-type stick rather than the normal 'spectacle' control column, which enabled Falk to throw this brand-new aeroplane around the sky in a superb manner.

In January 1953 VX770 was grounded to have fuel tanks installed inside its wings and 7,500lb (33.3kN) Armstrong Siddeley Sapphire engines fitted,

which would allow it to reach higher speeds and altitudes. As modified the aircraft flew again in July 1953, although it was still incapable of reaching the 50,000ft (15,240m) cruising altitude and could explore the high-speed part of the flight envelope only in a shallow dive. The rest of VX770's career is described in the section covering research and testing.

Second prototype VX777 came much closer to the required

The first Vulcan prototype attended Farnborough for three consecutive years. Here it is flying at the September 1954 event with everything down. Note the line painted across the underside of the fuselage level with the cockpit, giving the impression the aircraft is smiling!
Tony Buttler

production standard. It had more equipment including the H2S Mk.9A radar coupled with its NBC Mk.1 Navigation and Bombing Computer, the extended nose leg and a 16in (40.6cm) fuselage extension to make room for it, and the bomb-aiming blister underneath the nose. It also relied on 9,750lb (43.3kN) thrust Olympus 100 engines and as such made its maiden flight on September 3, 1953.

With Olympus units in place VX777 could get to grips with assessing the Vulcan's high speed, high Mach number and high-altitude characteristics/ performance. However, it was to be early 1955 before the aircraft could begin to explore these aspects in detail. At this stage it still sported the original wing and serious deficiencies were present, particularly in and above the cruising Mach number range, and for the time being these would prevent the Vulcan from being cleared for service use.

The additional thrust and performance provided by the Olympus engines also revealed the buffet and wing 'buzz' at high altitude as experienced by the 707A. Consequently, the compound sweep Phase 2 wing was fitted to VX777 from July 1955 and the aircraft performed its initial flight in this form on October 5. Then, with production

B.1s starting to appear, in July 1956 VX777 was allotted to serve as the aerodynamic prototype for the Vulcan B.2 with that version's bigger wing. In this configuration, and with 12,000lb (53.3kN) thrust Olympus Mk.102 units installed, VX777 made its next 'first' flight on August 31, 1957. This busy and successful prototype completed its flying career in 1960.

This A&AEE photo of VX777 shows how its wing changed with the introduction of compound sweep on the leading edge.
Tony Buttler

A glorious colour photo of VX770 at Farnborough in 1954. The all-white scheme contrasts beautifully with the near cloudless blue sky.
Terry Panopalis

This model of a Vulcan prototype has been included to show the space available inside the bomber's large wing section – to accommodate its fuel and engines.
Key Collection

Vulcan B.2 XH557 served as the Olympus 300 testbed and is seen here landing at Filton.
Bristol Siddeley via Key Collection

Production of the Avro Vulcan began with the B.1 version and the initial example, serial XA889, first flew on February 4, 1955. Covered by Specification B.129P the manufacturing run was to be based on the second prototype VX777, though the great majority would be fitted with the compound sweep Phase 2 wing.

In spring 1956 XA889 (with Phase 2 wing) was test flown by A&AEE Boscombe Down pilots. The ensuing report stated the aircraft was considered to have safe and adequate flying qualities in the high-altitude medium bomber role, but in some cases its operational capabilities came short of requirements. With its Olympus Mk.101 engines XA889 could

VULCAN VARIETY

achieve just 43,000ft (13,106m) over a target at the selected cruising speed of Mach 0.85 and it had an inadequate high-altitude cruising performance. This height was not enough for an unarmed bomber and needed to be increased very quickly. However, the radius of action with full fuel and a 10,000lb (4,536kg) bomb load was 1,500nm (2,780km). On completion of its A&AEE trials the Vulcan B.I was released for service to the RAF subject to certain conditions and limitations, though further extensive testing would be necessary to clear the various items of operational equipment.

Having completed several bombing trials in 1956, XA889 would become the first Vulcan to test installations ⏵⏵

Vulcan B.I XA895. In 1965 this aircraft was used to test the Mk.2 version of the Red Steer tail-warning radar.
Ian McDonald

The first picture to be released officially, in 1958, showing the Vulcan production line.
Tony Buttler

Manufacturer's section drawing of the principal components within the Vulcan B.1 airframe. Avro

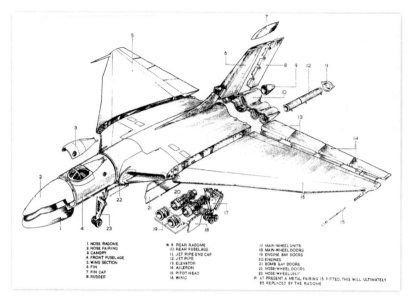

1. NOSE RADOME
2. NOSE FAIRING
3. CANOPY
4. FRONT FUSELAGE
5. WING SECTION
6. FIN
7. FIN CAP
8. RUDDER
✴ 9. REAR RADOME
10. REAR FUSELAGE
11. JET PIPE END CAP
12. JET PIPE
13. ELEVATOR
14. AILERON
15. PITOT HEAD
16. WING
17. MAIN-WHEEL UNITS
18. MAIN-WHEEL DOORS
19. ENGINE BAY DOORS
20. ENGINES
21. BOMB BAY DOORS
22. NOSE-WHEEL DOORS
23. NOSE-WHEEL UNIT
✴ AT PRESENT A METAL FAIRING IS FITTED, THIS WILL ULTIMATELY BE REPLACED BY THE RADOME.

A splendid nose view of a Vulcan prototype, with airbrakes open. There is also a fascinating array of aircraft in the background – all of which were developed and built by the British aircraft industry. Key Collection

of more powerful marks of Olympus engine. Between January and October 1958, it flew trials with the Olympus Mk.104. Then between August 1958 to July 1959 XA891 flight tested the updated Olympus Mk.200 for the forthcoming B.2 mark. For the record, B.2 Vulcans employed for engine development were XH538 (Mk.201 - 1963 to 1965), XH557 (Mk.300 - 1961 to 1964) and XJ784 (Mk.301 - 1961 to 1962). The Olympus Mks.200 and 300 were essentially prototypes for the B.2's Mk.201 and Mk.301 engines.

Other production B.1s used for

clearance and release work included XA892 (armament and landing trials and later nuclear weapons development), XA893 (avionics for the B.2 and Blue Steel), XA894 (auto-pilot) and XA895 (electronics including Red Steer Mk.2 in 1965). Finally XA890 trialled radio, radar and weapons and indeed would spend its entire career flying with either A&AEE or RAE, retaining in the process the original pure delta wing (trials covering weaponry are described in more detail in the relevant section).

Between 1959-62 those B.1s still

operational were fitted with updated electronics including a tail-warning radar similar to the type fitted to the B.2 (see later). Avro conducted a trial installation using XA895, but it was Armstrong Whitworth that carried out the rest of the conversions; this new sub-variant was designated B.1A.

In October 1952 Avro proposed a photo-reconnaissance version of the B.1, which had the bomb doors and various associated equipment removed and a camera unit installed in the bomb bay along with photoflashes for night work. An Air Staff requirement for a photo-recce Vulcan was raised in June 1956, but this version was never built.

Ultimate Vulcans

Although the Phase 2 wing provided some improvements, the weaknesses in the B.1's performance needed to be addressed. The outcome was a new version with more powerful engines and a larger mainplane, which became the Vulcan B.2.

The Phase 2 wing fitted to the B.1 had provided the maximum possible improvement in performance with the minimum alteration to the airframe structure (confined to just the outer wing ahead of the front spar). The

Airframe XA890 flies with airbrakes deployed at the 1955 Farnborough Show. Crown Copyright

addition of vortex generators had also maintained the buffet threshold at Mach numbers up to 0.89 and enabled engines of 12,000lb (53.3kN) thrust and more to be installed.

As knowledge was accumulated on the problems of Vulcan airframe buffeting at high altitudes, Avro was able to consider more extensive changes. Two wing developments were considered, Phase 2A and Phase 2B, before both were superseded by what was called the Phase 2C, which brought an extension to, and the addition of camber to, the leading edge. This made the outer wing thinner and increased both the chord and span, enabling local airflow to be kept subsonic up to a higher aircraft Mach number, thus delaying the buffeting as lift was increased.

The aerodynamics of this larger Phase 2C wing surface could also absorb much higher engine thrusts and, quite

conveniently, the time needed to complete the development of this wing meant it was introduced to the Vulcan production line at roughly the same time as suitable engines arrived, to take full advantage of it. The earliest Vulcan had been designed to reach Mach 0.95 in a shallow dive but Phase 2C was now stressed to cover Mach 1.

As noted earlier, in 1957 prototype VX777 became the Phase 2C aerodynamic test aircraft, but the B.2 introduced other improvements (detailed later in this section) and several B.1s served as trials aircraft to clear many items of equipment. Production Specification B.129P Issue 2 covered the new type and the first off the line, XH533, made its aerial debut on August 30, 1958. Controller (Aircraft) Release (C[A] Release) was granted on May 31, 1960.

The first seven B.2s were all used for development and equipment trials

at some stage, XH536 for example investigating radio and navigation, XH537 weapons testing, and XH538 in-flight refuelling, low-level role equipment and then electronic countermeasures (ECM). The second B.2, XH534, first introduced the extended and bulged end fuselage cone, which housed new ECM equipment, while Vulcans from **>>**

A maker's drawing showing the differing wing shapes of the first Vulcans built, the B.1 and then B.2. The substantial increase in wing area of the Phase 2C wing is clear. Avro

Vulcan XA889 was the first production aircraft and is seen here in the short-lived High Speed Silver livery. Key Collection

Vulcan pilots' instrument panel and controls. The two pilots would sit side-by-side on a raised platform at the forward end of the cabin.
Avro Heritage

The mass of dials, switches and instruments operated by the Vulcan's navigators and radio operator. The three crew members here were seated side-by-side facing aft, at this single table extending the full width of the cabin. Just pilots had ejection seats while, controversially, the other aircrew relied solely on parachutes.
Key Collection

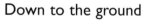

serial XJ784 onwards received the more powerful Olympus Mk.301.

In July 1959 Avro completed its assessment of the first B.2's flight characteristics. Trials with XH533 had in general shown that the flying qualities of the B.2 were far improved over the B.1. The change of wing aerodynamics had fulfilled the original predictions completely regarding high Mach number buffet, which meant

the increased thrust of the Olympus 200 engines could be utilised at altitude without affecting the aircraft's manoeuvrability.

The altitude performance was naturally superior to the B.1 and Avro reported that the change of wing aerodynamics alone had yielded a dividend of 2,000ft (610m) on the aircraft's cruise ceiling. Additional engine thrust had added a further

4,000ft (1,220m) so the target height of the B.2 would be some 6,000ft (1,830m) higher than the B.1 at comparable weights. The handling qualities of the B.2 had also been improved in several respects over the B.1. In particular, visibility and control on the approach were superior and the aircraft was sprightly in movement when cruising. The high Mach number characteristics of the B.2 also echoed those of the B.1.

Down to the ground

Following the cancellation of the American Skybolt missile the previous month (see weapons section), in January 1963 official approval was given to provide all three V-Bombers with the capability to perform strike operations at low level. Each 'V' type had been designed for high-altitude flight and so to do this they would need strengthened airframes, along with changes to the weapon choice and avionics, and particularly to the navigation aids. In comparison to high level flight, the buffeting normally expected lower down was likely to induce much greater crew fatigue over very long flights, along with increased airframe wear in general. Indeed, the switch to low level would bring an

abrupt end to the Vickers Valiant's career in 1964 through airframe fatigue and stress corrosion.

The low-level development programme would involve extensive flying trials, new protection against bird strikes, long range fuel tanks and the installation of terrain warning equipment. An interim clearance for Vulcans to operate at low level was issued in January 1964, the last ten B.2s to be built were completed in suitable green/grey camouflage and XM657, the last new-build Vulcan to fly, first flew on December 21, 1964. In August that year the B.2 was cleared to use overload fuel tanks for 'ferry' flights.

Two further versions of the Vulcan were produced, though both were modifications of the B.2. The B.2(MRR), at times called the SR.2 (SR signifying Strategic Reconnaissance), was a Maritime Radar Reconnaissance conversion made to Vulcans belonging to 27 Squadron from 1973 onwards. In these airframes the low-level terrain-following radar was replaced by LORAN C navigation equipment, the only change from the standard Vulcan avionics. On occasion B.2(MRR)s were also expected to carry atmospheric-sampling pods under their wings, so the first examples converted were

those still featuring wing hard-points fitted for carrying Skybolt missiles. Vulcans converted to B.2(MRR) standard included XH534, XH537, XH558, XH560, XH563, XJ780, XJ823 and XJ825, but just some of these could carry air-sampling pods.

The most high-profile alteration to Vulcan operations came right at the end of its career. This was in-flight refuelling. On service entry the Vulcan had no facility for receiving fuel when flying, but this capability had been added quite early in the bomber's career. Following trials at A&AEE Boscombe Down, held between June 1959 and April 1961 using B.1 XH478 operating as a receiver for fuel supplied by Valiant BK.1 tanker WZ376, a nose-mounted refuelling probe was fitted to the 16th production B.1 onwards and to all B.2s. Clearance trials for the B.2 were conducted at Boscombe Down between January-March 1961 using XH538. For the Vulcan, in-flight refuelling was vital to enable it to be ferried to and from overseas, but the most 'visible' role was its contribution to bombing missions during the 1982 Falklands War.

But Vulcans were not used as tankers themselves until 1982. The timing of the Falklands conflict was critical because the Handley Page Victor tanker fleet neared retirement and the new Lockheed Tristar and Vickers/BAC VC10 replacements were still being converted from their previous transport roles. The short notice Vulcan K.2 tanker conversion of 1982 was thus a stop gap, to provide more tankers for the long journey to the Falkland Islands, although they were not ready in time to take part in the conflict itself. Six Vulcans were converted, serials XH558, XH560, XH561, XJ825, XL445 and XM571, and the tanker programme proved ⊗⊗

Vulcan air display in September 1966. Evident here is the B.1 wing shape and open bomb bay. Note the bomb aimer's position under the nose, level with the RAF roundel.
Tony Buttler

ENTRANCE

Trevor Gardner, special assistant to the secretary of the US Air Force, boards a Vulcan at Farnborough on September 11, 1954, through the hatch beneath the nose of the fuselage. Entry was by means of this foldaway ladder, which was secured to the inside of the door and led to the intermediate level where the three rearward-facing seats were positioned. Once inside, a further ladder provided access to the pilots' floor.
Key Collection

Vulcan XH533 was the first production B.2, though when built it still had a B.1 tailcone.
Barry Jones via Terry Panopalis

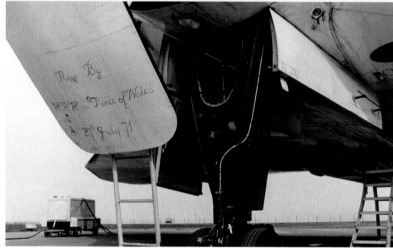

Forward detail for B.2 XL392, notably the access door and front undercarriage. The inscription on the door reveals that the Prince of Wales flew this aircraft on July 27, 1971.
Barry Jones via Terry Panopalis

ends, which extended slightly beyond the wing trailing edge. The air intakes were in the wing leading edge and on the B.2 these were enlarged to supply the more powerful Olympus units. One benefit of the thick delta wing was that installing different engines became relatively easy.

The two-spar wing itself consisted of a centre section made integral with the fuselage, and port/starboard outer wings. To delay the onset of compressibility, there was pronounced sweep back on the leading edges, and the trailing edges also had slight sweep back. The original true delta wing had its leading edge swept to an angle of almost 50°, but the B.1's Phase 2 wing introduced compound sweepback with the chord increased at approximately three-quarters span from the centreline. The inboard section was faired by a straight line swept 42° to a point at around semi-span, and then outboard at 53.5° sweep through to a larger tip chord.

The wing skin covering was light alloy and stiffened by stringers, and ten compartments were provided – five in each outer wing, to accommodate bag-type flexible fuel tanks holding most of the aircraft's fuel; with fuselage fuel the total internal capacity was 9,374 imp gal (42,623 lit).

The trailing edge of the outer wing had ailerons on the outboard part with elevators inboard. Each control surface was itself split into halves, each operated by its own separate power unit.

The Vulcan B.1's dorsal fin was swept to an angle of 49° 30' on its leading edge and was also built around two spars with closely spaced inter-spars, and light alloy sheet plating. Its fin fairing was extended along

successful. The first aircraft converted was XH561, which initially flew in this new form on June 18, 1982 – just 45 days after the go-ahead was given.

Under and over the skin

The Avro Vulcan B.1 bomber had a mid-position cantilever delta wing, single swept fin and no horizontal tailplane. It was powered by four Bristol Olympus turbojet engines located side-by-side in pairs in the wing centre section outboard of the fuselage, and between the front and rear spars. These were buried completely except for the jet pipe

The 101 Squadron B.2 XM602 deploys its drag chute when landing at London in Canada on June 7, 1981.
Terry Panopalis collection

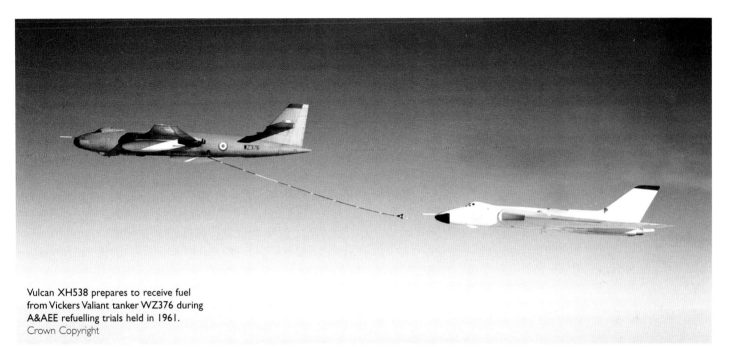

Vulcan XH538 prepares to receive fuel from Vickers Valiant tanker WZ376 during A&AEE refuelling trials held in 1961.
Crown Copyright

the fuselage to help the bomber's directional stability. The rudder was also power operated by duplicate units and airbrakes were provided on each side of the wing centre section, just aft of the front spar and on both top and bottom surfaces of the wing. Spring-loaded artificial feel units were provided for the pilots, simulating both wing and rudder loadings.

The main undercarriage was located outboard of the engines and comprised a pair of four-wheeled, eight-tyre bogie units, while the steerable nosewheel unit had twin wheels. The main units would retract forward and upward into their housings, the nose unit upward and backward into the fuselage nose. The fuselage was manufactured in four separate sections as a light alloy, stressed-skin structure of circular cross-section. It incorporated transverse formers braced by longitudinal stringers together with two fabricated ribs, creating support for the arch-shaped formers of the bomb bay. The four sections were as follows:

Nose – the upper portion housed the in-flight refuelling probe. Underneath was a dielectric structure forming the radome for the rotating H2S scanner.

Front – this constituted the crew's pressurised cabin. A prone-lying bombardier's station was also provided in a blister below the cabin and there were five crew in all (namely two pilots, two navigator/ bomb aimer/radar operators and one wireless/warning and protective device operator). Their entrance door

This aircraft, XA907, has been upgraded to B.1A standard with the new larger end fuselage pod housing improved ECM equipment.
Tony Buttler

opened downwards and was situated in the lower side of the fuselage nose, aft of the bomb aimer's blister and below the crew compartment. Early plans for a cabin that could be jettisoned were abandoned.

Centre – this was integral with the mainplane and extended from the rear of the crew's pressurised compartment to a point aft of the rear wing spar. Four fuel tanks were housed in the forward end, the remaining space forming the bomb compartment. On opening, the two bomb doors folded upwards inside the bay to minimise drag. The bay itself was 29ft (8.84m) long, 7ft (2.13m) wide and 6ft (1.83m) deep and was situated between front and rear wing spars. No defensive weaponry was carried.

Rear – this embodied the rear supports and outlets for the jet pipes and housed a cone-shaped fairing on its aft end. The rear fuselage supported the fin and housed the tail warning radar, and a 24ft-diameter (7.32m) ribbon braking parachute.

To increase the aircraft's range, provision was made for external slipper tanks to be fitted to the wing under-surface outboard of the main undercarriage units. These could ⏩

An atmospheric-sampling pod attached to the former Skybolt missile hardpoint of B.2(MRR) XH560.
Terry Panopalis collection

One of the Vulcans fitted with a single-point drogue during 1982 to serve as a tanker aircraft. Note how the jetpipes protrude beyond the wing trailing edge.
Avro Heritage

The Red Shrimp flat-plate ECM aerial fitted to a B.2 Vulcan underneath the engine pods.
Barry Jones via Terry Panopalis

A Vulcan spectacularly comes into land with everything down and airbrakes deployed.
Key Collection

hold 1,700 gal (7,730 lit) each and could be jettisoned in flight.

In its detail the Vulcan B.2 was generally the same as the B.1. However, the wing introduced the more pronounced compound sweep to the leading edge, which increased the span by 12ft (3.66m). The outer leading edge was taken further forward, and the aerofoil section showed a markedly drooped nose. In addition, the trailing edge control surfaces sported four elevons on each wing, their control configuration being quite different to the B.1. Thickness/chord ratio at the root for both B.1 and B.2 wings was 10%, at the tip on the B.1 it was 8% and on the B.2 5%.

The B.2's larger and more bulged tail cone housed a Red Steer tail warning radar and other avionics. The defensive ECM embraced a radar warning receiver, tail warning radar, powerful jammers, infra-red flares and chaff carried in the wing. A Green Palm communications jammer was accompanied by Blue Diver and Red Shrimp barrage jammers. A Blue Saga passive radar warning receiver was carried in the 1960s until replaced by the much better ARI.18228 receiver. B.2 avionics also included a general-

purpose high-frequency (HF) transmitter-receiver, two radio altimeters (high range and low range), an Instrument Landing System (ILS), Automatic Direction Finding (ADF) unit, Ultra High Frequency and a twin Very High Frequency installation. Radar gear comprised Gee navigation equipment, H2S ground-scanning, Identification Friend or Foe (IFF) and the Navigation Bombing Computer. Apart from the omni-type IFF and VHF aerials, no external antennas were fitted. The HF transmitter-receiver was fed with signals from a resonant slot in the aircraft fin and the ADF installation used parabolic and probe-type aerials in the fuselage. Metal strips and a box aerial in the mainplane supplied the ILS landing aids. Much of the B.2's avionics was housed between the crew cabin and bomb bay.

Converting B.2s into K.2 single-point tankers meant a hose drum unit replaced the avionics in the tail cone. A box-shaped cover went underneath, and this featured three lights on each side to help guide an

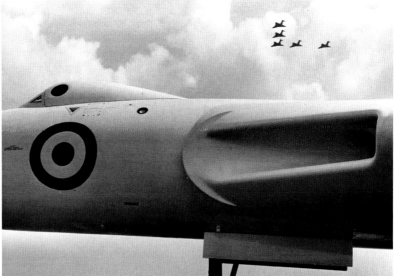

The air intake and side forward fuselage area of an early Vulcan. Gloster Javelin interceptors fly overhead.
Key Collection

aircraft that required fuel.

Early V-Bombers were painted 'anti-flash' white overall to protect them from the effects of a nuclear thermal flash generated by their own weapons (initially, the first production Vulcan B.1s were painted High Speed Silver). However, there was much discussion over the best choice of reflective colours for national, registration and other markings. For a while B.1s retained the standard shade red and blue roundels and fin flashes, but eventually all V-bombers had their roundels and markings reproduced in subdued shades for their nuclear role. In the 1960s the switch to low-level (non-nuclear) strike duties ensured Vulcans received disruptive green and grey tactical camouflage.

A photograph that provides considerable underside detail of a Vulcan B.1. The bomb aimer's position is particularly prominent.
Key Collection

A spectacular study of a Vulcan during an air display at Auf Den Dümpel in Germany during 1974. RAF Photo

The famous air show Vulcan XH558 enters a steep climb away during its career with the RAF Vulcan Display Flight. Key Collection

Vulcan deliveries to the RAF began with serial XA895 in August 1956 and the first unit to receive examples was the bomber's training unit, 230 Operational Conversion Unit (OCU). This provided aircrew ready to join frontline units. Airframe deliveries to the stations began with 83 Squadron, which reformed with the B.1 at Waddington on May 21, 1957. Next came 101 Squadron in October and another three would reform on the B.1, making five in all (see page 53 for a full unit guide). One of these, 44 Squadron, reformed in August 1960 having acquired B.1 airframes released by 83's conversion to the B.2. The final pair was 50 and 617 Squadrons, the latter being the famed 'Dam Busters'.

All five units and the OCU eventually converted to the B.2, along with

RAF OPERATIONS

another four squadrons new to the Vulcan. The RAF received its initial B.2 on July 1, 1960 and 27 Squadron became the first to form on type on April 1, 1961; the other 'new faces' were 9, 12 and 35 Squadrons. Between 1969-75 two of these, 9 and 35, were based at Akrotiri in Cyprus as part of the Near East Air Force. In November 1973, 27 reformed at Waddington in the Maritime Reconnaissance role with the B.2(MRR), in which form it survived until March 1982. Then, for the Falklands conflict in 1982, 50 Squadron became the Vulcan tanker unit flying the K.2 and, as such, became the last frontline unit to operate that famous wing shape. One further RAF unit to fly Vulcans, between 1961-66, was the Bomber Command Development Unit (BCDU) with B.1, B.1A and B.2 airframes.

Besides the individual squadrons the RAF's Vulcans, and indeed all the V-Bombers, were grouped together into official wings within their base airfield. These are not listed on page 53 but are summarised as follows:

Coningsby, Lincolnshire – 9, 12 and 35 Squadrons between 1962-November 1964, then Cottesmore, Rutland with the same units from 1964-69 (although 12 disbanded in 1967).

Finningley, South Yorkshire – 101 only from October 1957-June 1961 when it transferred to Waddington, Lincolnshire. 230 OCU and BCDU afterwards.

Scampton, Lincolnshire – 27, 83 and 617 during the 1960s, then 35, 617 and 230 OCU during the 1970s and into the 1980s. Between 1962-69, 27, 83 and 617 Squadrons operated as Vulcan Blue Steel units.

Waddington, Lincolnshire – quite a mix with 9 Squadron from 1975-82, 27 Squadron 1973-82, 44, 50 and 101 »

Three 230 OCU Vulcans fly in formation in September 1959. Top to bottom - XH503, XA896 and XH504. Crown Copyright

Scampton Wing B.2s with XJ783, XH554 and XH563 nearest in 1960. Terry Panopalis collection

Waddington Vulcans spread out at Cold War readiness. Key Collection

from 1960-61 until the 1980s, plus 83 and 230 OCU from the late 1950s to 1960-61. With the entry into service of the B.2, all B.1s were from then on concentrated at Waddington.

Akrotiri, Cyprus – 9 and 35 Squadrons from 1969-75. Both Squadrons based there to support the Central Treaty Organisation and were sometimes known as the Near East Air Force (NEAF) Bomber Wing.

High level nuclear deterrent

It cannot be stressed enough that, as a system for delivering nuclear weapons, the Vulcan was vital in the nation's defence network, primarily of course against the Soviet Union. As such the

first decade of the aircraft's career was dominated by the effort needed to carry out this role. To begin with the squadrons, which had just acquired this new warplane, flew extensive training sorties but, as they accumulated experience, became more active. That often meant numerous long practice deployments, goodwill trips overseas to 'fly the flag', and visits to other countries to compete in bombing competitions (usually in America) and participation in military exercises.

However, to open the Vulcan's service career the first frontline Squadron, 83, performed several high-profile flights across the world as part of a publicity campaign to boost the

image of the type, and the V-Force as a whole. On October 1, 1956, the 230 OCU aircraft XA897 crashed at London Airport on its return from a visit to Australia and New Zealand, generating adverse publicity. However, inside 18 months, 83's Vulcans had completed 'official' visits to Argentina, Brazil, Canada, Ceylon, Kenya, Malaya, Pakistan, the Philippines and Rhodesia. These trips also highlighted how the RAF could strengthen the UK's forces with a nuclear and heavy bombing capability, almost anywhere in the world… and at very short notice.

Due to the V-types being larger and heavier than the bombers they replaced, and thus requiring longer runways, many Bomber Command airfields had to be heavily modified and upgraded. The main Vulcan bases had 9,000ft-long runways but many other fields had special Operational Readiness Platforms built so that, in an emergency, groups of four bombers could be dispersed from their main stations. Each group could then scramble inside the four minutes expected to be available if there was a missile warning. Dispersal airfields so equipped included:

Vulcan B.1 line-up with XA902 nearest, then XA896 and XA895. All three have Waddington Wing badges on their fins. Barry Jones via Terry Panopalis

Vulcan B.1 XH481 of 101 Squadron is seen at RAF Church Fenton in September 1958. Terry Panopalis collection

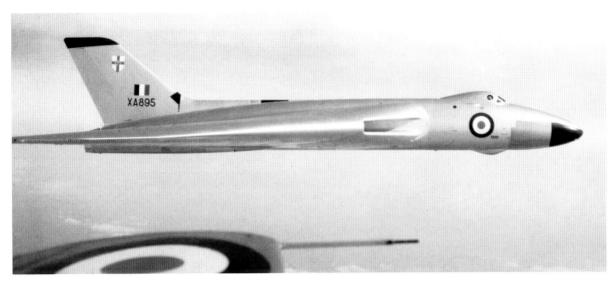

High Speed
Silver-painted
B.1 XA895
pictured early
in its career.
Phil Butler

Ballykelly, Northern Ireland; Bedford, Bedfordshire; Boscombe Down, Wiltshire; Brawdy, Pembrokeshire; Bruntingthorpe, Leicestershire; Burtonwood, Cheshire; Coltishall, Norfolk; Cranwell, Lincolnshire; Elvington, Yorkshire; Filton, Gloucestershire; Kinloss, Moray; Leconfield, East Yorkshire; Leeming, North Yorkshire; Leuchars, Fife; Llanbedr, Gwynedd; Lossiemouth, Moray; Lyneham, Wiltshire; Macrihanish, Argyll; Manston, Kent; Middleton St George, Co Durham; Pershore, Wiltshire; Prestwick, Ayrshire; St Mawgan, Cornwall; Stansted, Essex; Valley, Anglesey; Wattisham, Suffolk and finally Yeovilton, Somerset.

Each of these had a group of either two or four dispersals situated next to their take-off point. In the early days the regular exercises practised by Vulcans were:

Mayflight – a scheduled Bomber Command event involving the entire force held in dispersal, a period on standby and then a scramble, airfield by airfield. This was replaced later by the 'no-notice' Mickey Finn.

MICK – a Bomber Command 'no-notice' exercise that stopped short of dispersal.

KINSMAN – a station-sponsored mini-MAYFLIGHT affecting just one Vulcan squadron.

The name EDOM covered order changes in readiness state for ⏩

Vulcan
XA898 of 44
Squadron visits
Westover Air
Force Base in
Massachusetts,
USA in May
1961. Terry
Panopalis
collection

Aircrew rush aboard a Vulcan during a practice scramble. When the bomber first entered service, it had a T4 (Blue Devil) optical bombsight in the under-fuselage bomb-aimer's blister. However, the T4 was removed early in the type's career with reliance then passing to the Navigation and Bombing System or NBS, which comprised an H2S Mk.9A radar coupled to a Navigation and Bombing Computer.
Key Collection

An anti-flash white B.2, XJ824, with its Finningley Wing badge decorating the vertical stabiliser. Phil Butler

Vulcan B.1A XH478 is seen at A&AEE Boscombe Down in 1968 (with red tail bands) during bombing trials. Terry Panopalis collection

With the switch to low level, RAF Vulcans received camouflage on their upper surfaces. These B.2s, from top XM650, XM607, XL389 and XM648, are serving with 9, 44, 50 and 101 Squadrons, and inhabit alert platforms at Waddington. Barry Jones via Terry Panopalis

all aircraft on standby. With the arrival of Blue Steel in RAF hands during 1962, from then (until 1967) the three squadrons so equipped became Bomber Command's Quick Reaction Alert (QRA) force. The normal condition that applied to the peacetime QRA had one aircraft per squadron or the whole force ready to scramble inside 15 minutes (RS15 or Readiness State 15) with crews staying in ready rooms. Next came RS05 with crews at cockpit readiness, and then RS02, which involved starting engines and taxiing to the end of the runway; the latter covered gravity bomb loads only and not Blue Steel-armed aircraft.

Alert exercises could be called at any time, without warning, and were designed to simulate a real war. For a nuclear conflict, Vulcans would disperse to their wartime airfields across the UK to help prevent their destruction by concentrated enemy attacks. While living at these dispersal bases the crews were housed in caravans close to their aircraft, so they were ready to scramble at any time. Training flights for nuclear operations were also made as realistic as possible; for example, cockpits were blacked out with shields.

In October 1961, B.2s with 27 and 83 Squadrons flew with USAF bombers in a successful simulated attack against the USA, during which no Vulcan was attacked by the defending aircraft. At this time the latter were incapable of making effective interceptions at the Vulcan's cruising height of 56,000ft, because the bomber's big delta wing enabled it to out-turn and out-climb almost anything at altitudes above about 50,000ft. Subsequently, the delta-wing planform provided the Vulcan with such manoeuvrability at high altitude that it could avoid many NATO fighters taking part in other multi-national exercises.

The most critical moment during the Vulcan's ten-year-plus 'nuclear' career, when the force was taken to its highest ever state of alert, came with the 1962 Cuban Missile crisis. When the Soviet Union tried to install nuclear ballistic missile launchers on Cuba, the world situation became critical and

Vulcan XL320 with a Blue Steel in 1964. Although this weapon was retired in 1970, flying with it had ended rather earlier. Note the in-flight refuelling probe.
RAF via Terry Panopalis

the UK's V-Bombers were held at full cockpit readiness for three days. This was the closest the nuclear-armed V-Force ever came to being flown in anger.

During the early part of its tenure the RAF Vulcan's duties were closely allied to those of the USAF's Strategic Air Command (SAC), the two air arms having dovetailing plans. Later the Vulcans were assigned to Supreme Allied Commander Europe and, had the Cold War turned 'hot', the V-Bombers would strike targets in western Russia and the Baltic States, with SAC's Boeing B-52s following them from further afield.

Low level nuclear deterrent

In May 1960, when it used a guided missile to bring down an American Lockheed U-2 reconnaissance aircraft flying at more than 70,000ft, the Soviet Union demonstrated it had improved defences, which would make the high-flying V-Force extremely vulnerable when directly over enemy territory. Consequently, V-Bombers were forced to change their approach and to plan attacks where they flew in at low level 'under the radar', before delivering their Yellow Sun weapons, for example, with a so-called 'toss bomb' manoeuvre.

The operating profile for toss-bombing a nuclear store would have

the Vulcan approaching its target at tree-top level at speeds up to 415kts. On arrival the pilot would make a 2g pull-up to climb at 25°, open the bomb bay doors, release the weapon at 12,000ft altitude, within four seconds close the bay doors, and then initiate a 2g turn to have the aircraft tail-on to the explosion. The Vulcan would then dive to gain maximum speed before climbing away on full power. This method of weapon release was employed until the arrival of the parachute-retarded WE.177B. The Blue Steel stand-off missile was also modified to permit low-level launching, instead of the previous high-level

delivery for which the weapon was first designed.

After having completed low-level training, Vulcan B.1A units were declared operational in their new role on June 1, 1963, with B.2 squadrons following suit on May 1, 1964. One victim of this role change was the anti-flash white colour scheme, which was replaced by tactical camouflage on the Vulcan's upper surfaces. Normally, peacetime low-level training was performed at 500ft altitude and at 240kts but, as stated, for their war missions the Vulcans would have flown at tree-top height and at 400kts.

The change to low-level sorties ▸▸

An excellent photo of B.2 XL445 of the Cottesmore Wing taken in July 1968. The aircraft lacks any unit markings.
Terry Panopalis collection

The stylised fin badge on XL443 represents 35 Squadron.
Key Collection

A pleasing study of a B.2, XM575, from 101 Squadron. RAF via Terry Panopalis

missile submarines into service. However, from that point the V-Force was still required to be able to resume its alert status at short notice, to cover certain specified targets, and this capability had to be demonstrated in practice using Tactical Evaluations.

Conventional life

The change to low-level operations also affected the delivery of conventional stores. Standard 'iron' bombs received retarding tail units to ensure the bomber would be well clear of any shrapnel from their detonation. Despite having lost the nuclear deterrent, V-Bombers still supported NATO and CENTO (the Central Treaty Organisation covering the Middle East) with both nuclear and conventional weapons; the usual load for the latter comprised 1,000lb (454kg) retarded bombs. By the time Blue Steel was withdrawn, all Vulcans were serving with Strike Command's 1 Group (Strike Command was formed in April 1968 by the merger of Fighter and Bomber Commands).

Bomber Command exercises and training formed a major part of RAF Vulcan life, but V-Bomber sorties to British bases across the world became frequent and included so-called Lone Ranger deployments of one or two bombers to locations such as Butterworth in Malaya and Bahrain; the former was a trial reinforcement of the Far East Air Force. Later, these were followed by Western Ranger deployments to the US and Goose Ranger trips to Goose Bay, Canada for low-level exercises. Low-level training

also presented a major worry regarding V-Bomber airframes. Having been designed for flight at 50,000ft, where the level of turbulence was relatively low, flying in the rougher air at low level could at times dish out rough treatment to the airframes and seriously reduce their fatigue lives. In the case of the Vickers Valiant this problem brought forth premature retirement. For the Vulcan, however, a

very thorough fatigue-life assessment was undertaken, and airframe modifications were introduced that increased the fatigue life to 12,000 flight hours at low level. In addition, B.2 XM596 was taken from the production line to serve as a ground-based fatigue test airframe.

The Vulcan's primary nuclear deterrent role ended in 1969 when the Royal Navy introduced its Polaris

9 Squadron's XH562 on view at Ohakea, New Zealand after having been 'zapped' by the RNZAF. The Kiwi marks were removed after the Vulcan returned to the UK. Terry Panopalis collection

The second Vulcan B.2 to be built, XH534 of 27 Squadron, in flight over the North Sea in 1976 and wearing low level camouflage. RAF via Terry Panopalis

was also conducted over Libya, while those Vulcans based at Akrotiri flew low altitude training sorties over Iran, the Persian Gulf, Italy and Cyprus itself.

There were many Vulcan training flights to America, attending air shows and other specific events. In 1977 Vulcans and their crews began annual visits to Nellis Air Force Base for Red Flag exercises. Here aircraft from the USAF and other NATO air arms would fly against simulated Warsaw Pact targets, and these were designed to present realistic threats in that they were 'defended' by equipment developed to replicate Soviet air defences. Both RAF and USAF competitions involved dropping practice bombs against range targets (with marks awarded for accuracy) and navigation and electronic warfare exercises. In the later part of its career the Vulcan performed well in these wargames, although Victor squadrons took the prizes in some Bomber Command competitions. During the 1970s there was also an annual competition between RAF Vulcans and SAC B-52s, called Giant Voice. These events alternated between the UK and USA, and included both bombing and navigation sorties.

Other deployments to RAF bases involved batches of perhaps four Vulcans despatched to Malta, Cyprus, Bahrain, Singapore and Malaya. The most important of these appears to have been Operation Chamfrom in 1964-66, a reinforcement of the Far East Air Force during the Indonesian Confrontation over those years. Here the Vulcans (and Victors) did not take any active part in these troubles, but just made their presence and availability known.

The Near East Air Force Bomber

Vulcans (XJ784 far right) and Handley Page Victors at Akrotiri in Cyprus. Tony Buttler collection

The 230 OCU badge decorates the fin of B.2 XH559. Tony Buttler collection

Wing based at Akrotiri (9 and 35 Squadrons) operated primarily in support of CENTO, but also undertook other NATO duties and supported British interests in general in the Near and Middle East. The last RAF base in Africa was closed in 1970, after which the Soviet Union's influence in the area blossomed. These two Vulcan squadrons provided a

counter to this while considerably increasing the RAF's strike capability in the Mediterranean region. The Near East Air Force was disbanded in January 1975, 9 and 35 Squadrons returning to the UK.

A further V-Bomber role was to provide strategic reconnaissance using both conventional cameras and radar. The modified B.2(MRR) ▶▶

The drab camouflage on B.2 XM648 seems to match the wet weather on that day. Key Collection

Resplendent in wrap-around camouflage, 44 Squadron's XM575 breaks into the circuit after a training flight. *Avro Heritage*

A Giant Voice photo from 1974, showing XM606. *RAF via Terry Panopalis*

maritime reconnaissance Vulcan (with an F.95 camera in its bomb-aiming blister instead of the bombsight) eventually replaced the Victor on radar reconnaissance duties. As regards the Vulcan fleet as a whole, few B.2s were taken out of service prior to the early 1980s and some even found further

employment as ground instruction airframes.

In the early 1970s, 543 Squadron's Handley Page Victors were used to acquire samples of the debris and fallout from French nuclear tests in the South Pacific (this was known as Operation Attune). Later, Vulcans

belonging to 27 Squadron took on this work, though France ended its tests in 1974 and any subsequent air-sampling operations covered Chinese nuclear tests. It is understood that Vulcan sampling pods were based on the de Havilland Sea Vixen fighter's underwing drop tank. The Vulcan would carry a sample pod under each wing, on small pylons attached to former Skybolt missile hardpoints.

The April 1982 Falklands conflict is mentioned briefly here, since it receives deeper coverage in a later section. This famous campaign to recover the Falkland Islands from Argentine occupation, known in the UK as Operation Corporate, provided a quite spectacular farewell for the Vulcan – and in the process cemented the bomber's popularity in the eyes of the public. The aircraft's bombing contribution also became the first occasion it had been taken into battle and it brought a return to bomb delivery from high altitude.

At the time of the Argentine invasion of the Falklands, just three squadrons were still flying Vulcans, all based at Waddington. Two of these were due to disband but there was a pool of aircraft to on which to call for offensive operations; in due course six were picked as the best available (though just five would fly during Corporate). Five complete crews who had taken part in the most recent Red Flag exercise (February 1982) were chosen to fly them. A vital item was the restoration of these machines' air-to-air refuelling capability since their IFR probes had been inactive for quite some time. The chosen aircraft were also those that still had Skybolt attachment points and

Vulcan XM600 during Strategic Air Command's Giant Voice competition in December 1971. The aircraft is seen at McCoy AFB, Florida and has the 1 Group Panther badge on the fuselage just forward of the air intake. *Terry Panopalis collection*

internal 'plumbing' in position, since these fittings helped considerably in preparing them for Falklands duties; the modification work also involved the introduction of an improved inertial navigation system.

The Vulcan bombing campaign opened during the night of April 30-May 1, 1982 when XM607 attacked the airfield at Port Stanley, the capital of the Falklands Islands, using free-fall bombs released from 10,000ft. The aircraft had taken off from Wideawake airfield on Ascension Island and getting there involved a complex arrangement of in-flight refuelling operations, with no fewer than 11 Victor K.2 tanker aircraft also airborne. Twenty-one 1,000lb (454kg) bombs in all were unloaded diagonally across the Port Stanley runway to ensure that at least one would hit the hard surface. The objective was to try and restrict the basing of Argentine combat aircraft on the Islands, particularly fast jets.

This was the first of a set of raids codenamed Black Buck. On the night of May 3-4, XM607 completed a second attack but this time it did not hit the Port Stanley runway. On May 30 XM597 flew to the Falklands armed with AGM-45 Shrike anti-radar missiles with the objective of hitting Argentine radars, and on this sortie slight damage was inflicted on a main surveillance radar aerial. On June 2, XM597 made the long journey again and this time

launched two Shrikes to destroy one of the radars controlling an anti-aircraft battery near Port Stanley. However, during its return flight XM597 lost its capability to refuel and so the bomber was forced to divert to Rio de Janeiro,

Brazil, to land. The last 'Black Buck' sortie took place with XM607 on the night of June 11-12, 1982.

In the meantime, six more of the remaining operational Vulcans at Waddington were, as described ⟫

An atmospheric view of 44 Squadron's XM575 cruising over the English coast, near the end of the Vulcan's career in the early 1980s. The fin displays Waddington Wing and 44 Squadron badges. Tony Buttler collection

Vulcan XL388 provides underside detail during a publicity flight. Key Collection

A B.2, XM652, on the ground at Nellis AFB, Nevada, USA during Exercise Red Flag in 1980. RAF via Terry Panopalis

An RAF Phantom prepares to link with Vulcan XH560 for fuel on March 14, 1984, during the final Vulcan scramble by 50 Squadron. Key Collection

A 44 Squadron Vulcan departs Nellis AFB to begin an Exercise Red Flag sortie in early 1980. Key Collection

previously, progressively modified into the K.2 inflight refuelling tanker version to equip 50 Squadron. This short-term development brought an extension to the Vulcan's operational life until its final retirement from service on March 31, 1984.

Quite unlike the RAF's equivalent fighter squadrons with their bright fuselage bars, the V-Bombers did not display extensive markings and decoration on their airframes. Individual Vulcan squadron motifs were usually painted on the fin and at times on the under-fuselage entry door. Unit badges did sometimes appear on Vulcan noses to the rear of the roundel or again on the aircrew entry door. Finningley and Waddington-based Vulcans (and for a period Coningsby's machines) would often wear a 'wing' marking to denote their parent station. A further variation came for aircraft participating in competitions in America, with 1 Group Strike Command's 'Panther' marking appearing on Vulcan fins. BCDU aircraft carried no unit markings, though one example did have the unit's title on its fin.

As noted elsewhere, numerous Vulcans were flown by RAE Farnborough, RAE Bedford (with the Blind Landing Experimental Unit), A&AEE Boscombe Down, and 4 Joint Services Trial Unit in Australia, for all manner of trials and experimental work. Additionally, in 1965 the Royal Radar Establishment (RRE) at Pershore in Worcestershire received one Vulcan, B.1 XA895, for development flying of the Red Steer Mk.2 tail-warning radar; this aircraft served as the trials installation airframe.

When retired the Vulcan was undoubtedly out of date as a bomber, but it was an extremely popular aircraft with the public and its departure was expected to leave a (literally) big hole in airshow display programmes. Consequently, on April 1, 1984, the Ministry of Defence formed a Vulcan Display Flight at Waddington purely to demonstrate a surviving B.2 at air events (this had previously operated as the Vulcan Display Team within 55 Squadron at Marham with its HP Victors). Having operated both XL426 and XH558 during this period, the flight was finally disbanded in 1992. But XH558 would make a dramatic re-appearance in 2008 in private hands.

The B.2(MRR) Vulcan XH560 of 27 Squadron at McClellan AFB in California, during December 1975. This version was also known as SR.2 for Strategic Reconnaissance and here the aircraft carries air sampling pods. Terry Panopalis collection

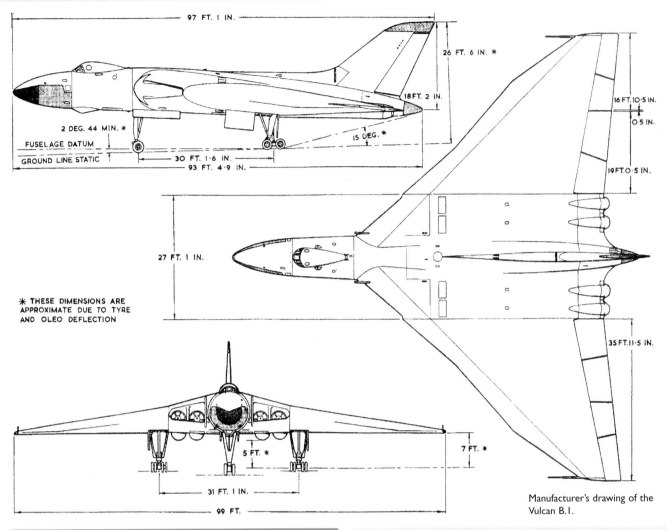

Manufacturer's drawing of the Vulcan B.1.

AVRO VULCAN DATA

Type: Avro 707 Scale Model Research Aircraft; Avro 698 Experimental Bomber Prototype; Avro Vulcan B.1 and B.2 Medium Bomber

Powerplant

707 and 707B 1 x 3,500lb (15.6kN) Rolls-Royce Derwent 5

707A and 707C 1 x 3,600lb (16.0kN) Rolls-Royce Derwent 8

Vulcan B.1 4 x 11,000lb (48.9kN) Bristol Olympus Mk.101, 12,000lb (53.3kN) Mk.102 or 13,500lb (60.0kN) Mk.104 turbojets

Vulcan B.2 4 x 16,000lb (71.1kN) Bristol Olympus Mk.200, 17,000lb (75.6kN) Mk.201 or 20,000lb (88.9kN) Mk.301 turbojets

Dimensions (span, length, height on ground, gross wing area)

707 33ft (10.1m), 40ft 2in (12.2m), 11ft 3in (3.4m), 366 1/2sq ft (34.1m²).

707B 33ft (10.1m), 41ft 3 1/2in (12.6m), 11ft 7in (3.5m), 366.5sq ft (34.1m²).

707A & 707C 34ft 2in (10.4m), 42ft 4in (12.9m), 11ft 7in (3.5m), 408sq ft (37.9m²).

698 Prototype and B.1 99ft (30.2m), 97ft 1in (29.6m), 26ft 6in (8.1m), 3,554sq ft (330.5m²)

B.2 111ft (33.8m), 105ft 6in (32.2m), 27ft 1in (8.3m), 3,964sq ft (368.7m²)

Gross Weight

707 8,600lb (3,901kg)

707B 9,500lb (4,309kg)

707A 9,800lb (4,445kg)

707C 10,000lb (4,536kg)

B.1 167,000lb (75,751kg)

B.2 204,000lb (92,534kg)

Fuel Load

B.1 75,056lb (34,045kg)

B.2 74,080lb (33,603kg)

Military Load

B.1 1 x 10,000lb (4,536kg) or 21 x 1,000lb (454kg) bombs, 1 x Blue Danube nuclear store

B.2 1 x 10,000lb or 21 x 1,000lb bombs, 1 x Blue Steel air-to-surface nuclear missile, 1 x 7,250lb (3,289kg) Yellow Sun Mk.2 nuclear store

Performance

Maximum level speed

707A & 707C: 403mph (648km/h)

B.1 620mph (998km/h) at height

B.2 640mph (1,030km/h) at height

Operational ceiling

B.1 55,000ft (16,764m)

B.2 60,000ft (18,288m)

Range

B.1 3,000 miles (4,827km)

B.2 4,600 miles (7,401km)

A remarkable photo showing Vulcan B.2 weapons options. Left to right: Blue Steel, Shrike, Martel, 3 x seven 1,000lb bombs on Seven Store Carriers, two 1,000lb Paveway IIs and 28lb practice bombs. It is thought this photo was taken at Waddington, near to the day when the Vulcan left RAF service. Chris Gibson

TOOLS OF DEST

From its inception the Avro Vulcan was designed to deliver Britain's nuclear deterrent. Until the mid-1960s the carriage of conventional ordnance was looked upon as a secondary role for the Vulcan, but this changed when the aircraft switched to low level operations, and when the nuclear deterrent passed to the hands of the Royal Navy.

Colour code stores

The first weapon specified for the V-Bomber fleet, and Britain's first atomic bomb or A-bomb, was codenamed Blue Danube (to hide its real purpose, documents from the period often called it a 'special bomb' or Target Marker Bomb). This 10,000lb (4,536kg) store could be carried in the Vulcan's normal bomb bay because its casing was based upon the conventional wartime 'Tallboy' high-explosive bomb, employed by the legendary Avro Lancaster.

The first Blue Danubes were delivered to the RAF in November 1953 and on October 11, 1956, a Vickers Valiant dropped the first live round, which was detonated over Maralinga in Australia. In August 1957, after full trials with XA892, A&AEE Boscombe Down cleared the Vulcan B.I to carry and drop Blue Danube; incidentally that same month the bomber was also allowed to carry and drop 25lb (11.3kg) practice bombs. It is understood that 58 Blue Danubes in all were produced but, such was

A Blue Steel missile with transporter at RAF Scampton. The missile's High Test Peroxide fuel demanded the utmost care in transferral to/from the weapon, due to its highly corrosive nature. T Panopalis

the pace and advancement of nuclear weaponry during this period, the atom bomb was very quickly superseded by the far more powerful, smaller and lighter thermonuclear or hydrogen bomb. Blue Danube was thus retired from service in 1962.

The development of Britain's first hydrogen bomb (H-Bomb) began in the 1950s and live rounds were dropped by Valiants both in 1957 and 1958 under the Operation Grapple test programme. As a short-term 'gap-filler' the Vulcan only carried the 9,000lb (4,082kg) Violet Club thermonuclear gravity bomb, of which just five were produced using Blue Danube casings.

Britain's first fully operational H-bomb was the 7,250lb (3,289kg) Yellow Sun gravity bomb. Vulcan B.1 carried Yellow Sun Mk.1 in its bomb bay from 1960 and clearance for the B.2 to field the updated Yellow Sun Mk.2 was given in August 1961. In addition, from 1958 the Vulcan

Britain's first nuclear bomb was Blue Danube. Chris Gibson

This Vulcan B.2, XL317 of 617 Squadron, is armed with Blue Steel. RAF via T Panopalis

RUCTION

Early production Vulcan XA891 demonstrated nuclear weapon delivery tactics at the September 1958 SBAC Farnborough show. Key Collection

Vulcan B.1 XA892 was used for several type-specific armament trials. Barry Jones via Terry Panopalis

was cleared to tote several American air-delivered nuclear gravity bombs supplied under the codename Project E; these weighed up to 7,500lb (3,402kg) but the US Air Force retained its control over their use. Carriage of these stores ended in 1962 and Yellow Sun was replaced in the late 1960s.

At the September 1958 Farnborough show, Vulcan B.1 XA891 demonstrated nuclear-weapon delivery tactics by flying into a LABS Toss Bombing manoeuvre directly after taking-off (LABS for Low Altitude Bombing System).

The nuclear weapon most associated with the Vulcan is surely the Blue Steel air-to-ground nuclear missile, which was another Avro product (built by its Weapons Division) replacing Blue Danube. All weapons described so far were gravity bombs, in other words they had to be dropped directly over a target. With the advances in the Soviet Union's defensive weaponry, particularly regarding surface-to-air guided missiles, by the late 1950s flying all the way to a target would make the V-Bombers extremely vulnerable. The solution was a weapon that could fly the last portion of the journey to the target by itself – in other words a store that would give the V-Bombers a 'stand-off' capability without them having to enter a well-defended area. The supersonic rocket-propelled Blue Steel cruise missile was the result.

Blue Steel was massive and could not fit inside the Vulcan bomb bay,

The only B.1 equipped to carry Blue Steel was XA903, which had to be specially adapted to operate as the development aircraft for this missile. Barry Jones via Terry Panopalis

The B.2 employed for most of the Blue Steel development work was XH539. In this March 1971 photo, the aircraft has a USAF Systems Command badge on its fin. Terry Panopalis collection

so carrying it required considerable alteration to the aircraft's lower fuselage for it to be attached underneath. The lower boom of the centre section front spar on B.1 airframes was not cranked, so on these Vulcans the missile could not be recessed sufficiently into the lower fuselage. Consequently, Blue Steel was only ever carried by the B.2, the modified variant being re-designated B.2A, and even these airframes still required changes to their main spars.

For the B.2A conversion the existing bomb bay doors were replaced by new contoured versions with a recess, which then formed a housing for the Blue Steel round. A pair of crutch frame assemblies and a carrier beam were installed in the bomb bay to hold the missile, and new separate upward opening doors were fitted in the bomb bay rear end, to accommodate the missile's upper fin. These doors would then close after the weapon's release.

This new and highly advanced missile had a span of 13ft (3.96m), its length was 35ft (10.67m) and weight 16,000lb (7,258kg). Power came from a 20,000lb (88.9kN) thrust Bristol Siddeley Stentor liquid-fuelled rocket motor, and for guidance the weapon featured a built-in automatic inertial navigation system. Maximum speed was Mach 2.5 and, if the weapon was flown in at high supersonic speed, a typical launch at around 50,000ft (15,240m) altitude gave a 100-mile (161km) range.

One early B.1, XA903, was modified substantially to enable it to serve as the Blue Steel development airframe and this aircraft first flew with a dummy round late in 1957. Development trials were conducted both in Britain and Australia, the latter at the Weapons Research

The caption: Airframe XA903 with a dummy Blue Steel displays at Farnborough on September 2, 1958, but only in the air... the aircraft did not land. Terry Panopalis collection

Establishment (WRE) at Woomera under the control of 4 Joint Services Trials Unit based at Edinburgh Field near Adelaide; the Australian testing began in August 1957 and releases were made over the Woomera ranges.

Vulcan XA903 itself went to Australia, but the B.2 used in most of this development work was XH539, which was based in Australia from December 1961 until January 1964. This B.2 was the first to be completed to Blue Steel standard – it had entered RAF service in September 1961, and it performed the first live Blue Steel firing in October 1963. Vulcan was cleared officially to carry Blue Steel ➤➤

Trials Vulcan XA903 departs for Australia on November 12, 1960, to conduct the next phase of the Blue Steel development programme. Tony Buttler

The B.2 XM599 of 35 Squadron shown dropping 21 x 1,000lb bombs in 1965. Crown Copyright via Terry Panopalis

July that year full operational low level carriage and pop-up release of Yellow Sun Mk.2 was cleared, followed in August by pop-up and release of Blue Steel. The latter was retired in 1970.

American influence

Several other nuclear stores were planned or proposed for the Vulcan during the early part of the aircraft's career but without being adopted. The example that came closest was the American Douglas AGM-87 Skybolt, which the British government wanted to buy to replace Blue Steel.

Skybolt was 38ft 3in (11.66m) long and weighed 11,000lb (4,990kg). Avro's first proposals for what was called the Vulcan Phase 6, or the Mk.3 long-endurance Vulcan, were made in May 1960. This would be a much modified B.2 with a larger outer wing and an extended dorsal spine, reheated Olympus engines or B.Ol.21 units with aft fans, more than double the previous fuel capacity, and four Skybolts carried on underwing pylons. Initially the aircraft had a span of 121ft (36.88m), length of 99ft 11in (30.45m), 4,215sq ft (391.995m²) wing area, all-up-weight of 344,300lb (156,174kg) and maximum range 4,730nm (8,765km). A further proposal introduced an extended pressure cabin that increased the overall length to 110ft (33.53m). One object of Phase 6 was to give the aircraft a far longer flight endurance, to well more than 11 hours.

Plans were laid down to convert two B.2s, XH537 and XH538, into Skybolt test airframes, though with far fewer physical changes than the Phase 6. And these would only carry two rounds, one under each wing.

in 1962, the limits for carriage being the same maximum speed, height and manoeuvring as for the aircraft itself, with release at Mach 0.84 indicated in straight and level flight (+/-5°) and at between 45,000ft (13,716m) and 55,000ft (16,764m) altitude.

The first fully operational Vulcan/ Blue Steel unit was 617 Squadron in February 1963 and, for a while at least, RAF Vulcan crews then no longer had to worry about penetrating enemy defences near a target. However, further progress in the development of new Soviet defensive weaponry soon nullified this advantage and, once again, the Vulcan became vulnerable when flying at high altitude over enemy territory. Consequently, in 1964 Blue Steel Vulcans were switched from high to low level operations with the missile released at around 30 miles (48km)

from a target and at just 250ft (76m) altitude; the weapon would then make a zoom climb to 17,000ft (5,182m) before diving onto its target. Interim clearance for Vulcans to operate at low level was passed in January 1964. In

A close-up of a Blue Steel installation on a 617 Squadron Vulcan. Key Collection

A Vulcan B.2, it's XL-prefixed serial partially obscured, demonstrates how snugly Blue Steel fitted underneath the bomber's fuselage. Terry Panopalis collection

The first flight by a B.2 with a pair of captive mechanical Skybolts aboard was made on September 29, 1961, the first dummy drops followed in December, and dummy trials were completed in February 1963. The first Skybolt Vulcan airframe was intended to have been delivered in March 1963, but the entire project was cancelled in December the previous year.

Early live Skybolt firings in America had been marked by a string of failures. The first fully successful flight took place on December 19, 1962 but three days later President Kennedy cancelled the Skybolt programme. This step created something of a crisis since it left the UK without a new nuclear weapon; it resulted in considerable disagreement between Britain and the US. The solution was the acquisition of the American submarine-launched Polaris ballistic system as a replacement, a move which ended Bomber Command's control of the British nuclear deterrent when it passed to the Royal Navy in 1969.

However, a by-product of Skybolt was the enhancement of inputs to the B.2's Military Flight System (MFS). The Sperry Heading Reference System, designed originally for Skybolt, was superior to the Vulcan's existing equipment and so its development was continued after the loss of the missile. This produced more accurate bombing from the Vulcan's navigation and bombing system (NBS), that is its H2S radar and navigation bombing computer (NBC); XH538 served as the trials aircraft.

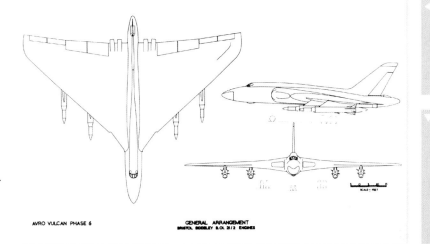

The Vulcan Phase 6 Skybolt carrier proposal of May 1960 also featured an extended dorsal spine. Avro Heritage

A Vulcan and Boeing B-52H Stratofortress bomber (60-0006) flying together, both carrying Skybolts. Douglas via Terry Panopalis collection

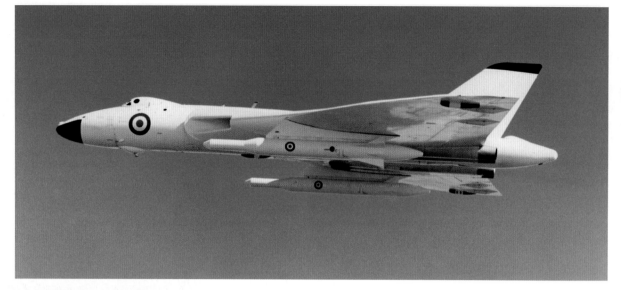

A superb image featuring one of the Skybolt trial Vulcans. Terry Panopalis via Chris Gibson

Airburst Mk.952 fuzes are fitted to these 1,000lb bombs being loaded into a Vulcan. T Panopalis

Despite losing its strategic nuclear role to the navy, the RAF did retain a tactical nuclear capability with the Atomic Weapons Research Establishment-designed WE.177B. This

622lb (282kg) laydown parachute-retarded nuclear gravity bomb entered service in 1966 and remained on strength until the 1990s. It was carried by Vulcan B.2s and was in fact a replacement for the 1,750lb (794kg) Red Beard gravity bomb, which had been Britain's first tactical nuclear weapon. This had entered service in 1962 and it too was carried by the Vulcan.

Mud moving

The Vulcan's secondary role was the carriage of conventional 'iron' bombs, and in quite large quantities.

In March and April 1956, A&AEE Boscombe Down assessed the first production Vulcan XA889 to release

to type for RAF use in the high-altitude medium bomber role. The aircraft was described as "an adequate bombing platform" and released to the service at a maximum weight of 167,000lb (75,751kg) and with a maximum 438mph (705km/h) Indicated Airspeed (IAS) between sea level and 30,000ft (9,144m) and 0.98 Indicated Mach Number (IMN) above that height.

Further trials needed to clear individual items of weaponry in relation to their use by the Vulcan. For example, during the first half of 1957 trials by A&AEE using XA892 green-lit the carriage and release of a 10,000lb (4,536kg) iron bomb at heights from 14,000ft (4,267m) to the maximum obtainable at 438mph

Vulcan XH535 flew to Edwards Air Force Base in America for Skybolt trials. Douglas via Terry Panopalis collection

(705km/h) or Mach 0.97, whichever was less. Then from February 1958 XA890 was used by RAE Farnborough for conventional trials with 2,000lb (907kg), 6,000lb (2,722kg) and 7,000lb (3,175kg) bombs.

For the Vulcan B.2, clearance of the 21 × 1,000lb (454kg) medium capacity bomb installation was conducted using B.1 XA892 between February 1958 and July 1959. Clearance was recommended for the carriage and release of 21, 14 or 11 × 1,000lb bombs under the following flight conditions; in both cases in straight and level flight +/-5°:

At heights from sea level to 20,000ft (6,096m) – 250 kts IAS; from 20,000ft to 50,000ft (6,096m to 15,240m) – 300 kts IAS or Mach 0.93, whichever was less.

Some additions to the Vulcan's conventional weapon inventory were made towards the end of the aircraft's career, and especially for the 1982 Falklands campaign. For example, late in its life the B.2 acquired the capability to carry the American Paveway II laser-guided bomb, three of which could be loaded into the bomb bay. Air-launched non-nuclear guided missiles, however, provided the most marked variation from previous practice.

Vulcans were involved in trial installations of the Anglo-French Martel TV-guided anti-radar missile,

which had entered service in 1972. This was never employed as operational ordnance, but tests were conducted in early May 1982 using XM597 and XM612, experimental launches being made over the Cardigan Bay range. One Martel could be loaded under each wing on pylons attached to the old Skybolt underwing hardpoints, but the American anti-radar AGM-45 Shrike was adopted instead.

The 390lb (177kg) Shrike did not enter regular UK service, but for the Falklands conflict examples were supplied covertly from America. Vulcans carried two per pylon (on twin adapters), four in all if required, to attack Argentine radar installations during Black Buck radar suppression missions. To complement the Shrikes the B.2 starboard underwing pylon

could carry an AN/ALQ101 ECM jamming pod for the Black Buck raids. This pod had been designed specifically to counter enemy radar-guided defensive weapons.

This review of the Vulcan's weapon arsenal has highlighted an aspect of the bomber often completely overlooked – that is how adaptable it was to accept alternative bombs and missiles. The range and different types of weapon described here is quite extraordinary, and the capability and sophistication of 1980s stores against those from the 1950s is also notable. The Vulcan design team could surely never have imagined back in the late 1940s, when the Avro 698 was first proposed, just how many different types of weapon their aircraft would eventually be asked to employ.

An unidentified B.2 releases a stick of 1,000lb (454kg) bombs fitted with No.117 retard tail units.
Tony Buttler

A Martel anti-radar missile on one of the Vulcans allocated for trials with this weapon in May 1982.
Key Collection

AVRO VULCAN B.2

Vulcan B.2, XM607, 44 Squadron, RAF Scampton, 1977. This unusual scheme was applied for one of that year's instalments of the Red Flag exercises at Nellis Air Force Base, Nevada, USA. Dark Green and Medium Sea Grey upper surfaces, with Dark Earth and Middle Stone below.

(Andy Hay/www.flyingart.co.uk)

XM607

The prototype VX770 pictured while serving as the Rolls-Royce Conway engine flight test bed.
Rolls-Royce via Terry Panopalis

Apart from those Vulcans used on clearance testing to pass the bomber for service use, further examples were employed as engine test beds and to assess other equipment. The most important of those are described here, although not included are the weapons and in-flight refuelling trials, which are detailed in their relevant sections.

Engine test beds

Including prototype VX770, four Vulcans were used to test alternative powerplants. The Armstrong Siddeley Sapphire and Rolls-Royce Spey and Conway units were mounted in the engine bays. However, the more powerful Olympus 22R and 593 developed for the TSR.2 strike aircraft and the Concorde supersonic airliner

respectively, and the Panavia Tornado's RB.199, were housed in special pods mounted in and beneath the centre fuselage bomb bay.

As noted in the development section, VX770 was flying with more powerful Sapphire engines by July 1953. In 1956, it was selected to serve as a test bed for the Conway, a low-bypass turbofan, not a pure turbojet, which had been specially designed to provide high cruising economy for bomber aircraft. Vulcan VX770 was delivered to Avro's facility at Langar for this conversion in August 1956; it initially had Conway R.Co.7 units installed, and the aircraft made its first flight in this form on August 9, 1957. The switch to a Conway powerplant required larger intakes and jetpipes within the Vulcan airframe, but VX770's wing planform was unchanged.

TEST BED TRIANGLES

Airframe XA902 with two Conway and two Spey engines undergoing ground testing at Hucknall. When the trial powerplants were housed in the normal Olympus positions, it was often difficult to tell from the outside if the alternative units were in place.
Rolls-Royce via Terry Panopalis

The Vulcan was delivered to Rolls-Royce at Hucknall on August 24 to begin flight trials to investigate the basic problems of engine handing and reliability. These flights primarily involved collecting data in readiness for the engine to go into service in other aircraft types. Later VX770 was fitted with 17,250lb (76.7kN) thrust Conway R.Co.11s to begin an intensive development programme with the newer variant. In this form VX770 attended the 1958 Farnborough Show but, because of its development role, the 'Conway-Vulcan' (as it was then called) only performed flypasts during the display itself and was not exhibited on static. On September 20, 1958, VX770 was destroyed in a tragic accident during the Battle of Britain display at RAF Syerston. The aircraft's starboard wing began to break apart during a low-level pass, it dived into the ground and all its crew were killed. The structural integrity had failed after the airframe had been over-stressed.

B.I XA894

In January 1956, XA894 joined the Ministry of Supply Air Fleet at Woodford for a programme of intensive de-icing and autopilot trials (see later). Afterwards it was used to test the Olympus Ol.22R (Mk.320) chosen for the British Aircraft Corporation TSR.2 strike aircraft. The Ol.22R nacelle positioned below the fuselage had bifurcated intakes, which were geometrically similar to the TSR.2 configuration itself, while the body of the engine was enclosed within a sealed sleeve, inside which boundary layer air would provide cooling. Airframe XA894 arrived at Filton for conversion in July 1960 and the first flight with the Olympus 22R aboard took place on February 23, 1962.

However, on December 3, 1962, XA894 was destroyed on the ground at Filton. An uncontained turbine failure occurred during ground running and the aircraft caught fire immediately. In fact, all five engines were running when the fire started, and it consumed the aircraft entirely (and one of the fire tenders that had rushed to the scene). A 22R turbine disc was discovered later some 100 yards (91m) from the scene.

B.I XA896

In May 1964 XA896 arrived at Rolls-Royce's Flight Test Establishment at Hucknall to serve as a test bed for the Bristol Siddeley BS.100 turbofan lift/thrust engine, then under development for the Hawker Siddeley P.1154 supersonic vertical-take-off fighter aircraft. The engine was to be housed in a pod beneath ➤➤

Vulcan VX770 flying during the September 1958 Farnborough airshow with Conway engines installed. Rolls-Royce Heritage Trust

The Olympus 22R installation under XA894 had a complex shape and quite large, extending for more than half the length of the Vulcan.
Key Collection

the fuselage, but the P.1154 was subsequently cancelled, the conversion was halted in February 1965 and XA896 was scrapped.

B.I XA902

Vulcan XA902 in late 1958 was allotted to replace VX770 and complete the planned Conway trials programme. It was converted at Woodford from December 1958 to take R.Co.11 engines (the Mks.102 and 103). In fact, the Conway came under serious consideration as a

replacement for the Olympus in further developments of the Vulcan, but its main military application was to be the Handley Page Victor B.2, the Vulcan's great rival.

After conversion XA902 arrived at Hucknall on July 17, 1959, and the programme included flights at a cruising altitude of 40,000ft (12,192m). However, at this height the cruise rpm for the Conway meant that the Vulcan's maximum speed would be exceeded, thereby taking this B.1 beyond its airframe

limits. Consequently, it was decided to run the Conways at Boeing 707 airliner ratings, slightly lower than that for an R.Co.11; actually two of the engines were operated at high rpm (9,370rpm) with the other two at a lower figure. But it was this structure/power limitation problem that had been responsible for VX770 breaking up in the air in 1958, because the prototype's structure had been nowhere near as strong as that used in production aeroplanes, and its Mach number limit was correspondingly less.

Another Farnborough 1962 study, this time showing XA894's Olympus 22R with reheat on (and airbrakes deployed). The Vulcan's standard Olympus units were noisy – but having the TSR.2 version in reheat as well must have been deafening!
Terry Panopalis

With the four Conways in position, XA902's maximum all-up-weight was around 160,000lb (72,576kg). In January 1960, Flight magazine recorded that XA902 had frequently flown for 18 hours a day, and in all it would record 1,021 hours airborne with Conways installed. Much of the programme was carried out from Hucknall, but hot weather sorties were flown from Malta during January-March 1960.

Airframe XA902 had been earmarked to test the RB.163 Spey engine, which was to power the then new Blackburn Buccaneer naval strike aircraft. With the Conway programme out of the way, XA902 was modified to take Speys in the inboard engine positions only, with Conways retained in the outer bays. The aircraft made its first flight in this latest form from Hucknall on October 12, 1961, and after just two trips test pilot Jim Heyworth reported favourably on the new engine's handling qualities. It is understood that Spey testing occupied just 88 flight hours over a period of four weeks, the main objective being to check a new all-speed engine control system in flight (all other Spey testing was performed on ground test beds and in rigs).

Rare colour view of the Conway-powered XA902 at Farnborough in 1959. Tony Buttler

Vulcan XA902 was finally retired in October 1962, after which it was carefully dismantled and then taken by road to RAF Dishforth, North Yorkshire on March 7, 1963. This final exercise was used as a feasibility study to see if it would be practical to transport Vulcan airframes in such a manner, should the need ever arise.

B.I XA903

The BAC/Aerospatiale Concorde's Olympus 593 engine – developed from the Olympus 22R – was tested by Vulcan XA903, which had arrived at Filton for conversion in January 1964. Previously, XA903 had been used for Blue Steel development trials. Again, the test engine was installed underneath the fuselage, but this time in the form of a Concorde engine pod with a single 'straight-through' intake. In this configuration the Olympus 593 thrust line was a full 7ft (2.13m) below that of the bomber's standard Olympus units. The maiden flight with the additional engine took place on September 9, 1966, and the trials involved 219 flights and 417 hours airtime, plus a further 24 hours' ⏩

The Vulcan engine test beds featured regularly at Farnborough shows. This view portrays XA894 during its display at the September 1962 event. Terry Panopalis

ground running. *Flight* reported that a total of 2,665 ignitions, 18 hours of reheat testing and 1,279 reheat lightings were also recorded. In March 1971, a water spray rig was fitted under the Vulcan's forward fuselage to permit water and ice ingestion tests.

A key element of the programme involved XA903 being landed repeatedly at above its maximum design landing weight, and it was also flown beyond its service limit speed. Remarkably, the handling qualities of the Vulcan/593 combination revealed that no significant pitch-trim changes were induced over the complete throttle range of the SST powerplant. The Olympus 593 programme ended

in 1971 after six standards of engine and three intake configurations had been flown, in ten phases of testing. The final phase involved the installation of a -4 engine representative of the units installed in pre-production Concorde 01. The Vulcan proved ideal for assessing the Olympus 593, in part because of the ease with which flight conditions could be altered.

The final engine tested by the Vulcan was the Rolls-Royce/Turbo-Union RB.199 developed for the Tornado multi-role combat aircraft and again XA903 served as its testbed. Here, the supplementary nacelle conformed to the starboard side of a Tornado fuselage and in due course would

receive the additional fitting of a Tornado gun pod complete with a Mauser 27mm cannon. Again, this would enable engine relighting, windmilling and reheat lighting to be carried out in a realistic environment.

In August 1971 XA903 was flown to Cambridge for Marshalls to undertake the conversion. It was delivered to Rolls-Royce in February 1972, and then made its maiden flight with an RB.199 in position on April 19, 1973. A unique feature of the programme occurred in January 1976 when XA903 was flown to A&AEE Boscombe Down to undergo firing trials with the Mauser cannon. These were performed on the ground with the object of determining

The Olympus 593 test bed XA903 pictured in 1966. The conversion did not just involve fitting the nacelle; the bomb bay contained water and fuel, as well as avionics and instrumentation for the trials. The bomb aimer's blister and tail cone were removed. *Rolls-Royce via Terry Panopalis*

Test Bed XA902 landing at Rolls-Royce Hucknall. *Key Collection*

whether the ingestion of the products from shell propellants might affect the engine's performance. A total of 285 flying hours were accumulated with the RB.199 before XA903 was finally retired in March 1979 as the last Vulcan B.1 to fly. Its nose survives at the Wellesbourne Wartime Museum.

A helping hand

An early modification earmarked for the Vulcan B.1 was the application of rocket-assisted take-off (RATO) – in fact all three V-Bombers were at one stage expected to acquire this facility. RATO gear would permit the bombers to launch at their maximum weights from shorter length runways or, alternatively, in tropical conditions (where take-off performance might be degraded by high ambient temperatures). For the Vulcan the installation would comprise two 8,000lb (36.6kN) thrust de Havilland D.Spe.4A Spectre motors; these could be jettisoned and would be attached underneath the bomber's wings.

In May 1959 B.1 XA889 was allotted as a RATO trials aircraft, the programme opening with a set of dumping trials of the rocket motor's High-Test Peroxide (HTP) fuel. These were held at Woodford to assess the likelihood of the airframe being contaminated by the discarded fuel. The next stage would be the fitting of dummy RATO nacelles for jettison trials, and then ground firing would be concluded at A&AEE Boscombe Down. A total of 25 test firings were conducted at the de Havilland Engine company's Hatfield facility using a large Vulcan structural test specimen, but the Vulcan RATO programme

A view of the Olympus 593 test bed performing at the September 1968 Farnborough.
Terry Panopalis

The Rolls-Royce/ Turbo-Union RB.199 engine mounted in its 'Tornado Fuselage' housing on the underside of XA903. This view was taken at the SBAC Farnborough Show in September 1974.
Tony Buttler

was cancelled in August 1959, despite 65 modification kits having already been ordered.

'Hands-off' development

An automatic landing capability for the V-Force was to be introduced on Vulcan and Handley Page Victor B.2s, and development work for the Vulcan

B.2's Mk.10B autopilot lasted several years. Integrating the original Mk.10 autopilot with the bomber's existing Navigation and Bombing System began with XA894. This equipment was then fitted into B.1 XA899 for trials conducted from A&AEE Boscombe Down and RAE Bedford (Thurleigh) under the control of the Blind ❷❯❯

The B.1 XA889 was selected to serve as the RATO trials aircraft, but this programme was never completed.
Tony Buttler

Landing Experimental Unit, the trials continuing from February 1959. A first fully automatic landing was achieved at Thurleigh on December 22, 1959, using a modified Mk.10A unit, and then a Mk.10B was installed in XA899 in September 1960.

Official clearance trials of the Mk.10B autopilot and the associated Military Flight System Mk.1B were finally underway in May 1963, using the first B.2 XH533. Many automatic landings were performed both at Boscombe and Bedford, but the requirement for an Automatic Landing System or 'Autoland' for Vulcan and Victor was then cancelled in 1967. However, by then the work carried out by both V-types had laid the ground for Autoland systems that followed in civilian airliners.

Tuning the delta

Another programme involving a Vulcan was the 'Take-Off Director' trial. This research programme was part of development work for the Concorde supersonic transport, and in particular for approving its slender delta wing. For Concorde, a totally new and difficult problem was the certification of the airliner's slim delta. Previously all civil airliners had been certified on their stalling speed, but this delta did not stall like a conventional surface. So, instead of the stall speed, a feature called the 'zero rate of climb speed' was set as the new reference point. However, a worry was if Concorde lost an engine when flying at this speed.

An engine flameout on a

This view shows Concorde Olympus XA903 with the special spray rig, and its piping fitted beneath the forward fuselage for water and ice ingestion tests. Water could be sprayed in at different concentrations with the nacelle's de-icing system running. A tail cone has been refitted and the first flight with the grid installed was made on March 12, 1971. Bristol Siddeley via Terry Panopalis

conventional airliner at its stalling speed would not make much difference, but at the zero rate of climb speed, Concorde's nose would have to be lowered and the drag reduced immediately to enable it to accelerate to the new and rather higher zero rate of climb speed for the three remaining engines. This problem was overcome by the creation of the Concorde Take-Off Director instrument or TOD, which would provide pilots with an easy guide to maintaining the optimum climb performance after an engine had been lost when flying at low speed.

Early B.1 XA890 flew the TOD

development and demonstration programme, which started in 1964 and was conducted by the Aerodynamics Research Flight (Aero Flight) at RAE Bedford; by then XA890 had already been used for radio, radar and armament trials. The Vulcan's normal right-hand seat flight instruments were replaced by a panel that closely resembled that of a Hawker Siddeley Trident airliner. After around 100 hours' development flying by test pilots, airline pilots were taken aloft to experience the new equipment in operation. A typical demonstration would start with a

normal take-off to get them used to the Vulcan, but on the second take-off the RAE aviator would cut a throttle on the initial climb out. The civilian pilot could then see how the TOD would immediately take the Vulcan to the new correct attitude and speed. Two and even three throttles could be closed during a take-off but the TOD would put the Vulcan into a climb at around 200ft/min (61m/min) even on one engine. Airframe XA890 was one of the few Vulcans to retain the original straight wing leading edge – and was perfect for the TOD programme. ◖▬

Vulcan B.1 XA903, the RB.199 test bed, about to make the final landing of its career, at RAE Farnborough on March 1, 1979. RAE via Terry Panopalis

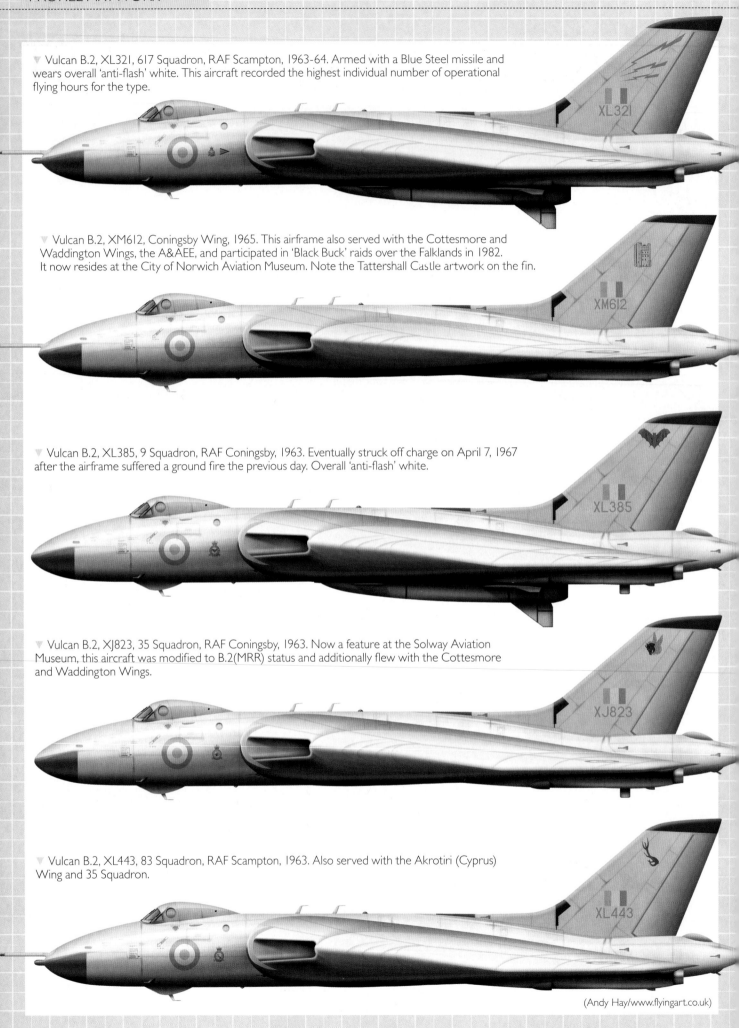

▼ Vulcan B.2, XL321, 617 Squadron, RAF Scampton, 1963-64. Armed with a Blue Steel missile and wears overall 'anti-flash' white. This aircraft recorded the highest individual number of operational flying hours for the type.

▼ Vulcan B.2, XM612, Coningsby Wing, 1965. This airframe also served with the Cottesmore and Waddington Wings, the A&AEE, and participated in 'Black Buck' raids over the Falklands in 1982. It now resides at the City of Norwich Aviation Museum. Note the Tattershall Castle artwork on the fin.

▼ Vulcan B.2, XL385, 9 Squadron, RAF Coningsby, 1963. Eventually struck off charge on April 7, 1967 after the airframe suffered a ground fire the previous day. Overall 'anti-flash' white.

▼ Vulcan B.2, XJ823, 35 Squadron, RAF Coningsby, 1963. Now a feature at the Solway Aviation Museum, this aircraft was modified to B.2(MRR) status and additionally flew with the Cottesmore and Waddington Wings.

▼ Vulcan B.2, XL443, 83 Squadron, RAF Scampton, 1963. Also served with the Akrotiri (Cyprus) Wing and 35 Squadron.

(Andy Hay/www.flyingart.co.uk)

SQUADRON AND UNIT LIST

9 Squadron
Vulcan B.2: 4.62 to 4.82; Coningsby, Cottesmore (from 11.64), Akrotiri (Cyprus 2.69), Waddington (1.75)

12 Squadron
Vulcan B.2: 7.62 to 12.67; Coningsby, Cottesmore (11.64)

27 Squadron
Vulcan B.2: 4.61 to 3.72; Scampton

Vulcan B.2(MRR)/SR.2: 11.73 to 3.82; Scampton

35 Squadron
Vulcan B.2: 1.63 to 2.82; Coningsby, Cottesmore (11.64), Akrotiri (1.69), Scampton (1.75)

44 Squadron
Vulcan B.1/B.1A: 8.60 to 11.67; Waddington

Vulcan B.2: 11.67 to 12.82; Waddington

50 Squadron
Vulcan B.1: 8.61 to 11.66; Waddington

Vulcan B.2: 12.65 to 3.84; Waddington

Vulcan K.2: 4.82 to 3.84; Waddington

A B.2, XM575, landing at Waddington. The vertical fin carries both 44 Squadron and Waddington Wing badges.
Key Collection

83 Squadron
Vulcan B.1: 7.57 to 8.60; Waddington

Vulcan B.2: 12.60 to 8.69; Scampton

101 Squadron
Vulcan B.1/B.1A: 10.57 to 1.68; Finningley, Waddington (6.61)

Vulcan B.2: 1.68 to 8.82; Waddington

617 Squadron
Vulcan B.1: 5.58 to 7.61; Scampton

Vulcan B.2: 9.61 to 12.81; Scampton

230 Operational Conversion Unit
Vulcan B.1: 8.56 onwards; Waddington

Vulcan B.2: 7.60 to 8.81; Waddington, Finningley (6.61), Scampton (12.69)

Bomber Command Development Unit
Vulcan B.1/B.1A: 6.61 to 11.66; Finningley

Vulcan B.2: 7.65 to 1.66; Finningley

4 Joint Services Trial Unit
Vulcan B.2: 12.61 to 2.64; Woomera (Edinburgh Field, Australia)

Vulcan Display Flight.
Vulcan B.2: 4.84 to 9.94; Waddington

DELTA-WING

Dr Robert Pleming FRAeS explains how he and his team put Vulcan XH558 back in the air, making it an airshow stalwart once again before its final grounding

Vulcan XH558 arrives at Eastbourne on Saturday August 11, 2012. Thomas Webers

On October 28, 2015 Avro Vulcan XH558 landed for the final time at Doncaster Sheffield Airport. Not only was she the final example to fly, but also the last airworthy all-British four-engined jet. However, the airframe's story started 56 years earlier.

Construction of XH558 commenced on Wednesday March 25, 1959; its first test flight took place 14 months later to the day, on May 25, 1960; '558 was the tenth Vulcan B.2 to be completed, the previous nine being used for trials and test work. Test pilot Tony Blackman flew XH558 from Woodford to RAF Waddington, Lincolnshire on July 1 that year, as the first B.2 to enter RAF service.

The aircraft then moved to RAF Finningley, South Yorkshire in 1961,

serving with 230 Operational Conversion Unit (OCU), training Vulcan aircrew for squadron service. Between 1968 and August 1973, the aircraft served with 44, 50 and 101 Squadrons at Waddington, before being converted to maritime radar reconnaissance (MRR) standard, remaining in this role with 27 Squadron at Lincolnshire's RAF Scampton until March 1982, when she was returned to Waddington's 44 Squadron. With the outbreak of the Falklands conflict in April 1982, XH558 was converted again, this time to a stop-gap tanker version, designated K.2. Although '558 took no part in the campaign, Sqn Ldr Martin Withers DFC, who captained Vulcan XM607 and carried out the first 'Black Buck' bombing raid on Port Stanley airfield, was chief pilot for most

of '558's second display flying career.

By 1984 the Vulcan fleet had been retired from RAF service, the final official sortie being flown on March 26, 1984 when XH560 carried out a refuelling mission. Soon after, XH558 was flown to RAF Marham, Norfolk, on September 17, 1984 to see out her final days on the station fire dump. Two aircraft were to be kept in service for public displays: Vulcan XL426 continued on the Vulcan Display Team, and XH560 was initially chosen as the back-up aircraft until it was found that XH558 had more flying hours remaining and was duly rescued from the dump. XL426 gave its last display with the team in June 1986 and was then replaced by XH558, which made its airshow debut just two weeks earlier at RAF Mildenhall, Suffolk, on

ED PHOENIX

May 24, 1986.

XH558 remained with the renamed Vulcan Display Flight until September 20, 1992 when she flew her final display in RAF hands at Cranfield's Dreamflight airshow. Defence budget cuts at the end of the Cold war – the so-called 'Peace Dividend' – meant there was no funding available to keep her flying. Despite a huge petition to save the aircraft, in February 1993 the Ministry of Defence put XH558 up for auction. With the aircraft's subsequent sale to C Walton Ltd, the last Vulcan left the RAF, flying into Bruntingthorpe Airfield, near Lutterworth, Leicestershire, on March 23,1993 for what everyone thought at the time was her final landing.

Start of the return

Having followed the fortunes of XH558 during her final years in the RAF as one of my favourite display aircraft, I decided to look more deeply into the history of the Vulcan, and was amazed by the leap in aviation technology in the immediate post-World War Two years that the aircraft represents. Conscious of the massive public support for XH558, and aware that the machine was retired before its time, in early 1997 I resolved to explore the feasibility of returning XH558 to flight.

The initial challenge was to discover whether the civil aviation regulatory regime would allow an ex-military aircraft that heavy, powerful and complex to fly. The key to a positive response was to gain the formal support of the then British Aerospace (now BAE Systems), which had inherited design responsibility from A V Roe. With the aid of a project plan built by a small, expert team I had formed to investigate the feasibility of a return to flight, and the enthusiasm ⏩

The engineering team underwent Vulcan technical training at Marshall Aerospace, Cambridge, before on-aircraft work could commence.
Robert Pleming

Members of the engineering team at Bruntingthorpe as work starts on the restoration in August 2005. Vulcan Operating Company

Many components and systems were sent to specialist firms for overhaul – the nose undercarriage leg here is at aerospace engineering specialist Kearsley Airways. Robert Pleming

of some senior British Aerospace personnel, this support was granted in May 1999 – theoretically, the Vulcan could fly again.

In September 1999, a three-day Project Definition Workshop was held, with design representatives from BAE Systems and our retained Engineering Authority, Marshall of Cambridge Aerospace. The outcome was the specification for a detailed technical survey to determine whether there were any insurmountable technical issues with a return to flight – not the least of which was to find a way of

extending the airframe fatigue life – and the scope of the restoration work needed to place XH558 back in the air. The latter turned out to be a 'Major Service' – the most in-depth form of Vulcan maintenance – with some additional inspections because of her age and time since the last flight.

By Spring 2000, the aircraft had undergone the technical survey, which verified that its airframe and systems could be restored to full airworthiness at reasonable cost. In addition, the availability of an almost complete library of original documentation and

design data, and several hundred tons of spares – including, vitally, eight zero-time Rolls-Royce Olympus 202 turbojet engines – meant that in practical terms the restoration to flight was feasible.

Several hundred Original Equipment Manufacturers who made the thousands of individual Vulcan systems and components were painstakingly sought and contacted – many had been taken over – and each one agreed to assess and service their components as required. This major commitment meant that, with the appropriate Civil Aviation Authority (CAA) regulatory approvals and technical support by BAE Systems, work could start on the return to flight.

It was already clear from project costings that funding of some £3.5m would be required. This was a mammoth task, one not easily undertaken by engineers, but we had gained the voluntary support of Mrs Felicity Irwin, an experienced fundraiser. Many supporters from the public came forward, and promises were made, but with millions to be secured and the clock ticking, it was apparent that a major financial backer was vital. The Heritage Lottery Fund (HLF) was the obvious funding body for such a valuable British heritage asset: a grant application was made in March 2002, but sadly was rejected in late November that year. Following a vigorous reaction from the public to this decision, the HLF provided specific and detailed feedback on how our application could be enhanced to emphasise the long-term public advantages.

This revised application was submitted in May 2003, including additional public educational benefits. Despite openly having a policy not to support projects whose aim is the restoration of aircraft to flight, in December 2003, HLF Trustees announced to my team and our supporters that they had made an "exceptional decision" to earmark a grant of £2.5m for the project.

On June 23, 2004, the Heritage Lottery Fund confirmed it would award £2,734,000 to the Vulcan to the Sky project, with the rest to be raised by ourselves. The scope of the grant included not just the restoration of XH558 to flight, but the provision of

public access to her on the ground, and the creation of educational activities to tell the story of the Cold War – and to provide lessons for schoolchildren in technology, engineering and maths based on the aircraft and its operation. Over the coming months, details were thrashed out and contracts signed and, in February 2005, the HLF gave the go-ahead for the purchase of the aircraft from C Walton Ltd by the Vulcan to the Sky Trust, a Registered Charity, and the commencement of restoration. The first task was the recruitment and training of the technical team needed to work on the aircraft – a total of some 18 people, spread across the aircraft trade skills of airframe, propulsion, electrics and avionics. A detailed 13-week Vulcan technical training course was devised and delivered to the technicians, turning them from trade generalists into Vulcan specialists. Restoration work finally started in August 2005.

Devil in the detail

Initial project planning estimated that the restoration would last for 14 months and consume about 50,000 man-hours. Because of their experience in one-off aircraft projects and their CAA accreditations,

engineering control of the project was passed to Marshall of Cambridge Aerospace. The restoration was to have four phases: a detailed 'Inspection' of the aircraft for faults, followed by 'Rectification' of those faults. During this period, hundreds of systems components were overhauled and returned in time for the 'Recovery' of the aircraft to the correct configuration for flight. 'Test' followed, first on the ground and then, with ticks in all the boxes, the aircraft was to be released to its aircrew for its trial flights.

In preparation for the inspection, virtually everything that could be removed from the aircraft was removed, requiring a major logistical exercise to track each one of these valuable components. Inspection of the aircraft's structure was very detailed; every aspect of the structure was examined visually, and various non-destructive techniques were employed to discover any underlying problems, including X-ray (more than 450 X-ray pictures were taken), ultrasound, eddy current and borescope. Numerous minor repairable faults were found, including skin and rib cracks, missing rivets and corrosion, but none so significant as to generate serious concern.

A structural fatigue life extension modification on the rear spar of each wing was embodied; this involved removing the main bolts that secure the bottom of the wing spar to the centre section of the aircraft and adding a steel reinforcing plate – a risky task because, if a mistake was made, the aircraft would have been grounded.

The complete hydraulic, pneumatic and oxygen systems were removed for inspection and overhaul. All flexible pipes and seals were replaced, which was a significant and expensive effort on its own. The Vulcan has many ⟫

All components that could be removed for overhaul, were removed – this is the starter from an engine. Vulcan Operating Company

XH558 in the hangar at Bruntingthorpe in July 2006 as the restoration gathers pace. Vulcan Operating Company

August 31, 2006: XH558 rolls-out of her hangar for the first time since 1999, to the news that the project could continue, owing to many people's generosity. SAC Ben Stevenson

critical systems powered by electricity, including the flying controls, so the integrity of the aircraft's wiring and electrical supplies is vital: an early decision – the aircraft would be rewired, this in itself a major exercise.

Twelve months after work started on the project, it was clear that tasks were taking much longer than initially estimated, the result being that manpower costs were rocketing. Not only were jobs taking longer, because of the learning curve associated with work on this unique aircraft, but some problems were more difficult than anticipated. For instance, significant corrosion was found on magnesium alloy skins and structure of the flying control surfaces, requiring rebuild of these units. Another example: it was

known that some 47 of the aircraft's original systems would not be needed in our operation of XH558 under civilian regulations, ranging from the analogue Navigation and Bombing System to the crew's ration heaters. Late in the day, it was decided that each system's deletion would require its own safety case, needing extensive and unplanned design analysis.

However, a major media-led campaign in August 2006 raised the £1.2m required to complete the project, including a significant donation of £500,000 from British businessman the late Sir Jack Hayward.

Recovery and Testing

With aircraft structural rectification nearing completion in the Spring of

2007, attention focused on refitting the aircraft's systems. One by one the components removed for overhaul were reattached: radome, ejection seats, canopy, landing gear, wheels and brakes, fuel tanks and pumps, the engines (each with its attached constant speed drive and 60kVA alternator), elevons and rudders, powered flying control units and motors, artificial feel units, yaw damper, auto-mach trimmer, undercarriage doors and hydraulic rams, air conditioning system, cockpit instruments, the fifth engine in the airborne auxiliary power pack… the list went on.

Apart from modern avionics, the restored XH558 is almost completely authentic, with just a few material substitutions being required because of the unavailability of the originals. The safety case for flying the aircraft was based on the in-service safety record of the Vulcan fleet; it was therefore vital that XH558's specification was as near as possible to the original airframes, with each deviation requiring a separate risk assessment.

With much of the recovery complete, ground testing started in early summer 2007 with the application of electrical power – initially the 24v DC vital supply, followed by the 200V 400Hz 3-phase AC and subsidiary supplies. One by one the various systems were put through documented procedures to ensure correct set-up and operation. Possibly the most time-consuming and messy was the fuel

Beagle Aerospace in Christchurch, Dorset rebuilt XH558's elevons and rudder – this is the rudder being re-skinned. Robert Pleming

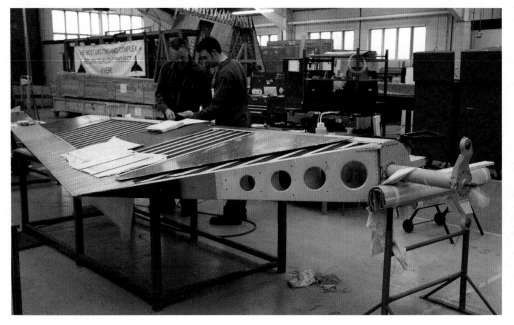

system, with its 14 fuel tanks (holding almost 8,579 imp gal in total), 29 fuel pumps and associated pipe work. On the Vulcan, fuel is used to maintain the fore-and-aft centre-of-gravity in the correct position, so it is vital this system works correctly.

With recovery completed in August 2007, it was time to light the fires! On an airfield 'pan', one by one, the four new Rolls-Royce Olympus 202 engines were started and, on test, performed perfectly – more than 25 years since they were last test-run.

It would be wrong to imply there were no problems found during testing – there were – but that is what the process is all about. Two faults were spectacular, both arising from component failures in the 3,000psi hydraulic system. But all 'snags' were fixed and, by that October, XH558 was ready to move under her own power for the first time since the start of the project. Slow and fast taxiing tests followed, including deployment of the brake parachute.

Finally, after 26 months, more than 100,000 man-hours and £7m spent, a restored Vulcan XH558 was ready to fly again. Thursday October 18 was a perfect day for flying, and in front of the expectant crowd of those who had made it happen, XH558 roared down the runway and leapt into the air. There were shouts, cheers, and

tears of joy; so much effort by so many people. I myself felt awed, stunned, but remember thinking 'I can't relax until she's safely back on the ground'. After a full 30-minute flight, our test flight crew brought her back to the airfield for a perfect landing – we had done it. Safely. The return of the Vulcan to the air prompted national media coverage, a British aviation achievement the like of which had not been seen for many years.

Challenges

Despite its size, the Vulcan features a straightforward design, the main complexity being in the original valve-based analogue electronic navigation systems. The materials used, while modern in their day, were latterly discovered to have unsatisfactory corrosion modes such as exfoliation and stress corrosion cracking. Fortunately for XH558, because of good stewardship, this was not too much of a problem. However, supply of identical materials for repairs did pose challenges, and while Imperial sizes can still be found in the USA, substitution by newer metric measurement materials was often required, needing design approval. ◆》

Recovering the Vulcan to its full configuration included refitting the overhauled elevon powered flying control units. Robert Pleming

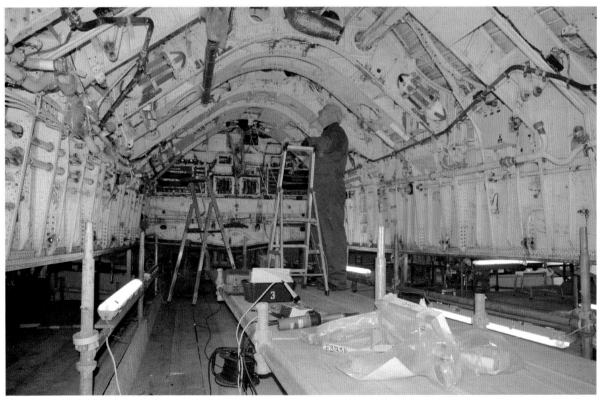

Rewiring the aircraft with bomb bay cable runs. Robert Pleming

Vulcan XH558 bows out of the Royal International Air Tattoo on Sunday July 19, 2015, escorted by the Red Arrows. Robert Pleming

The major challenges in the restoration, however, arose during the overhaul of various critical systems such as the powered flying control units, and the chassis-mounted fuel systems for the engines. The companies responsible for these sub-assemblies had luckily retained the original drawings and testing gear, but not necessarily the skills – several firms found themselves re-hiring retirees just to work on XH558's systems.

One major update was made, to replace the aircraft's 1950s military flight systems with modern equipment, not just because the originals were deemed unreliable and unmaintainable at reasonable cost, but also to ensure compliance with current Air Navigation Order requirements. A new 'Horizontal Situation Indicator' (aka Compass) and Artificial Horizon was provided for the pilots, with additional navigational equipment such as GPS, transponder and height-encoding altimeter – each requiring new aerials to be installed.

Aircraft Operations

Following a series of further test flights required to iron out minor problems with the aircraft's new avionics suite, XH558 was finally awarded her 'Permit to Fly' on July 3, 2008. Two days later, she flew her first display for an enthralled public at the RAF Waddington Airshow. Over the eight years of her second flying life, XH558 flew for more than 344 hours in 229 sorties, in front of 15 million-plus people, at over 200 events around the UK and Europe. She has been seen by countless more as she has transited around the country; in all that, '558 proved to be remarkably trouble free. To keep the aircraft in top condition, there was a rigorous servicing schedule: regular checks on the engines, landing gear and critical structure are driven by flying hour milestones. Every winter, the aircraft underwent a thorough inspection and lubrication; critical components that have a calendar life, such as the ejection seats, fire extinguisher bottles and oxygen regulators, were overhauled or replaced. This is not cheap; to keep this 'one-aircraft airline' going costed around £2m per annum, for 40-50 flying hours.

Retirement

At the start of 2015, I received a letter jointly signed by BAE Systems, Rolls-Royce and Marshall Aerospace, announcing the withdrawal of their design and engineering support at the end of that year, citing the loss of skills to continue. Despite a vigorous rear-guard action, we could not get them to change their minds – 2015 was to be XH558's final flying year. She went out in style, flying 50% more hours than in previous years, with her final sorties being tours of the UK.

It is worth noting that the enthusiasm shown by the original manufacturers for the project in 2000 appears to

Press call following the debut test flight on October 18, 2007, left-to-right: Alistair McDicken (captain/test pilot), David Thomas (chief pilot), Barry Masefield (AEO), Kevin 'Taff' Stone (crew chief), Robert Pleming (VTST chief executive), Andrew Edmondson (engineering director). Jon Windover

have been overtaken by the risk-averse corporate governance of today. I feel this culture of risk avoidance means that if were we looking to start restoring XH558 to flight now, the project would in all probability not get off the ground.

Unlike modern commercial airliners, which are built to a damage-tolerant design policy, the Vulcan was designed to a 'safe life' principle: XH558 had a well-defined limit to her structural fatigue life, beyond which she cannot fly. At the end of 2015, there was sufficient airframe and engine life available to be airborne for perhaps two more seasons, but the end was indeed nigh.

Vulcan XH558 is now being maintained in ground-running condition at Doncaster Sheffield Airport, with plans to make her the centrepiece of a major new tourist attraction, the Vulcan Experience, where visitors will be able to hear the story of XH558's history, her restoration to flight and the part played by the RAF's V-Force aircraft in preserving the peace during the Cold War. The Vulcan Experience will include a National V-Force Memorial, honouring those who served during the Cold War.

Central to the attraction will be an exciting new Green Technology Hub, which will feature explanations of the reasons for climate change, and in particular, aviation's contribution,

For his work on the Vulcan project, in May 2016 Dr Robert Pleming was presented with the Air League's Scott Farnie Medal by its patron, HRH the Duke of Edinburgh… who flew in Vulcan XA900 in 1958! Beaumont Photography

descriptions of the engineering solutions being devised to counteract climate change, and demonstrations of the technologies being developed to eliminate its causes. The Green Technology Hub will offer hope by showing there are solutions for more environmentally friendly aircraft design and the engines that power them, but also inspire the future generations to pursue careers in aerospace and engineering.

The success of the Vulcan project was in my view due to three things: the determination and perseverance of the small team that made it happen; the enormous support coming from the public's desire to see the Vulcan fly again; and the assistance from many, many firms in the British aviation

industry. Sincere thanks must go to all these constituencies, from everyone who has experienced the feeling of pride upon seeing this marvellous example of British engineering heritage in the sky.

The restoration and aerial display of Vulcan XH558 has demonstrably confirmed that engineering heritage, especially of the working variety is able to communicate with the public on several levels: telling the historical story, exemplifying engineering innovation, inspiring the young, and generating pride in successful endeavour.

For further information, and details on how to support the Vulcan to the Sky Trust's new initiative, Operation Safeguard, please visit: www. vulcantothesky.org

XH558 returns to the public, who wanted to see the aircraft so much… debuting here for her second display career at the RAF Waddington Airshow on July 5, 2008. This photograph was taken from the rear gunner's position of BBMF Avro Lancaster PA474. Mark Arnold

BLACK BUCK: 1982

Gp Capt (ret) Alastair Montgomery was detachment commander at Ascension Islands for the Vulcan raids during the Falklands conflict. Here, he provides a retrospective view of the type's part in the campaign

Vulcans XM607 and XM612 arrive at Ascension on April 29, 1982. The front of the ALQ-101 ECM pod is just visible under the starboard wing of '612.
Both RAF via T Panopalis

The Falklands War is further away from us now than World War Two was in 1982. Since then, the technology of air warfare has changed dramatically. Vulcan missions in '82 probably had a more direct lineage to those flown by Lancaster, Stirling and Halifax crews in 1945 than to the stand-off and unseen attacks flown by Typhoon pilots today. No different, however, is the attitude and determination of the aircrews groundcrews, and support teams.

There are numerous books, articles, films, views and opinions on the

Falklands campaign and Operation Black Buck, many by individuals who did not speak directly to crews and got no nearer the South Atlantic than the Isle of Wight. This short piece is not definitive and, in honesty, some of the authors derided know more about the Vulcan than I ever did. We are all a little more stooped now and not just from time spent squeezing into our various seats in 'Avro's Finest'.

A tense spring

In early 1982, the Vulcan force was part way through its drawdown to final disbandment. At its peak, the organisation comprised more than 70 Vulcan B.2s operating with nine

squadrons in the nuclear free-fall or Blue Steel missile role. By April 1982, four units were still in service, IX (B), 50, 10, and 44 (Rhodesia) Squadrons with disbandment dates already

announced. However, there was no atmosphere of 'wind down'; instead, there was a sense that, while it was the end of an era, plenty of good flying was to be had while the going and weather were good. For some years, the aircraft had suffered fatigue problems and had to be flown more gently than many of us wished, to conserve life. With less than a year to go, our low-level trips were more adventurous – even if this information did not always excite the engineers or the senior management, the latter usually known as the station commander.

Out of the blue, at least as the UK Foreign Office was concerned, ➠

The patch worn by Vulcan aircrew based at Ascension Island.
All Alastair Montgomery unless stated

The view from a Victor while it refuels a Vulcan. Note the small under-wing fairings indicating this is a Skybolt aircraft – but before the addition of the 'Pye Pylons' to carry ECM pods/AGM-45 Shrike. Via Alastair Montgomery

Argentina's General Galtieri and his colleagues decided to improve their domestic popularity by waving the Malvinas flag and whipping up anti-British sentiment. In the UK, the political aftermath of the invasion was swift, and an early decision was made to form a task force to undertake what became known as Operation Corporate. Inevitably, given the distances involved, this was to be led by the Royal Navy. The Task Force was to sail as soon as possible while much of the logistics would be sorted out en route and principally at Ascension Island, lying half-way between Africa and South America.

Vulcans called up

The Chief of the Air Staff, Sir Michael Beetham, commenced an immediate review of what RAF assets should be involved. Clearly, the transport and maritime forces would be required from the outset. Finding a platform that could be used to attack the Argentine forces was more difficult. It was decided that the Vulcan was an option, should be considered and training started immediately. Thus, the action moved to RAF Waddington in Lincolnshire.

Despite the fortuitous position of Ascension Island, even the long-range Vulcan would have to refuel in the air to manage a round trip. However, no Vulcan pilots were current in air-to-air refuelling – indeed, it was 13 years since a Vulcan had undertaken this task, which we had been led to believe was the strict preserve of intensely skilled fighter pilots. The priority was to select three crews. Four crews had recently completed the renowned Red Flag exercises in Nevada, USA, and thus were the most experienced at nocturnal low-level flying and two were selected, those led by Flt Lt Martin Withers and me, Sqn Ldr Alastair Montgomery. The third crew chosen was that of the irrepressible

A Twin Shrike Carrier with said stores attached. The AGM-45 anti-radar missile was a USAF weapon, at that time usually more at home on an F-4G Phantom II 'Wild Weasel' aircraft. Key Collection

and determined Sqn Ldr John Reeve.
A fourth team, led by Sqn Ldr Neil
McDougall, was added later.

Training and airframes

Three Victor air-to-air refuelling
instructors (AARIs) were selected,
using the straw procedure, to teach
us the dark art. Each had a short
simulator trip and the next day off
we set. At this point, there was very
little sense that we might go off to do

The wing pylon
(so-called 'Pye
Pylon') following
modifications to
make it more
aerodynamic.
Via Alastair
Montgomery

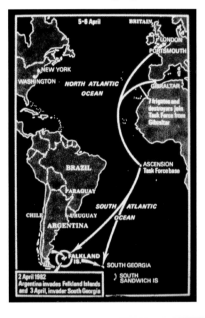

anything whatsoever – and the exact
whatsoever had not yet been decided.
Consequently, there was a reasonably
relaxed atmosphere, which lasted until
we got behind our first Victor tanker.
No-one paid much attention to the
fact that we were launching with a
stranger in our right-hand seat to teach
us to refuel an aircraft in which he'd
never sat previously.

We all rendezvoused with a single
tanker, which allowed us to watch
each other's high jinks. The AARIs
found the Vulcan delightful and easier
to handle than the Victor. There were
mixed fortunes on the first attempts,

although Martin made a contact
before his AARI. From the Vulcan,
it was impossible to see both probe
and drogue in the latter stages of the
approach, which led to a few misses.
The next day (everything is easier
the next day) we gradually settled
down and made decent progress. It
was quite possible if you overcooked
things to get the refuelling basket
banging off the side of the cabin, which
was not particularly dangerous but
did get the rear crews quite excited.
Within two days we were let loose on
our own before hitting a major snag:
the probes leaked. We could all >>

A period graphic
showing military
movements on
April 2, 1982.

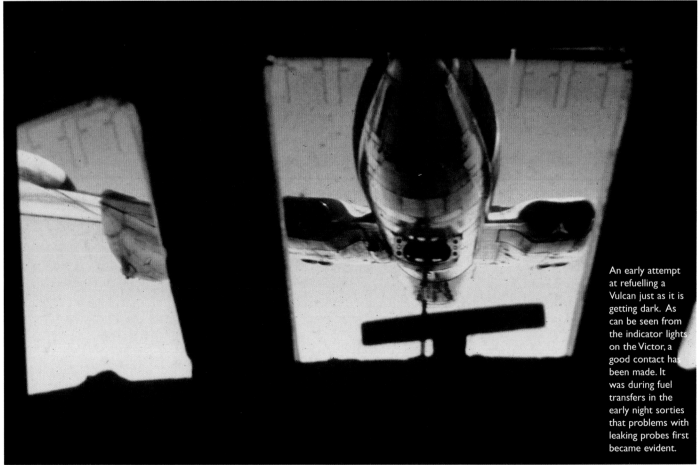

An early attempt
at refuelling a
Vulcan just as it is
getting dark. As
can be seen from
the indicator lights
on the Victor, a
good contact has
been made. It
was during fuel
transfers in the
early night sorties
that problems with
leaking probes first
became evident.

View from a cockpit on the runway at Ascension Island. This is inside a C-130 but clearly shows the rather interesting hill to the right. Vulcan and Victor crews avoided worrying about it by only taking off in the dark! Via Alastair Montgomery

attack, much needed to be done. For starters, the conventional bombing system had to be reactivated. Seven Store Carriers for 1,000lb bombs were put into the bomb bay and a 90-Way Bomb Control Unit was plumbed into the navigator radar's station. Electronic countermeasures (ECM) protection was required. Imaginative local engineering meant a pylon was fixed to each wing, on hard points designed to carry the Skybolt missile, and Westinghouse AN/ALQ-101D ECM pods were borrowed from the Buccaneer force.

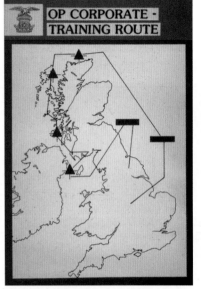

▶ The final UK training route for the Vulcan crews before they deployed to Ascension Island.

cope with this by day – but by night it was proving just too difficult and, without solving this, we were going nowhere. Initial attempts at a solution were mechanical and various devices were fitted to probe and windscreen to deflect the leaking fuel, none of which did any good whatsoever. Next, us clever pilots asked for vortex generators to be attached to the nose to aerate and therefore evaporate the fuel – which proved as much use as the deflectors. Finally, as is now well

known, by stripping down a Vulcan probe and comparing it to that from a Victor, it was found internal shims had been miss-fitted. Ground crew 1- Aircrew 0.

While the pilots jousted with the baskets, Wg Cdr Simon Baldwin, OC 44 (Rhodesia) Squadron, had been put in charge of operational planning and selecting the most suitable target. It was quickly decided this would be the runway at Stanley. To achieve even the likelihood of launching such an

◀ Most of the Victor fleet on the ramp at Ascension. Note that all wear tactical camouflage rather than the Hemp and Light Aircraft Grey scheme applied later in their RAF service. Via Alastair Montgomery

refuelling and back to Waddington. Additionally, seven live 1000lb retarded bomb drops were carried out on Garvie Island off the north coast of Scotland. During the run in to the day drop (in extremely turbulent conditions just off the Thurso cliffs) sheep were spotted on the top of the island. So impressed were they with our abilities, they did not even bother looking up! We then bombed in the dark to fool the sheep.

The plan

While the crews trained, Wg Cdr Baldwin was considering the targeting profile including the Argentine threats. These latter concerns were not insignificant. The Argentinians had been sold Oerlikon anti-aircraft cannon by the Swiss; Roland missiles by the French and even Tigercat missiles by, er, the British. These all created a significant menace and more problems for the good wing commander who was probably working harder than the aircrew. The crews had initially expected to attack at low level from the north using the shielding of the sea lochs around Stanley – after all, this was the core of many years' training. Attacking aircraft would have to over-fly the target and, if detected, could expect a lively reception. However, releasing 1000lb retarded bombs from around 300ft would have very little penetrative effect on the runway. Consequently, at a late stage the plan was altered to a low-level direct run-in, with a pop-up to a height to be ⦿»

Twenty-one 1,000lb bombs on Seven Store Carriers being loaded at Ascension Island; keen-eyed readers will spot the chalked 'good wishes' from the groundcrews.

Groundcrew start the task of loading 1,000lb free-fall bombs. Alastair Montgomery's navigator radar, David Stenhouse, is on the aircraft door.

The long-range navigation system was resolved by fitting Litton Carousel inertial navigation (INAS) kits taken from redundant civilian VC10s. The first night these were flown, a helpful engineer from the Aeroplane and Armament Experimental Establishment at Boscombe Down remarked that proper trials would take six to nine months. Some six hours later we were able to report that it worked just fine!

Crew training progressed in a little over ten days to a composite sortie, which consisted of refuelling over the North Sea; low level over the Western Isles – where the terrain is remarkably similar to that of the Falkland Islands; an attack at Jurby range off the Isle of Man with practice bombs; another

A rather dramatic view of the take-off hazard on Ascension Island. For a few days in May 1982, this was the busiest runway in the world!

A very busy Ascension Island ramp on April 30, 1982. It is worth noting the presence of a USAF C-141 Starlifter on the left.

decided after detailed consideration of the threats, thus increasing survivability and the likelihood of cratering the runway. This late change of tactics provided little opportunity to practise the new profile.

To bring a long story and a short time-frame into perspective, between first being told we 'might be required for something' and deploying two Vulcans to Ascension Island were 13 days (and nights) of intensive flying; 13 sorties/38 hours, 20 of which were in the dark. And, perhaps more significant than the crews' efforts were the remarkable achievements of the engineers and groundcrew who had to complete an enormous range of tasks: reconfiguring the aircraft systems for conventional bombing; fitting INAS; re-installing a working AAR system; designing, building and fitting two pylons to carry a 'jamming' pod and, later, the AGM-45 Shrike anti-radar missile. This list does not do their efforts justice.

There were mistakes and surprisingly few mishaps. The latter included a lost probe nozzle, followed by fuel spilling over a windscreen and into engine intakes and a double engine flameout. A principle concern would prove to be rate of fuel burn. Prior to deployment, each team had never flown in a formation of more than two aircraft: one Vulcan and one Victor tanker, which provided inadequate fuel data. However, time ran out and, on April 28, after one cancellation due to lack of sufficient tankers for the transit, two Vulcans deployed to Wideawake airfield on Ascension Island while the groundcrew, essential spares and the third Vulcan crew deployed by VC10 and C-130.

Ascension Island

What a remarkable place and, without it, the plans to re-capture the Falkland Islands could not have gone ahead. It was vital to the re-supply of the fleet; as a last land-training ground for troops and, of course, as an airhead for Victor, Nimrod and Hercules operations. Ascension had been established as a British naval

The ramp at Ascension during the conflict, with most of the Victor fleet in view. The Nimrod MR.2s display their refuelling probes, and two Harrier GR.3s from 3 (F) Squadron are fitted with probes and armed with AIM-9L missiles prior to their long transit to the fleet.
M·F·C James

detachment during Napoleon's exile on St Helena. It was utilised in both world wars as a naval outpost and, during World War Two, as a staging post for maritime air operations. Latterly, the Island was used as a civil and military communications base and a potential emergency landing ground for NASA's Space Shuttle. It has a long runway and, at 7 degrees south of the equator and a near constant daytime temperature of 28°C, it needs it.

Crew accommodation was spartan. The smart Nimrod personnel, first on the scene, had nabbed the only permanent accommodation. By the time the Vulcan operations crew arrived, the cupboard was bare. However, as the adjutant, a naval lieutenant commander, banned us from a location known as Two Boats, that's where we headed. A long-empty hut was the best on offer and that was shared with a Hercules crew who were, I think, still looking for the local hotel. It was basic, but good enough.

The imperative was to engage with the RAF Marham and I Group planners to work out a fuelling plan, which proved extremely challenging.

They were experts at formulating deployment trails and calculating the amount of tanker support necessary. However, new parameters were added: it was deemed essential (and popular with the crews) that, at any stage, if a failure or disaster of any kind occurred, all the aircraft could

make it back to Ascension – there were no diversions except Brazil's Rio de Janeiro in extremis. Secondly, we were struggling to calculate the Vulcan's fuel consumption. While some information would be gleaned during the transit of the aircraft to Ascension, a plan had to be put ●》

The track of the bomb line across the Stanley runway… the classic 30° cut being clearly visible.
MoD

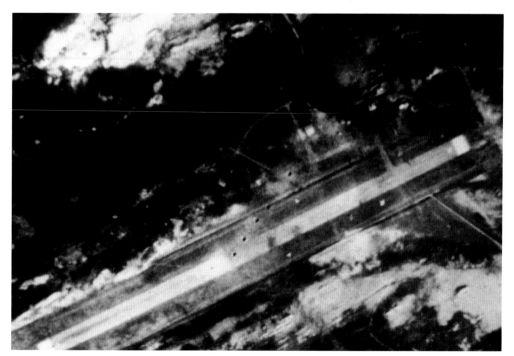

▶ Crew brief for Black Buck 7. Neil McDougall is on the extreme right. Bill Perrins is in the centre, and Alastair Montgomery and Pete Ford are next to Neil. Chris Lackman is against the tent wall. Via Alastair Montgomery

▼ Vulcan XM607 about to land at Ascension Island on the afternoon of May 1, following the Black Buck I mission of 15hrs 45mins.

in place. The Vulcan's take-off weight was going to be 10% higher than the normal maximum of 203,000lb and, accounting for the need to be able to recover to Ascension from any point, the weight would remain close to maximum throughout the journey south, thus significantly increasing fuel consumption. These calculations are normally made using the Operating Data Manual (ODM). However, for the transit height of around 28,000ft (the maximum for the heavier Victors), there were no such tables for our operating weights. The key to the mission was to be able to move enough fuel down to the South Atlantic. Graph after graph was re-drawn and extrapolated and, every time a figure was given to the Victor/1 Group team, heads were shaken in disbelief. To give perspective, at these heights, the Vulcan normally burnt 10-11,000lb of fuel. Our calculations

Martin Withers and crew touching down at Ascension Island at the end of Black Buck 1 on May 1, 1982. Readers might note that the vortex generators fitted to disperse leaking fuel (and which did not work) are still on the nose.

were panning out at 15,000lb per hour. This was the figure we went with… and, as will be seen, it was somewhat low.

We stuck with this plan and needed just about the whole Victor fleet to make it work. There were 18 sorties flown by 15 Victors, two Vulcans and one Nimrod, which used two million pounds of fuel. As the years have passed, my admiration for the Victor crews and their planners has grown enormously. Quite frankly, we, the bomber crews, knew our own job and we had enough skill to refuel and a talented rear crew to get us to the target. The mysteries of the refuelling plan were beyond us and without the talents of our individual AARIs, we would have struggled on the early sorties. The decision to include them as an integral part of our crews for the initial sorties was wise.

Execute!

On April 30, 1982, the execute order for Black Buck was given.

The final hours before launch were a flurry of engineering and crew activity, rising tension and excitement, culminating in the crew briefing in a tent which, somehow, gave the impression we should be supporting the Desert Rats. Thankfully, the AARIs understood the mysteries of the refuelling plan. Half an hour later, as

darkness fell (almost instantly on the island) I climbed up the ladder of both Vulcan cockpits to speak to the crews, but they were glad as the doors closed and they were on their own. The noise rose as engine after engine started

and Victors began to move out in line toward the runway in a sandstorm of dust. Minutes later, the volume increased to a roar as Victor followed Victor down the runway; and then, the noise changed dramatically to the ⏩

Argentine land based Exocet missiles in Stanley. This threat was part of the reason for Shrike attacks against the island radars.
Via Alastair Montgomery

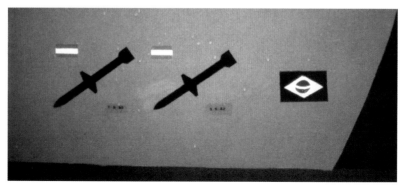

Two Shrike emblems on the nose of XM612 following two successful sorties for Neil McDougall and crew. The Brazilian flag denotes the unplanned diversion to Rio de Janeiro.
M F C James

Alastair Montgomery and Neil McDougall's crew in the purloined bungalow at Two Boats, Ascension Island. Left to right: Rod Trevaskus, Neil McDougall, Barry Smith, 'Monty', Chris Lackman, John Hathaway, Dave Castle, Pete Ford, Dick Arnott, Dave Stenhouse.
Bill Perrins

'Monty' (left) and Martin Withers transiting Ascension Island in 2007, en route to the Falklands for the 25th anniversary of the end of the war. They were travelling on what was, at the time, the oldest flying Boeing 747 in the world.

familiar Vulcan howl as John Reeve's aircraft started its roll, followed a minute later by Martin Withers and his crew. Moments later, dozens of us stood in amazement at what we had just seen: and suddenly there was silence, and just the island darkness.

The drama for Black Buck One was only just beginning. Shortly, after take-off, John Reeve's aircraft suffered a pressurisation failure and was replaced by the Withers crew, who

continued the long-haul south. The story is well documented elsewhere; however, it is no exaggeration to state that it was touch and go and lady luck lent a hand more than once. It was difficult in the conditions for crews to find each other and join with the Victors, and flares had to be used. The transit was bedevilled by thunderstorms and extreme turbulence, which dramatically extended refuelling brackets; the

Victor intended for the long haul lost a probe and time was spent re-transferring its fuel to Bob Tuxford's aircraft, which took on the long slot. The net result was that, at the end of the final transfer, both Withers and Tuxford were considerably lower on fuel than intended: in the case of the Vulcan – despite Tuxford passing more than the planned amount of fuel – 8,000lb short. And the Victor had insufficient fuel for the return to Ascension without the assistance of an emergency tanker. It was the determination, doggedness, and bravery of these two men and their crews – and the wisdom of the Tanker Team in re-launching an extra recovery wave – that ensured the success of the mission. As Vulcan '607 left the final refuelling, Martin thought: "Well, we are finally on our own now: it is up to us". At 300 miles to go, the Vulcan descended to 300ft over a dark and foggy sea to avoid the Argentine TPS-43 radar at Stanley and, at about 40 miles, it eased up to around 500ft to allow Bob Wright to check his radar before dropping back down under cover. The Vulcan then climbed to 10,000ft for the run in and release of the 21 × 1000lb bombs on their way to open the engagement… and close the runway to fast jets. As they were approaching the target the aircraft was illuminated

by an enemy Fireguard radar, which Hugh Prior, the air electronics officer, successfully jammed.

The Vulcan then faced the long flight home after rendezvousing with a Victor, vectored to them by a Nimrod. Thankfully, Bob Tuxford's Victor also returned safely. At a duration of 15hrs 45mins (and seven fuel transfers) it was, at the time, the longest bombing mission in history.

Follow up

Black Buck One was followed by further runway attacks and a change of role to anti-radar work using the Shrike missile, flown on the wing pylons. The primary crew for this mission was Sqn Ldr Neil McDougall. With the experience gained from Black Buck One, the refuelling plan was revised; tankers were sent into two distinct waves thus getting more fuel further down the South Atlantic. I flew

And, once the first Shrike missile had struck, the enemy switched off radars immediately when they detected a high-flying aircraft. The Vulcan attacks and the enormous Victor

effort in the South Atlantic had a permanent effect on the future of air warfare: AAR became mainstream. The ability to project power has changed dramatically.

Following the end of the campaign, Martin Withers and Neil McDougall were awarded the Distinguished Flying Cross; Martin's crew were all awarded Mentioned in Despatches. Bob Tuxford received the Air Force Cross.

Finally, the mission was not called Black Buck at all! Our authorisation came via a garbled line and, as Black Buck did not sound right, the sorties were authorised as Black Bull. Two days afterwards, I re-wrote the sheets. If you do not believe me, I still have the original… ▬

• Alastair Montgomery took early retirement at the age of 50 as Group Captain Operations HQ Strike Command

A retired Gp Capt Montgomery beside one of Martin Withers' bomb craters at Stanley in 2007.

Martin Withers (left) and Alastair Montgomery visited Government House in Stanley during 2007. Alan Huckle, the governor, holds a copy of Rowland White's best-selling book 'Vulcan 607'.

reserve on the final Black Buck sortie. As we approached the first refuelling bracket there were five Victors and a Vulcan ahead of me; meanwhile, high above, another formation of five Victors passed beyond us to let down hundreds of miles south to set up the next rendezvous. We had learned.

In subsequent years, many have dissected what took place and whether it achieved the desired objectives. Here are the facts. From the moment the first 1000lb bomb left XM607 there was no turning back. When that bomb hit the runway, Stanley Airport could never be reconfigured for fast jet operations.

Martin Withers DFC (left) at Newark Air Museum in 2015, with a visiting Argentine officer who was part of the air defence team at Stanley in 1982.

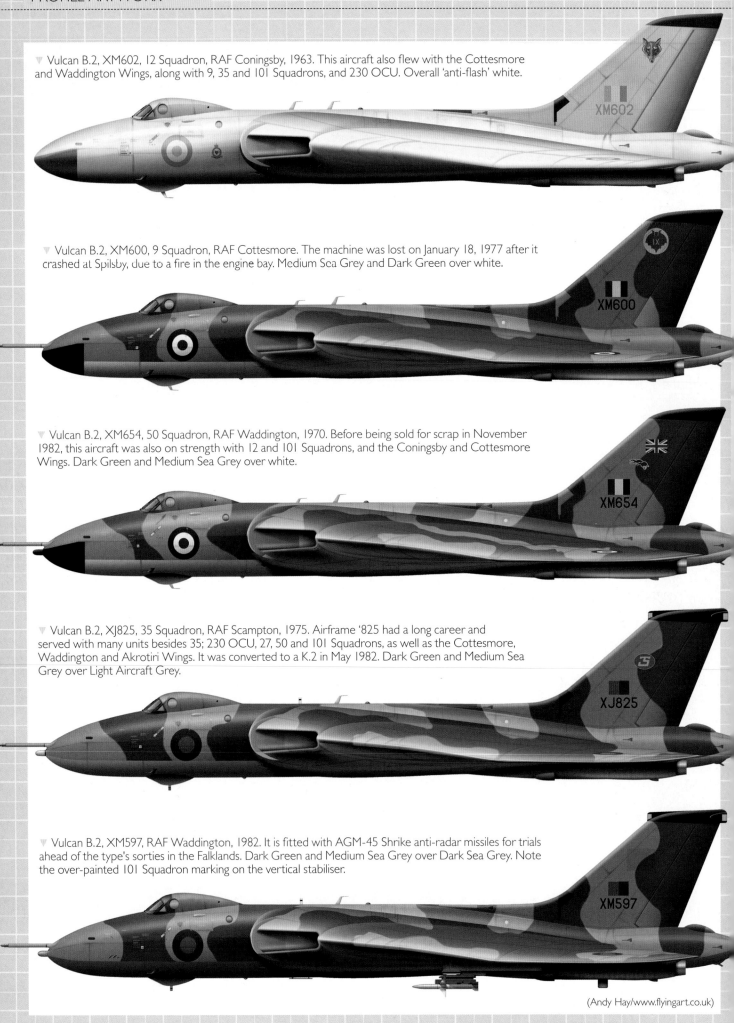

▽ Vulcan B.2, XM602, 12 Squadron, RAF Coningsby, 1963. This aircraft also flew with the Cottesmore and Waddington Wings, along with 9, 35 and 101 Squadrons, and 230 OCU. Overall 'anti-flash' white.

▽ Vulcan B.2, XM600, 9 Squadron, RAF Cottesmore. The machine was lost on January 18, 1977 after it crashed at Spilsby, due to a fire in the engine bay. Medium Sea Grey and Dark Green over white.

▽ Vulcan B.2, XM654, 50 Squadron, RAF Waddington, 1970. Before being sold for scrap in November 1982, this aircraft was also on strength with 12 and 101 Squadrons, and the Coningsby and Cottesmore Wings. Dark Green and Medium Sea Grey over white.

▽ Vulcan B.2, XJ825, 35 Squadron, RAF Scampton, 1975. Airframe '825 had a long career and served with many units besides 35; 230 OCU, 27, 50 and 101 Squadrons, as well as the Cottesmore, Waddington and Akrotiri Wings. It was converted to a K.2 in May 1982. Dark Green and Medium Sea Grey over Light Aircraft Grey.

▽ Vulcan B.2, XM597, RAF Waddington, 1982. It is fitted with AGM-45 Shrike anti-radar missiles for trials ahead of the type's sorties in the Falklands. Dark Green and Medium Sea Grey over Dark Sea Grey. Note the over-painted 101 Squadron marking on the vertical stabiliser.

(Andy Hay/www.flyingart.co.uk)

AVRO 707 AND VULCAN PRODUCTION LIST

Scale Model Research Aircraft
Avro 707s (5 + 1 cancelled)

707: VX784 (built at Woodford); 707B: VX790 (Woodford);
707A: WD280 (Woodford) and WZ736 (Bracebridge Heath);
707C: WZ744 (Bracebridge Heath), WZ739 cancelled

Avro 710s (2 cancelled)

VX799 and VX808

Full-Size Bombers
Avro Vulcan Prototypes (2)

VX770 and VX777

Avro Vulcan B.1 Production (45)

XA889 to XA913, XH475 to XH483, XH497 to XH506 and XH532

Avro Vulcan B.2 Production (89)

XH533 to XH539, XH554 to XH563, XJ780 to XJ784, XJ823 to
XJ825, XL317 to XL321, XL359 to XL361, XL384 to XL392,
XL425 to XL427, XL443 to XL446, XM569 to XM576, XM594 to
XM612 and XM645 to XM657.

Note: XM596 used as ground-based test specimen and never flown.

Total Vulcans completed with prototypes = 136.
All built at Woodford

◄ Vulcan B.1 XA891 first flew in September 1955 but it
never joined an RAF Squadron. In 1957 it was used as a
B.Ol.6 Olympus 200-series trials aircraft before crashing
in July 1959. Tony Buttler

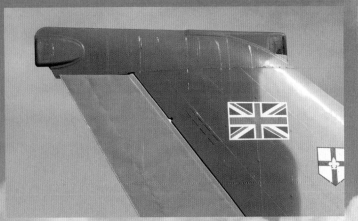

▲ Vertical stabiliser top with passive ECM fairings front and aft.

▲ Starboard air intake with FOD guard in place.

WALK AROUND

Combat Machines was kindly granted access to Vulcan XH558 at Doncaster Sheffield Airport for our walk around photos. Thanks go to Dr Robert Pleming and his team. The aircraft is to be the centrepiece of a new attraction, the Vulcan Experience, which will also feature a Green Technology Hub (see p.61). All Key-Jamie Ewan

▲ The refuelling boom mount and nose extremity. On XH558, a blanking plate covers where the terrain-following radar blister was attached on service aircraft.

Port air intake with boundary layer splitter plate. The black panther head badge is that of RAF 1 Group.

▲ The windscreen glazing, wipers and rain guard.

▲ Engine breather outlets. Note the red and white fire extinguisher doors.

▲ Aerial fairing for the I Band radar jammer, attached to the underside of the ECM bulge at the aircraft's rear.

▲ Tailcone ECM gear housing, with dome for the Red Steer X-band radar at the extremity. The upper bulge is for the braking parachute.

Engine exhaust nozzles
with blanking plates fitted.

▲ Main landing gear unit.

▲ Bomb bay looking forward. Note the black and white oxygen bottles, and grey domed inspection lamps on each side.

▲ Bomb-aimer's fairing with frontal glazing.

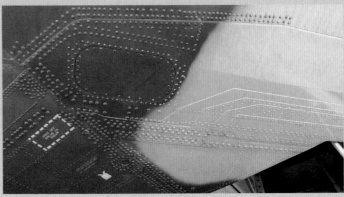

▲ Strengthening plates ahead of the port main undercarriage bay.

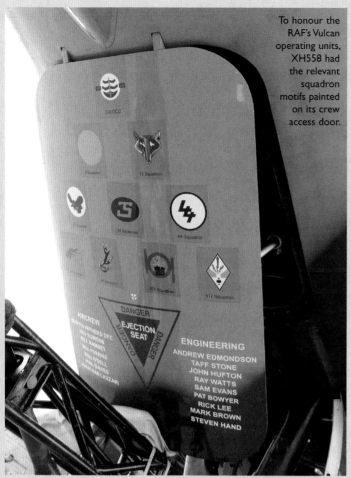

Crew boarding ladder and access hatch

At the top are covers for the chaff dispenser housings, and below is the square, pale green Decca doppler panel. Both are situated under the port wing, behind the wheel bay.

The spring-loaded tail strike indicator.

To honour the RAF's Vulcan operating units, XH558 had the relevant squadron motifs painted on its crew access door.

Vulcan XH558's instrument panel. The aircraft's civil registration is shown on the upper right-hand section.

KITOGRAPHY

This guide to Vulcan and Avro 707 model kits, accessories and decals is not exhaustive and focuses primarily on products that are currently available via retail, but also explores some out-of-production items that can still often be found on Internet auction sites or at model shows. Compiled using Hannants' website and stock numbers where appropriate: www.hannants.co.uk. Item numbers in parentheses are the maker's own.

KITS

1/200

Cyber Hobby

Avro Vulcan B.2 (2011)

Avro Vulcan B.2 Ascension Island 1982 (2016)

1/144

Anigrand Craftswork

Avro Vulcan B.2 (AA-4028)

Great Wall Hobby (GWH)

Vulcan B.2 (L1001)

RAF Vulcan K.2 Tanker (L1002)

Trumpeter

TU03931 Avro Vulcan B.2

144th.co.uk

Avro 707A Straight Wing (144001)

Avro 707A Kinked Wing (144002)

Avro 707C (144003)

1/96

Lindberg

Avro Vulcan (70530)

Revell

Avro Vulcan (4331)

1/72

Airfix

Avro Vulcan B.2 (09002)

Avro Vulcan B Mk.2 XH558 Vulcan To The Sky (A50097)

Avro Vulcan B.2 (A12011) new tool due 2021

Olimp Models (also boxed under Pro Resin)

OLPR7228 Avro 707A

OLPR7245 Avro 707B

OLPR7229 Avro 707C

ACCESSORIES

1/144

Aircraft in Miniature Ltd

GE144054 Avro Vulcan B.2/K.2 Towbar

TWC144022 Douglas Skybolt missile conversion (GWH)

Armory

ARAW14402 Vulcan wheels with weighted tyres (Anigrand/GWH/Trumpeter/Welsh Models)

Master

AM144010 Vulcan B.2/K.2 refuelling probe (Anigrand/GWH/Trumpeter/Welsh Models)

Peewit

PEE144029 Avro Vulcan canopy masks

RetroWings

Vulcan K.2 Conversion (RW44054 – GWH)

Vulcan Bomb Bay (RW44076 – GWH)

Scale Aircraft Conversions

SAC14410 Avro Vulcan B.2 Landing Gear (GWH)

Shelf Oddity

Vulcan B.2 detail set (SO214402 – GWH)

Top Notch

TNM144-M185 Avro Vulcan B.2 paint masks (standard upper surfaces only – Trumpeter)

TNM144-M186 Avro Vulcan B.2 paint masks wraparound upper/lower surfaces – Trumpeter)

1/72

Aircraft in Miniature Ltd

GE72054 Avro Vulcan Towbar

Armory

Vulcan wheels with weighted tyres (Airfix)

Flightpath

FHP72050C Avro Vulcan K.2 Tanker Conversion (Airfix)

FHP72052 Avro Vulcan Mk.2 Upgrade (Airfix)

FHP72056 Avro Vulcan Mk.1/Mk.1A Conversion (Airfix)

Master

MR72098 Avro Vulcan Mk.2 Refuelling Boom (Airfix)

Mastercasters

MST72004 Avro Vulcan weighted wheels (Airfix)

Scale Aircraft Conversions

SAC72020 Avro Vulcan Landing Gear (Airfix)

Top Notch

TNM72-M185 Avro Vulcan B.2 paint masks (standard upper surfaces only – Airfix)

TNM-72M186 Avro Vulcan B.2 paint masks wraparound upper/lower surfaces – Airfix)

White Ensign Models

Avro Vulcan Interior PE Detail Set
(PE7255A – Airfix)

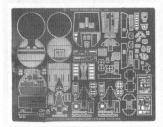

Avro Vulcan Exterior PE Detail Set
(PE7255B – Airfix)

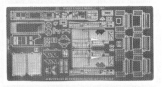

Avro Vulcan Bomb Bay PE Detail Set
(PE7255C – Airfix)

Wolfpack Design

Avro Vulcan B.2 Update Set (WP72047
– Airfix)

Avro Vulcan B.2 Seamless Intake Set
(WP72048 – Airfix)

Avro Vulcan B.2 Wheel Bay Detail Set
(WP72049 – Airfix)

Avro Vulcan K.2 Conversion Set
(WP72062 – Airfix)

Avro Vulcan B.2 Super Update Set
(WP72087 – Airfix)

Avro Vulcan Refuelling Probe Set
(WP72089 – Airfix)

DECALS

1/144

Cut then Add

CTA-002 V-Bombers in Anti-Flash White

fündekals

Avro Vulcan B Mk.2s

Print Scale

PSL14423 Avro Vulcan B.2 Part 1

PSL14424 Avro Vulcan B.2 Part 2

PSL72252 Avro Vulcan B.1/B.2 Part 1

PSL72256 Avro Vulcan B.2/K.2 Part 2

1/72

Freightdog Models

Gods of Sea and Fire – The Neptune
and Vulcan in RAF Service
(FSD72001S)

fündekals

The Mighty Vulcan B.2

Kits-World

KW172214 Avro Vulcan

Model Alliance

RAF V-Bombers Part I (MA-72178)

RAF V-Bombers Pt II (MA-72179)

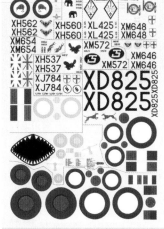

Modeldecal

Royal Air Force Vulcan B.2 (No.70)

Royal Air Force Vulcan (No.71)

Xtradecal

X72208 The History of 12 Squadron
1015-2014

Airfix's original 1/72 Vulcan B.2
built by Jan Forsgren (*Airfix Model
World* – September 2018 issue)

WEYMANN'S

*"It is not the individual or the army as a whole
But the everlastin' teamwork of every bloomin' soul."*

(The Weymanthem)

© 2002 John A Senior - Section 1: The History of the Company
© 2002 Alan Townsin and John Banks - Section 2: Design Development
ISBN 1 898432 36 8

A Weymann's flexible-bodied Leyland Cub, see page 31.
Courtesy Leyland BCVM.

The British Bus and Truck Heritage

WEYMANN'S

of Addlestone

A history of the Company

and its products from 1923 to 1945

by

John A Senior MCIT

Venture *publications*

FOREWORD

The seeds for this book were sown as long ago as 1976, when the writer interviewed Norman Froggatt, Weymann's last General Manager, in the drawing office of the former Burlingham company in Blackpool. Burlingham had by then been taken over by Duple and Norman was working for the latter company, having moved there after Weymann's closed, and subsequently moved north when Duple left London.

The purpose of the interview was to find out more about Hall, Lewis, (later Park Royal), where Norman and his father had both worked in the late 1920s. I was researching Park Royal's history for publication though was actually in Blackpool to finalise arrangements with the late Martin Montano – Duple's Sales Manager – to publish the Duple history which I duly did in 1976.

We arranged to meet again and in one of those meetings Norman began to tell me something of Weymann's chequered history. I was fascinated but saw no opportunity to publish anything at that time since I was fully committed for some three or four years with work on the surviving major bodybuilders of whom there were still ten in those halcyon days.

To many students of transport, the name Weymann is synonymous with distinctive bus bodies built in the home counties until the mid sixties. Indeed, to the casual observer (and also to some of the workforce), the name itself might have come from the proximity of the factory to the River Wey, or the town taking its name from that river which runs through the same part of Surrey. The name Weymann was in fact that of the Frenchman who founded the company, but who had no interest at all in building buses.

Bodywork by Weymann, sometimes described as being by MCW, begins to hint at a story that was not quite as straightforward as at first may have seemed. MCW was in fact the initials of Metro-Cammell-Weymann, the sales organisation which during the lifetime of this narrative built no buses at all, despite popular belief to the contrary. And then there was the question of ownership . . .

Here Norman really caught my interest with the most unusual background to the ownership of the Company, not something that then usually rated very highly in our researches. I duly recorded the information and saved it for the future.

The opportunity to pursue matters came only comparatively recently after enforced early retirement following a heart attack. It seemed just the sort of therapeutic puzzle I might enjoy to pass the time away. Some therapy! Some puzzle!

Assuming you stay the course, and I most sincerely hope you will, for there is more to Weymann's than elegantly designed buses with flared skirts and beautiful paintwork, you will read a fascinating story which I suggest can have no equal in the bus industry.

How a group of well-heeled racing men put money into a venture to build aeroplanes, cars and, later, buses. How they were supported by a London bank which, in partnership with a South African gold mining company, financed and built a railway in Spain. How the fall of the Spanish Government and subsequent exile of the King led to the nonpayment of the greater part of the £2million bill. How the bank fell and the Mining Company only survived because South Africa followed Britain's lead and devalued its currency, abandoning the gold standard which until then linked the value of currencies throughout the world to the price of gold.

Later we read how a major British financial institution – The Prudential – bought the Weymann shares as a promising investment, only to sell them to a shipping company – United Molasses – wanting to take advantage of a wartime government grant for developing electric motor cars at precisely the time that the financial institution was short of ready cash following huge losses in supporting the British Cinema industry.

So what at first might be expected to be a relatively simple story turns out to be an extremely complicated one, with almost John Buchan-like overtones of Government influence, together with that from the armaments and ship building industries, but one which I hope you will enjoy and to which I hope I have done justice largely thanks to the many hours of interviews with patient former employees who frequently interjected with the same expression – "but how on earth did you find out that when I worked there and had no idea what was going on?"

All the above will become clear as the story unfolds, but the reader is warned that there are many twists and turns which make it far from straightforward. Some of the more abstruse answers came from the archives of the companies which had at one time or another owned Weymann's; one of those companies lost its offices and records when it was bombed out during the London blitz of 1940. The project became the most fascinating jigsaw puzzle I have ever encountered and I wouldn't have missed it for all the world. Thank you Norman!

CONTENTS

This book spans the production of buses from the Addlestone factory between 1929 and 1945 and also follows the fortunes of many of Weymann's customers. In 1942 Lincolnshire, who operated this Leyland single-decker TS8, changed owners, something Weymann's were not unfamiliar with, and became a Tilling company, painting its buses in that group's green livery as seen here, and buying its vehicles from the in-house Eastern Coach Works. Early signs of a changing world in which Weymann's – and others – could not survive, try as they might.

GHF Atkins

The story of Weymann's bus building years is a fascinating one. It follows the Company's earlier life as a builder of aeroplanes and motor cars, and encompasses the Second World War years with manufacture concentrated on output for the war effort. Taxis, lorries, vans, fire engines and even an infamous boat are all part of the story, though they appear in Volume 2 covering the post-war years. The relationship with Metropolitan Cammell Carriage and Wagon Company of Birmingham, and the joint sales organisation – Metro-Cammell-Weymann – all broaden the scope of the work. The interplay among Weymann's and other companies is interesting, particularly with Park Royal who provided so many valued and long-serving Weymann's employees in exchange for others who became equally important to the north London competitor.

The changes in ownership of the Company, extensions and expansion, big contracts and small ones, all played their part in the growth of Weymann's. But the changing face of the bus industry in the sixties, coupled to an unfortunate but true reputation for militancy, meant that the Addlestone factory could not survive in the more competitive world. Metropolitan Cammell's purchase of the Company, in order to close it completely, may or may not have been unavoidable. Certainly it made sense in Birmingham where the loss-making Addlestone plant was by then seen as a competitor more than a partner and its troubled industrial relations ensured it would play no part in future plans.

This book represented both a challenge and a change in emphasis for the author. For more than a quarter of a century as a transport book publisher I have been encouraging and assisting others in the production of histories of the British bus manufacturers and in so doing have seen the demise of a once-great industry. Since I published their histories AEC, Bedford, Bristol, Duple, Eastern Coach Works and Park Royal have ceased production whilst Alexanders, Plaxtons and Northern Counties have all changed ownership, though in all cases I disclaim responsibility! Even the once mighty Leyland empire is no more and the much-vaunted Leyland National plant at Workington is just a memory. Venture's history of East Lancashire Coach Builders published in 2000 represents one of the few survivors whilst Metropolitan Cammell Carriage and Wagon Company, Weymann's eventual owner, will form a companion volume in this series. Brush and Willowbrook are two more almost forgotten bodybuilders whose histories are in course of production.

Weymann's was always an obvious candidate for a book, but 25 years ago we lacked the various resources to tackle it thoroughly, as it clearly deserved. Each project depended in the early days on financial input from the Company concerned and Weymann's had already been closed for a decade when I began my publishing venture. Now, in semi-retirement, I found the time and enthusiasm to tackle this title as a balanced manufacturing and social history in a way which I hope will give satisfaction to those who worked for the organisation, in addition to the many bus enthusiasts and others in the industry who are always interested in detailed histories of the former manufacturers.

My good colleagues in Venture looked surprised at my determination to finally investigate Weymann's – some thirty-three years after the factory closure. My only direct connection with the Company had been the interviews with Norman Froggatt in 1976 when he worked for Duple in Blackpool, after the closure of the Addlestone plant by Metropolitan Cammell. Would I really be able to find enough material to satisfy the wider social and financial aspects involved – which we all agreed we wanted to see included – they wondered? Would I just! Bob Rowe, recognising the vast amount of material I was amassing, offered to help with various aspects, particularly the production analyses which took the two of us many hours to sort out and I thank him for this and for generally helping the project along as also has my son Mark.

One lunchtime I mentioned the idea of researching Weymann's history, with a view to publication, to my good friend the late Mike Harris, who lived in Addlestone a stone's throw from the Otter, where the Annual Reunions now take place, and his quiet conviction that there were hundreds of ex-Weymann's employees just waiting to tell their story encouraged me to make a start. A letter to the local newspaper set the ball rolling when Dave Humphrey subsequently rang to find out, ever so tactfully, what a fellow from North Derbyshire was doing researching a defunct Surrey bus manufacturer. I sent Dave a copy of the Duple book to establish my credentials and from that conversation has grown a friendship without which this book could not have been produced. Dave has assiduously worked his way through all sorts of connections to find people who worked in the factory with him, before him, or after he left, in order to give me the opportunity to find out just how Weymann's ticked and what it was like to work in the Addlestone factory.

As the months passed more and more former employees have made contact, and I have spent many fascinating hours with the tape recorder setting down their memories and experiences. I think their enjoyment has been every bit as great as mine and I have made many new friends in the process.

Another good friend, again without whose help the book could not have produced, is Bob Smith. Bob has meticulously provided the body details for all known Weymann buses and coaches, and also has provided some background information on the early directors, shareholders and financial matters for which I am extremely grateful. Our mutual friend Geoff Lumb has also helped greatly in this area as also has Chris Taylor.

As we delved deeper into the Company history Gareth Jones took on board some diligent work at Companies House in Cardiff. It took a Welshman to find what existed in their cellars against the previously adamant conviction that everything had been destroyed under the thirty year ruling.

Other companies involved include the Prudential, and United Molasses, both one-time owners, and Clare Bunkham and Les Mollison at their respective companies have been tremendously helpful here, giving me access to material I could never otherwise have traced.

ACKNOWLEDGEMENTS

And then we have those stalwarts who were involved directly or indirectly with Weymanns itself. It gives me great pleasure to thank them all, publicly, for their unstinting assistance. Starting with the ladies I thank Gillian Axtell, the late Edna Bubb, Margaret Colman, Beryl Froggatt, June Guarnori, Marcelle Healy, Val Humphrey and Lily Partridge. The men include Joe Allen, Reg Allen, Don Arthur, Keith Barkham, Ron Barrett, Bunny Beaver, Peter Bovingdon, Maurice Bullivant, Brian Burton MBE, Henry Colman, Albert (Chubby) Cox, Ray Cox, John Davies, Walter Healy, the late Frank Higgs, Frank Hooker, Dave Humphrey, Raymond Proudfoot, Cyril Smith, Bob Smith, Vic Smith, Keith Todman, Gordon Whindle.

John Banks, Venture's Production Director, agreed to look after the second part of the book, looking more closely at the design of the vehicles, with Alan Townsin, leaving me free to concentrate on researching the previously largely unrecorded history and finding sufficient 'new' material to illustrate it. My thanks to them both. Many of those mentioned read the manuscript or proofs, also including Roy Marshall and Eric Ogden in addition to Venture's indefatigable in-house reading team of David and Mary Shaw, and I thank them all, though any errors are mine and not theirs.

I hope as you read this book that you will begin to understand just what made the company the way it was. The people who founded the company, the directors, management and workforce; the shareholders and customers; the good times and the bad all feature. Here I must point out that, whilst I have tried to be fair and objective in reporting the story as told to me by former employees, the conclusions drawn, and any inaccuracies which may appear, are my responsibility alone. I hope there will not be many, for I have tried hard to capture the flavour of Weymann's as they spelled it out.

But throughout shines the spirit of a Company which, despite the activities of a small minority, grew and operated like a huge family concern. EG Izod's conviction that *"It is not the individual or the army as a whole, But the everlastin' teamwork of every bloomin' soul"* may have an old fashioned ring nowadays but is there really any other way?

Success only comes through a combined determination to succeed. I have, sadly, researched too many companies where militancy wrecked an otherwise prosperous concern. And who gained? Not those whose jobs disappeared, nor those whose prospects of a good job in the local area, following their fathers and grandfathers, evaporated with their P45. Weymann's was an early casualty in a changing bus world – indeed the very first to benefit from the Labour Government's Redundancy Act (a significant but not perhaps the most sought-after epithet?) – but no one has convinced me that it could not have continued if the tail had stopped trying to wag the dog.

Nor has anyone ever criticised the quality of the product, the skill of the craftsmen or the pride in their ability to build buses as good as – or better than – any others in the country. Let this book be a tribute to that memory.

John A Senior
Glossop
Derbyshire
February 2002

Over thirty years after the Company closed down an annual reunion still takes place each May. Here former employees meet for the 1998 event, ready to enjoy a ride round on a preserved London Transport RLH bus, built at Addlestone in 1953, and to swap reminiscences before retiring for a drink at a local hostelry. Left to right: Phil Hutchins, Brian Burton MBE, Gillian Axtell, Tony Wiggins, Marcelle Healy, Vic Smith, Keith Barkham, Dave and Val Humphrey, Bob Smith, Don Carver, Walter Healy.

The photographs and other illustrations used in the two parts of this first volume in the History of MCW have come mainly from the Author's *Senior Transport Archive*, with original Weymann's official prints to fill gaps being loaned by Keith Barkham, Brian Burton MBE, John Davies and Amy Partridge during the course of interviewing former employees.

Fellow enthusiasts who have loaned material, also including original Weymann's and prints from other manufacturers include John Banks, Peter Gascoine, Robert Grieves, Robin Hannay, Keith Healey, Geoff Hyde, John Kaye, Geoff Lumb, Roy Marshall, Ron Maybray, Chris Taylor, David Toy and Alan Townsin.

Official manufacturers' prints from defunct companies including AEC, Daimler, Guy, Karrier, Leyland (courtesy of the British Commercial Vehicle Museum, Leyland), Ransomes Sims & Jefferies, (courtesy of the Rural Life Studies Unit, Reading University), and Sunbeam have also assisted in providing variety in the illustrations.

The Geoffrey Atkins collection has provided many splendid contemporary views of vehicles in service in the thirties and forties, often when new or nearly so, helping to bring the pages to life. John Banks has been particularly helpful here in locating and electronically converting these and all the other images.

Personal items from family collections have been invaluable and here I particularly record my thanks to Joe Allen, Bunny Beaver, the late Edna Bubb, Beryl Froggatt, Walter and Marcelle Healy, the late Frank Higgs, Shirley Moon (nee Page) and Vic Smith.

The Birmingham Central Library; the Central Reference Library, Manchester; the Midlands Motor Museum, Bridgnorth; the Museum of Transport, Manchester; the National Motor Museum, Beaulieu; the

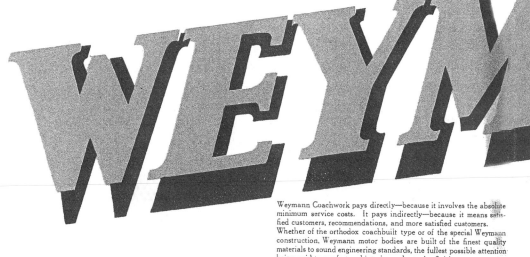

Weymann Coachwork pays directly—because it involves the absolute minimum service costs. It pays indirectly—because it means satisfied customers, recommendations, and more satisfied customers. Whether of the orthodox coachbuilt type or of the special Weymann construction, Weymann motor bodies are built of the finest quality materials to sound engineering standards, the fullest possible attention being paid to comfort and interior and exterior finish.

Double page advertisement from
THE COMMERCIAL MOTOR
February 10th, 1931.

WEYMANN'S MOTOR BODI

National Tramway Museum, Crich; the Prudential Assurance Company; the Public Record Office, Kew; and United Molasses have also all been most helpful. Gareth Jones found the key to opening the vaults at Companies House in Cardiff, and the fruits of some of his labours will appear in the next volume.

Articles and advertisements have been culled from the various magazines of the transport press including Bus & Coach, Commercial Motor, Electric Tram, Railway and Bus Journal, the Leyland Journal, Motor Transport, the Motor, the MPTA Journal, Old Motor, Passenger Transport, the Railway Gazette, Tramway & Railway World (later Transport World), and, of course, last but by no means least the Company's own House Magazine **The Weymag** which was invaluable in pinning down dates. Local and National newspapers have also provided most useful material. Financial and other related matters came from many sources but the Motor Transport Year Books were particularly helpful.

Histories of bus operating companies, too many to list, but mainly published by the former Transport Publishing Company, more recently by Venture Publications and also by Ian Allan Ltd and Robin Hood Publishing together with the records of the PSV Circle have provided further information about the vehicles. Official Company Histories which have been absolutely invaluable include that of Vickers Ltd from my own collection, United Molasses kindly loaned by Jack Curwen, and, the real gem, Golden Years, the history of the Corner House Group in South Africa, parent company of Central Mining and Investment Corporation, found and loaned to me by Bob Smith who also provided the detailed body production lists to which all the above material was painstakingly linked.

I offer my sincere thanks to everyone mentioned and apologise if I have inadvertently missed out anyone.

WEYMANN EVERYTIME!

for COMFORT SILENCE AND MINIMUM RUNNING ,,COSTS,,,,,,,,,

30-Seater Green Line Coaches,
Bodywork by Weymann's Motor Bodies
(1925) Ltd.; Chassis, A.E.C. Regal

25) LTD., Addlestone, Surrey

CHAPTER ONE: 1889 – 1928

THE FRENCH CONNECTION

Charles Terres Weymann was already used to taking chances – and living dangerously – by the time he was twenty-one. Some twelve years later he had become a successful international businessman and manufacturer.

Born in Haiti in 1889 to an American father and French mother he was brought up in France and in due course given French nationality. A penchant for living life in the fast lane developed and he made a name for himself with his racing exploits. In 1911 he took part in the Daily Mail Round Britain Race, competing amongst others against WF Cody, better known as Buffalo Bill, and in that same year won the Gordon Bennett air race racing in a Nieuport monoplane. In 1913 he took part in the Schneider Cup Trophy, again racing in a Nieuport, this time in Monaco. His accomplishment as a skilled aviateur would have stood him in good stead during the First World War; he joined the French Air Force and, as Capt. Weymann, fought for his country against the Germans.

After the end of hostilities he was, like many others of his time, unsettled and looking for a better future. He had already designed a method of flexible construction for motor car bodies, based it is believed on aeroplane designs in which he had been involved, and launched his prototype at the Paris Motor Show in 1921. It was an instant success and on the strength of this he opened a component manufactory in Paris in 1922. There he had all the necessary fittings made: locks, hinges, catches, handles, brackets and so on. All were fully covered by patents.

He then licensed various car manufacturers to produce his bodies and, with the revenue so generated, expanded further by creating a British component manufacturing company.

These three strands of aircraft, motor cars and various international connections were to recur throughout his relatively short-lived post-war career in England, as we shall shortly see.

Advertisement for the Nieuport monoplane in which Monsieur Charles Weymann won the Gordon Bennett Air Race in America in 1911.
James Gordon Bennett Jnr, provider of the cup, was the son of the founder of the New York Herald. He followed his father as Editor and gained a reputation for gilding the lily in his reporting. His name duly became a byword as a mild expletive when expressing incredulity or annoyance. It was Bennett who sent Henry Stanley to Africa to find Dr. Livingstone.

Weymann seen in a genuine 'hands-on' situation on a Farmann airplane probably around 1910-11. Fashion accessories such as cockpits and windscreens had yet to make their appearance – this was clearly not a sport for the faint-hearted.

UNSETTLED TIMES

WHY CHOOSE BRITAIN FOR CAR MANUFACTURE ?

Since Weymann was French, and had already established himself as a very successful business man in his own country, why should he want to brave the unknown by coming across the English Channel?

The answer almost certainly lies in the obstacles which our Government was putting in the way of imported goods after the end of the First World War. In order to protect jobs, and also to discourage imports for trade balance reasons, punitive trade tariffs were thus being levied throughout the 1920s.

Weymann could see a market in Britain for his cars but the imposition of an import tax of 33.3% would make his already expensive cars prohibitively so. Had he been importing from Germany the tax would have been even higher. Only by building in this country could he avoid this protectionist taxation. This would seem to be the most likely explanation for him choosing to establish a major factory here.

The cessation of the so-called Great War left perhaps more problems needing resolving than it had been hoped to end. Millions had died, great deprivation had been caused, resentment and injustice were rife. Before there was any real chance to start to get back to normal a catastrophic worldwide outbreak of 'flu killed even more people than the whole of the war casualties; an estimated and unbelievable 20 million fell victim to this virus.

Here in Britain further misery was caused by a strike of coal miners resulting in widespread problems hitting factories and homes alike in a desperately cold winter, and even forcing curtailment of railway services due to non-availability of coal. The railway's problems were to assist the growth of many new businesses operating charabancs, some of which later became bus operators and as such customers for Weymann's bus bodies. Perhaps it is indeed an ill wind . . . ?

To launch a new business into this situation must have required much courage, especially for a man who wasn't even British, and, according to the record, had difficulty with our language. That a short-lived slump around 1920-1 had affected small manufacturers of cheaper model cars more than those at the top end of the market – 'his end' – must have encouraged Weymann considerably at a time when he was planning his future expansion.

Captain Weymann (CTW) was, of course, far from being alone in facing up to problems of supply and demand after the war. On a somewhat larger scale the great armament manufacturers were also facing up to hard truths; in peacetime, and certainly just after such a dreadful war, orders for big guns and battleships were going to be rather thin on the ground. Substantial profits had been made by the wartime munitions and armament industry but now, with orders having dried up, there was over-capacity, a requirement to rationalise production, and, above all, a need to diversify. These factors would play a part in Weymann's future, even if he could not have foreseen it at the time.

Another external factor he could be forgiven for not taking into account was the unsettled market for gold. South African mining corporations were facing up to the fact that with the price dropping and mining costs rising it was an uneconomic time to sell gold, and it was better to invest some of the huge reserves many companies had accumulated during the good years. More of this shortly.

Finally, perhaps, in this tale of forthcoming doom and gloom, three men whose names were to become known throughout Britain and most of the developing world, were also implementing plans which would bear directly onto Weymann's own ambitious scheme for his specialised car building business. William Morris, Herbert Austin and Henry Ford would influence the demand and methods of manufacture for motor cars in a way which, together with social changes in society, would decimate the market for bespoke limousines which had been associated with the motor car trade since before the Great War. Even some of the less expensive cars they would replace would have been Weymann-bodied . . . as such their loss would represent a real threat to the future core business of both in-house manufacture and also in licensing. The latter point would later prove crucial to Weymann's personal finances when, as numbers built dropped, his income also fell.

As if all this wasn't enough, and just for good measure, events overseas later led to the failure of the bank which had financed Weymann's English company in 1925. We anticipate our story, however, and we shall now see how CT Weymann and his backers walked into a minefield from which only a set of most unusual circumstances led them to temporary safety, though in a rather different manner and direction than had been originally envisaged or intended. It is a complex tale with many twists and turns to spice the plot.

CTW BECOMES A MOTOR CAR BODY MANUFACTURER

Weymann had patented a method of construction for motor car bodies whereby the unevennesses of the roads of the time could be somewhat alleviated by the flexing of the wooden body. A further advantage was the elimination of squeaks and rattles whilst the method of assembly and construction resulted in weight reduction and a product which could be assembled by semi-skilled labour. His first car body, on a Talbot-Darracq chassis, was displayed at the Paris Motor Show in 1921 and was an instant success. Such was the popularity of Weymann bodywork that licences to build were soon issued to a wide variety of international motor car manufacturers and coachbuilders.

One year after opening his French company in Paris, Weymann formed a private company in England in August 1923, Weymann's Motor Body Ltd, and opened his second factory, this time in north west London. His business partners were the Aron brothers, Hermann and Eugen, directors of Rotax Motor Accessories (instrument and lighting set manufacturers). Again this factory was for component manufacture only. The first licensee amongst British manufacturers was Rover; amongst many others building bodies to his patent designs were Sunbeam, Riley, Park Ward, and, of later significance, Chalmer & Hoyer, later called Hoyal.

The future appeared bright and it seemed logical to look at expansion through manufacture, alongside appointing further licensees. There was, however, a fundamental difference between the two arrangements. Manufacture required a factory, a significant number of employees, and a considerable amount of cash. Weymann was already wealthy, however, and his various patents were bringing in a substantial income. Demand for licences was ever-increasing and it seemed sensible to go ahead.

It was decided to take the plunge and, fortuitously, an opportunity arose to acquire a ready-made fully-operational factory in south west London – the premises of The Cunard Motor & Carriage Company – based in Putney and having skilled staff competent to carry out such work.

To provide the necessary capital a new company – Weymann's Motor Bodies (1925) Ltd – came into existence on 25th November 1925, with Weymann as its Chairman and Managing Director. On the same day it was agreed at an Extraordinary General Meeting that the 1923 Company be formally wound up, and in due course all debts were cleared in full.

A contemporary advertisement from *The Motor* magazine after Weymann's move to Addlestone in 1928, drawing attention to the virtues of the construction and also to the Trade Mark which continued to be used on buses at least until 1943. It also appeared on the Menu Cards for the 1950 Silver Jubilee celebration lunches and on the 1000th Weymann's RT bus. The prestigious sales and showroom address at 47 Pall Mall, London SW1, was the home of the former Cunard Company whose assets Charles Weymann purchased following its demise and which the 1925 company continued to use until they came out of the car market. Cunard later resumed car body manufacture after being purchased by Stewart & Arden; by 1938 they were advertising themselves as commercial body builders.

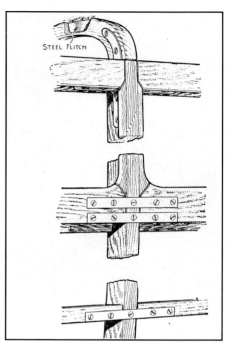

Note the spaces, 2-3mm wide between the components of the framing, where greased paper gaskets were inserted in the gap to eliminate squeaks.

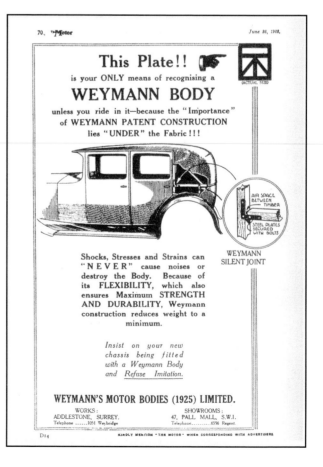

Unlike the earlier, private, company this new venture was a Public Company whose shares could be traded on the stock market. The £66,000 capital for the new Company was raised through 55,000 £1 preference shares taken by a London bank, Bernhard Scholle, with whom CTW had good relations through a friendship with one of the Directors, Maurice Dollfus, and 220,000 one-shilling (5p) ordinary shares of which Weymann himself was allocated 88,000. Dollfus was head of Ford's French operation. Another of the Bank's Directors was Lt. Col. Llewellyn Evans, MIEE., CMG., DSO who, as one of Weymann's new Directors initially took charge of the day-to-day running of the company, implying that this was a major investment for the bank, or a high risk venture, or both. The Registered Office of the new company was at 22, Austin Friars in the City, home of the Bank. The ability to sell the Company's shares on the open market would, in due course, result in some strange changes of ownership.

In October 1926 it was announced in the trade press that Rootes Ltd, of Devonshire House, Piccadilly, London W1 had been appointed as 'Sole Distributors for Great Britain and the Irish Free State for Weymann bodies manufactured by Weymann's Motor Bodies (1925) Ltd'.

Other manufacturers whose chassis carried Weymann bodywork also invested in the business, and a significant part was played by Louis Coatalen, the leading light behind Sunbeam cars. Coatalen's importance was recognised by his position as a Director of the Weymann company. According to CTW, 60% of the saloon bodies built in the Sunbeam factory in 1928 were produced with Weymann flexible patented bodies. How the two men shared the royalties is not recorded. Amongst other manufacturers, Mark Birkgit of Hispano-Suiza was a shareholder, whilst Lord Montagu of Beaulieu was apparently a Director – for two days.

A close friend was Henry Segrave, Sir Henry after taking the land speed record in his racing car Golden Arrow. He also put money into the new venture and took a position with responsibility for motor car sales. His death in 1930 on Lake Windermere whilst attempting to take the water speed record was a great blow for Weymann. Segrave's chauffeur Tim Healy, however, was to remain in the story for another 20 years or so.

This was not Weymann's only venture into manufacturing finished cars with Bernhard Scholle's support. A third plant was opened in Indianapolis in 1926 but it was not successful and had closed by 1931. Among many reasons given for the failure were American protectionism tariffs, the over estimate of the number of bodies which would be taken by the Stutz Motor Car Company – 'thousands' actually turning out to be 'hundreds'. The American market also wanted the high gloss finish which the fabric-bodied Weymann cars could not produce. There were some very badly burned fingers after this failure.

Sir Henry Segrave obtained the World Land Speed Record of 231.445 mph at Daytona in the USA in 1927. (His mechanic and chauffeur was Tim Healy, father of Walter Healy who joined the company in 1941 in the Wages Department and helped in the research for this book.)

Born in 1896 in Baltimore as Henry O'Neal Dehane Segrave he was, like CTW, a pilot. After the war he joined the Sunbeam Talbot Darracq works team, winning 31 out of 49 races in Sunbeams.

His association with Weymann was thus at least threefold: through Coatalen of Sunbeam; through a common interest in racing for speed records; and, clearly, through involvement in the first Weymann car – built on a 1921 Talbot-Darracq chassis.

Through one or more of these associations he became a major Weymann's shareholder and Director and was in charge of the Sales Department for cars.

Knighted in 1929 he died the following year in a tragic accident on Lake Windermere, hitting a submerged object whilst trying to better his own water speed record of 98.76 mph in his craft Miss England II.

If his shareholding was indeed a substantial one it could well have exacerbated the financial and other problems which culminated in the major 1932 reorganisation and withdrawal from the car market.

Motoring magnificence. A splendid Weymann patent flexible body on a Hispano-Suiza chassis. Mark Birkgit of Hispano was a shareholder in the 1925 Weymann company.

THE CUNARD MOTOR & CARRIAGE CO. LTD

The Cunard Motor Company had been formed in 1911 to manufacture motor cars and other mechanically propelled vehicles, soon becoming a subsidiary of Napier cars. It had been involved in Government contracts for the War Office but, by 1925, Napier was ready to cease car manufacture, and thus had no further need of the Cunard company. Cunard was one of probably over a hundred such companies operating in and around London at the time, and with over-capacity in the industry pricing was ruinously competitive; it was an equation we shall meet again some 40 years later.

CT Weymann could afford to be optimistic, however, with the constant demand for additional licences to build his bodies, and doubtless saw this as a golden opportunity. Having raised the capital to expand as previously mentioned, Cunard's operation and its premises were purchased from Napiers for £3500 in cash, £900 less than Weymann himself had put into the new company, and production of his car bodies began in Putney. Orders gained were sufficient to outgrow the available space and before long a move to bigger premises was being considered. Everything seemed very promising.

It has not so far been possible to find out to what extent the former Cunard Company was expanded in terms of management or staff by the formation of the 1925 Weymann's company, for although we have a record of some of the people who transferred to Addlestone from Putney we don't know whether they were 'Cunarders' or 'new Weymann's' people. One person who worked in the Mill at Putney was the grandfather of Dave Humphrey who has, through his enthusiasm and assistance, helped enormously in this project. Dave's uncle worked in the Paintshop in pre-war days whilst Dave was, in much later years, employed in the Panel Shop from Christmas 1955 to mid-1963.

However, although confidence in the flexible bodies had clearly been justified in 1925, only two years later and just as preparations for the move were being finalised, as is often the way of these things, the market was changing. The peak of the popularity for the flexible body had just passed. The increasing numbers of more affordable mass produced small cars, and the gradual increase in pressed metal bodies, were eroding into Weymann's market. Another factor was the popularity of the recently introduced faster drying cellulose paints which reduced build times, and overnight made Weymann's fabric-bodied cars with their leathercloth-type finish seem outdated and unfashionable. The timing could not have been worse.

A First World War 'Dental Motor' for the War Office, built on an Albion subsidy chassis by The Cunard Motor and Carriage Co. Ltd. at its Putney works whose premises were situated between Lower Richmond Road and Feltham Road, with access from Lower Richmond Road. Note that the vehicle has been presented by De Trey & Co Ltd – clearly sponsorship is nothing new.

VICKERS OF CRAYFORD

The Cunard connection was straightforward and easy to follow. The Vickers connection was neither, but its ramifications were to affect Weymann's future for the rest of the company's existence, and led ultimately to its extinction. For this reason it is important to understand what had happened to Vickers after the end of the war, why it had become involved in building commercial vehicles and buses, and why it would, at very short notice, stop production completely. JD Scott in his book *Vickers - A History* graphically spells out the sorry story.

The Crayford (Kent) factory was a good example of the change of use necessitated by the return to peacetime conditions – the factory had previously produced a variety of armaments including Maxim machine guns. After the war a 'Peace Products Committee' was set up to determine future product policy. Yet this was a hopeless task. Vickers were, had been and would have to remain, armament manufacturers. Their Chairman pointed out, however, that that placed them in a difficult position in a country (Britain) which had just decided to be non-belligerent and have no re-armament commitment!

Furthermore since Vickers' lifeblood was steel, any peacetime products would have to make use of that commodity. Crayford, home to the design and production of precision naval gun-sights for battleships, machine guns and the ordnance to feed those guns, and manufacture of aircraft such as the Vimy bomber, was to be reduced to making, amongst other things, domestic sewing machines. It does not need a skilled mathematician to work out that you need to sell an awful lot of sewing machines to equal the value of one small aeroplane, let alone equip a battleship with gun sights. And sewing machines don't use bullets. Where would Vickers' future income come from?

Commercial Motor visited the bodybuilding section of the Crayford factory in 1924 and reported that it had been reorganised for peacetime output and laid out on American lines for mass production. A capacity of some 12,000 bodies per year was quoted, of which 2,000 would be buses of up to 35 different types. It was already doing sub-contract bodywork for Leyland Motors as shown in the illustration below. It was offering a variety of services, including the production of complete framing for other builders wishing to complete the vehicles themselves. This was no under-funded or half-hearted enterprise.

A report of a further visit, also by *CM*, in November 1928, included a view of a Leyland Titan TD1 built under sub-contract to Leyland by Vickers for Bradford Corporation. Leyland PLSC Lions were also bodied, at a time when Leyland could not meet the demand its advanced new models had created. The Crayford complex was described as England's largest motor body works and Vickers' General Manager at Crayford was William Black.

Interviewed by the writer at his Claygate home in 1980, after his retirement, the then Lord Black recalled those days. He had been responsible for the bodybuilding plant, and in his own words "had bodied thousands of Fiats and

In addition to specialist steel manufacture, hacksaw blades and files were amongst the items produced by members of the Vickers Group.

Amongst its many other contracts Vickers had been building Leyland-designed bodies as sub-contractor to Leyland Motors of Lancashire since 1924 and this work continued until the end of production at Crayford. This full-fronted body is of the 'Crosville' type, so named because it was first supplied to that customer. This example, on a Leyland SG chassis, was for a Scottish operator. This connection was but one of the many facets of Bill Black's attraction to Weymann's new management – see overleaf – as the company prepared to change its direction.

Citroens". He went on to explain that he had seen an opportunity to get into buses, "but hadn't asked, and just got on with it."

Vickers promoted its bodybuilding plant vigorously and secured business which made others take note. Mr Black subsequently received a most significant phone call. "I was invited to have dinner with Capt. Weymann, the Managing Director of Weymann's, by Mr Izod, and offered the job of General Manager at their new Addlestone plant" (see pages 19 & 21). He accepted the offer and the appointment took place around mid-1928.

Izod had explained that although Weymann's had a skilled team "and were doing well" they now saw their future in bus building, of which they had no experience, and so also needed someone to take on sales responsibility to facilitate this change of direction. Black suggested CW Reeve, a high-flyer then in charge of contracts for the Underground Group (UERL). Although Reeve did not join Weymann's "Bill" Black duly moved, and took with him some of his key people who we shall meet later. We can surmise that as he could not have foreseen the forthcoming upheavals at Vickers, he might have declined the offer from Izod if he had known what would happen some 18 months later. We can also deduce that Black and Reeve were known to each other since Reeve was indeed seeking a career change at that time, but chose instead to go to AEC as personal assistant to Lord Ashfield, later becoming Managing Director of that Company before Ashfield took charge of the newly formed London Transport in 1933. This apparent closeness may partly explain why Weymann's and AEC were clearly working together to some extent after Black moved to Addlestone.

It was what happened next that was to change Weymann's future. Both Vickers and north east England shipbuilders and heavy engineers Armstrong Whitworths were in dire financial trouble, such that Armstrongs literally could not have survived more than a few months longer. Both were crucial to any future (unspoken) need to re-arm to safeguard Britain's independence, but

An advertisement from the *Railway Gazette* dated April 1920 listing the various companies which formed The Metropolitan Carriage, Wagon and Finance Company Ltd. This was the company which Bernard Docker had created in 1902, and sold to Vickers in 1919. Note the prominence of the Dockers Paint portion of the advert. The joint Managing Director of this company was then, and remained until its reconstruction in 1929, Percy Wheeler JP. Mr Wheeler was from 1921 until his death in 1936 also an active and prominent Director of AEC, illustrating the inter-connections and diversification of interests which often explained why contracts went in certain directions between otherwise apparently unrelated companies.

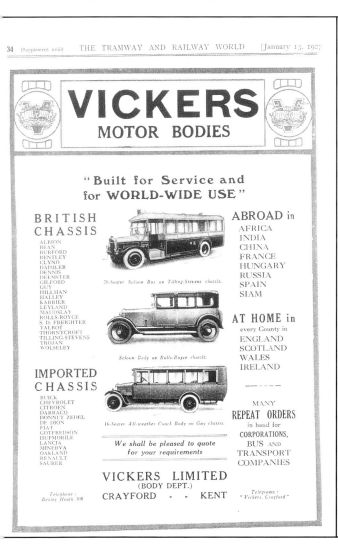

VICKERS
MOTOR BODIES

"Built for Service and for WORLD-WIDE USE"

BRITISH CHASSIS

ALBION
BEAN
BURFORD
BENTLEY
CLYNO
DAIMLER
DENNIS
DEEMSTER
GILFORD
GUY
HILLMAN
HALLEY
KARRIER
LEYLAND
MAUDSLAY
ROLLS-ROYCE
S. D. FREIGHTER
TALBOT
THORNYCROFT
TILLING-STEVENS
TROJAN
WOLSELEY

20-Seater Saloon Bus on Tilling-Stevens chassis.

Saloon Body on Rolls-Royce chassis.

IMPORTED CHASSIS

BUICK
CHEVROLET
CITROEN
DARRACQ
DONNET ZEDEL
DE DION
FIAT
GOTFREDSON
HUPMOBILE
LANCIA
MINERVA
OAKLAND
RENAULT
SAURER

16-Seater All-weather Coach Body on Guy chassis.

We shall be pleased to quote for your requirements

ABROAD in

AFRICA
INDIA
CHINA
FRANCE
HUNGARY
RUSSIA
SPAIN
SIAM

AT HOME in

every County in
ENGLAND
SCOTLAND
WALES
IRELAND

MANY
REPEAT ORDERS
in hand for
CORPORATIONS,
BUS AND
TRANSPORT
COMPANIES

VICKERS LIMITED
(BODY DEPT.)
CRAYFORD - - KENT

Telephone:
Bexley Heath 300

Telegrams:
"Vickers, Crayford"

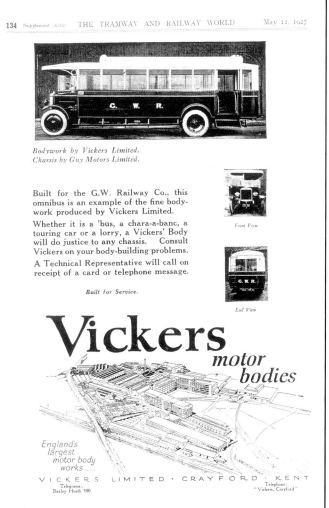

Bodywork by Vickers Limited.
Chassis by Guy Motors Limited.

Front View

Built for the G.W. Railway Co., this omnibus is an example of the fine bodywork produced by Vickers Limited.

Whether it is a 'bus, a chara-a-banc, a touring car or a lorry, a Vickers' Body will do justice to any chassis. Consult Vickers on your body-building problems.

A Technical Representative will call on receipt of a card or telephone message.

Built for Service.

End View

Vickers
motor bodies

England's
largest
motor body
works....

VICKERS LIMITED · CRAYFORD · KENT

Telegrams:
Bexley Heath 300

Telephone:
"Vickers, Crayford"

Vickers' advertising was both eye-catching and forceful. Shortly after these two appeared, in January and May 1927, a double-page spread in a 1927 issue of Commercial Motor – almost unheard of for a bus bodybuilder – reinforced the message they were helping to get across. They must also have formed a very useful part of Black's cv when he was having dinner with Capt. Weymann. The Tilling Stevens bus in the upper position in the left advert was one of eight supplied to Blackpool Corporation Tramways, whilst the Guy in the upper right position was supplied to the Great Western Railway Company.

ironically in addition to shortage of orders both were suffering cash-flow problems whilst waiting to be paid by the British Government for war work, and in particular the supply of munitions a decade ago during the First World War. Cutting a long story short, the two were forced to write down capital, to partially combine, and to divest themselves of various interests and subsidiaries which were holding them back or could be sold to raise cash.

Vickers owned the Metropolitan Carriage, Wagon and Finance Company, (see opposite) based in Birmingham, which it had bought in 1919 from Bernard Docker (of Dockers Paints, BSA and Daimler fame). Docker was appointed by the Government to oversee the rescue package which, as an interim step, resulted in Vickers creating a new company – Vickers (Crayford) Ltd – in July 1928. The crunch came in 1929, when Vickers was forced to reorganise its rolling stock interests. It was obliged to relinquish its electric traction and railway interests and to form a new company, Metropolitan Vickers, to handle that part of its former empire whilst its other non-electric road and rail interests were to be channelled into a new company, jointly owned with Cammell Lairds, and now named Metropolitan **Cammell** Carriage, Wagon and Finance Company, but still located in Birmingham. Crayford's bus works was immediately surplus to requirements and notice of its complete withdrawal from coachbuilding was announced in September 1929. How this new company came into partnership with Weymann's will be seen in the next Chapter.

Notwithstanding the enormity of Vickers' financial problems which had brought the need for these dramatic changes, Black must have been aghast that such a vast organisation, previously under his command, could be wound up in short order at the dictate of a group of financiers. He must at times have wondered whether, if he had stayed to the end, he would have become the king-pin at Birmingham. However, he and some of his senior men now had the opportunity to continue where Vickers were about to leave off.

Black's contacts throughout the growing bus industry, but especially with AEC, with whom Weymann's clearly developed a close relationship, and with Leyland Motors and some of its customers for whom he had produced bodywork, would have been vital, as Izod clearly realised. Especially so was his detailed and first-hand knowledge of the precise method of constructing what had just become amongst the most popular bodies on the bus market – the new Leyland range. He was able to use this expertise to show the Addlestone men how to produce fully-fledged coachbuilt (or to use the more common name 'composite') bodywork to complement the flexible patented variety which would now be used for single-decker bus construction as car production was phased out.

The flexible body was suitable only for single-deck vehicles, whereas the coachbuilt construction was suitable for single- or double-deckers. However from now onwards Weymann's would be principally a *bus* building plant, and until the Fanfare model in the 'fifties, coaches would, in the main, be what in later years would be classed as dual-purpose vehicles with more comfortable seats and higher specification fittings and trim in what was in essence still a bus shell. Interestingly, the first order for coachbuilt-bodied coaches was apparently sub-contracted to Burlingham of Blackpool to complete the interior appointments. It will also become apparent that the bulk of the Addlestone factory's passenger output was for full-sized vehicles, with only a limited number of smaller vehicles such as Leyland Cubs in the 20-seat range.

It should not be thought that Vickers and Amstrongs were alone in their troubles or that Metropolitan Cammell Carriage, Wagon and Finance Co. was a unique amalgamation. All the major engineering, shipbuilding and steel manufacturers were facing similar difficulties and making arrangements to protect or expand their interests and markets. Geoff Lumb records in his history of the English Electric Company's trams that the Board of that Company (set up in December 1918, only a month or so after the end of the war by people from within the John Brown Group of steel makers and shipbuilders) encompassed a wide spectrum. Not surprisingly, its Chairman came from John Brown, with Directors from electrical manufacturing and tramcar building backgrounds. That others came from Fairfield Shipbuilding, Thomas Firth, Cammell Laird, Harland and Wolff and the London & North Western and Lancashire & Yorkshire Railways reveals a network of some considerable influence. During the 'twenties and 'thirties many firms were purchased, factories closed and orders moved around within the remaining members to protect the shrinking market, prices and shareholders' dividends.

Even this pales somewhat when compared to Lord Ashfield's grandiose attempts to form a national consortium of transport manufacturers – to have been called British Vehicles – as reported in 'The Leyland Papers' by former BBC man Graham Turner. Between 1929 and 1933, whilst Ashfield was Chairman of the mighty Underground Group, manufacturers of trams, trolleybuses, buses and underground railway rolling stock for London, he attempted to persuade Leyland and AEC to merge as the opening shot in his scheme. Though he was unsuccessful, the breadth of his plan was breathtaking.

With hindsight we can see that Weymann had chosen a time of great upheaval to enter the coachbuilding industry, with grand plans and no little scheming to attempt to combat the huge problems facing the old-established steel and shipbuilding manufacturers. If he was aware of them, perhaps he felt he would fare better in America but, as we have seen, he was to be disappointed there also.

Lord Ashfield, the former Albert Stanley, was born Albert Knattries in 1874 at New Normanton, near Derby. Brought up in Detroit USA he was General Supt. to the Detroit Street Railway by 1902. In 1903 he joined the New Jersey Street Railway, becoming General Manager by 1907. Later that year he moved to London as General Manager of the Underground Electric Railways Co. becoming Managing Director in 1910. He was, additionally, appointed Managing Director of AEC on its formation in 1912.

Knighted in 1914, he was appointed President of the Board of Trade by Prime Minister Lloyd George in December 1916. He resigned all offices in the UERL Group until he relinquished the Government post in May 1919. He returned to UERL as Chairman and Managing Director, being appointed to the same two positions in AEC in June 1919.

Sir Albert Stanley was elevated to the Peerage in 1920.

On 1st July 1933, now as Lord Ashfield, he became first Chairman of the new London Passenger Transport Board, a position he held until 1947.

In 1940 Ashfield took a 'spare time' position in the Ministry of Aircraft Production acting as personal assistant to Lord Beaverbrook. This would be a logical position for him since he was already involved in wartime aircraft manufacture through London Transport's position in London Aircraft Production Group (LAP) an organisation set in being to co-ordinate bomber production from Duple, Park Royal, Chrysler, Express Motor & Body Works Ltd and LPTB.

During the war he took a keen interest in the welfare of the thousands of people who used the London tube stations as air raid shelters, visiting them nightly during air raids. He died soon after retiring in 1947, aged 73.

Edwin Gilbert Izod, the man charged with the task of taking Weymann's into pastures new.

Educated at Rugby he left this country to gain experience abroad in the manner common before World War 1. A consultant mining engineer with Central Mining and Investment Corporation in South Africa by 1921 he returned to England around 1928, taking charge at Addlestone soon after the move there from Putney.

His job for CM & I was to assess the requirements for equipment and manpower for new projects, making him an ideal choice for the bus factory.

Following the death of Sir Henry Segrave, he took on Tim Healy, Segrave's chauffeur, as his own chauffeur.

The Company's Silver Jubilee brochure of 1950 correctly records him as being Managing Director in 1929. He became Joint Managing Director (with Homfray-Davies) in 1932 after the major re-organisation (qv). In 1937/8 he was appointed Chairman by new owners The Prudential Insurance Company, (alternating with Homfray-Davies) when the Central Mining Company ceased to have any interest in Weymann's.

Remembered for his drive in the factory, enthusiasm for sport, and his speeches from the balcony to spur on the workforce, he also held several patents in his own right including the one carrying his name which is still used for testing the hardness of metals.

Married with a family, he chose to make Edith Cottage, in the factory grounds, his base, regularly entertaining customers, the trade press and selected members of staff there with the assistance of his secretary and companion Miss Hilda Nash. For several years he was Hon. Treasurer of the Sports & Social Club and Hon. Secretary of the Weymann's National Savings Group.

EG Izod died in October 1946.

WEYMANN'S FINANCIAL STRUCTURE: 1925-1937

Readers wishing to follow the detailed financial machinations of the Company are referred to Appendix 1, but the following summary will enable an overall view of the situation to be obtained. It should be noted that information on shareholdings in the period 1928-37 is still being researched, but with difficulty since Companies House have apparently destroyed all papers from the 1925 Company. Any information regarding this aspect will be welcomed and may allow amplification in the Second Volume of this history.

We have seen that up to and including the formation of the 1925 Company the capital came from CTW's racing friends and fellow car manufacturers and, through their connections, the Bernhard Scholle bank. The 1925 Company, as previously noted, was a Public Company financed by this bank.

To understand what would happen to Weymann's factory, personnel and to some extent its order book, we need to look more closely at this bank. Our investigations take us to South Africa, where, in the early 'twenties the vast mining corporations were finding cause for concern, since the price of gold was dropping whilst the cost of mining was steadily increasing. One company in particular comes to our attention, The Central Mining and Investment Corporation, a company within the Corner House Group.

Central Mining had decided to diversify by investing some of its huge reserves into other areas, and chose transport as one of them. It invested in Cape Town Tramways, Port Elizabeth Tramways, Charabancs of Jo'burg, and others of whom Lisbon Tramways would later become very important to the Weymann's factory. It also invested, heavily, into a London Bank which was financing transport development in the UK and elsewhere – Bernhard Scholle.

Central Mining sent one of its senior managers to look after one company which the bank was financing with its money – Edwin Gilbert Izod, an engineer, and the man who was to be in charge at Addlestone until he died in 1946.

From the move to Addlestone in 1928 cars, as noted, became less important to the Company's future. The change of emphasis to concentrate on buses was announced to the trade press in December 1930 and finally confirmed when, in January 1932, in view of the change of direction for the Company, Weymann resigned. Coatalen and Dollfus then left the board of Weymann's Motor Bodies (1925) Ltd, and the production of complete motor car bodies at Addlestone ceased soon afterwards. Weymann's pay-off and the need to value the late Sir Henry Segrave's shares for probate may have been the catalyst for a new valuation of the worth of the Company in 1932, but for whatever reasons the outcome was a dramatic writing down of the value of the shares. Sir JL Napier, Bart. was appointed to the Board around this time whilst the Registered Office moved to Number One, London Wall.

Bernhard Scholle had continued to be involved with CTW's car manufacturing activities as we have seen, and as recorded the American venture was an utter failure. In 1929 the bank increased its capital in line with increasing commitments but it came to grief through no fault of its own over a defaulted £3million Spanish railway contract and in 1935 it went into liquidation.

As the Bank had run deeper into trouble so the involvement of the Mining Company – which was half-owner of the Bank – had increased. As part of the reconstruction, in 1932, Central Mining's London Manager, AW Rogers, was appointed Chairman, succeeding CTW, and alternating with RA MacQueen, the Mining Company's Secretary. The eventual outcome was the sale of the Bernhard Scholle bank's shareholding in the Weymann's company by the liquidator of the Bank in 1937 to the Prudential Insurance Company. Rogers and MacQueen then disappeared from the Weymann's scene.

How Weymann's fared under the 'Pru, and what the 'Pru's eventual solution to disposing of its acquisition became, we shall see in a later chapter.

CHAPTER TWO: 1928 – 1932

THE ADDLESTONE FACTORY

In the previous Chapter the purchase of Cunard and the start of car production was described. Weymann's next expansion was once again built on the back of another business which had been in difficulty but this time the move was to much bigger premises, in Station Road, Addlestone, a town situated some seven miles south of Staines, two miles from Weybridge and approximately 25 miles from central London. It was an address to become familiar to thousands who worked there and to those legions of famous bus companies – throughout the world – who bought the vehicles which were arguably the factory's most famous products, even 40 years later. Had a previous purchaser – Callenders Cables – who bought the building from the liquidator for £16,000 in 1927 actually moved in, our story would have been quite different. In the event they evidently had a change of heart and apparently sold the building to Weymann's for £21,000 later that year.

The Cunard Company had provided manufacturing capacity and know-how, with a skilled workforce able to build Weymann cars as one part of its previously wide repertoire, though no record of anything other than Weymann flexible car production taking place between 1925 and 1928 has been found. The Addlestone factory – strangely with another aeroplane connection – was required for a different market, though, being empty at the time of purchase, it provided no workforce. In an area abounding with precision engineering, aircraft, motor car, bus and van manufacture, that was not a hindrance, staff could always be poached. Norman Froggatt commented to the writer many years later that the presence of Hoyals, on what became known as the Weybridge Trading Estate, was almost sufficient justification in itself for the choice of Addlestone as the company's new home.

The aeroplane connection was no more than a coincidence, but an interesting one nevertheless. The previous occupant of the factory had also been a Frenchman, and an aircraft builder. He was Louis Blériot, the first man to cross the Channel in powered flight, in 1909. His factory, built in 1916 with British Government finance, was now empty because of the lack of demand for his products which, latterly, had included bicycles – and motor cars. He had, in better days, been very successful in producing acetylene motor car lamps.

By chance, late in 1927, a young lady in Addlestone found herself in conversation with an aunt who had worked for Blériot until the factory closed. The aunt was friendly with the caretaker in the now-empty factory and knew that a new company was only a matter of weeks away from moving in. They needed a temporary telephonist to hold the fort until the troops arrived from the old Cunard works at Putney. Our intrepid fourteen year old – Miss Margaret Whindle – offered her services, was shown how to work the switchboard by the caretaker, and became the first employee in the 'new' factory. By an almost incredible stroke of good fortune the writer was able to interview her 73 years later and to obtain, first hand, a record of many events which took place during those crucial early days. She remained with Weymann's until 1942.

She was interviewed for her temporary position by Major Ross, one of the Weymann management team who was in the factory making arrangements for the Putney staff to move in. The Major played no other part in the day-to-day affairs at Addlestone and is thought to have been based at the former Cunard offices at 47, Pall Mall, visiting Addlestone only occasionally.

BLERIOT WHIPPET
(CHAIN DRIVE)
LIGHT CAR.

LARGE CAR COMFORT -- SMALL CAR PRICE.
Dynamo Lighting and Spare Wheel.
Most Economical Running.

£125

THE AIR NAVIGATION & ENGINEERING CO., LTD.,
ADDLESTONE, SURREY.

Advertisement for the Blériot Whippet car, manufactured briefly at Addlestone before Blériot went out of business. The Air Navigation & Engineering Co. Ltd. was the successor to Blériot's earlier company Air Navigation Co Ltd, which had been registered on 1st January 1918.

THE MOVE FROM PUTNEY IS COMPLETED

Early in 1928 the move from Putney took place and amongst the first people to arrive was the manager, AH Walker. The Company Secretary and Accountant, Francis C Webb, then arrived, interviewed Miss Whindle and quickly converted her temporary appointment into a permanent one. Miss Sansom in the buying office became a good friend of the new telephonist and in due course married an up-and-coming man at Weymann's who later became Park Royal's Managing Director. We shall meet him again shortly.

Cunard's Managing Director RI Musselwhite had left in 1923 before the Weymann takeover, as had Arthur Froggatt (ATF), the former General Manager at Putney. It is believed both went to Windovers at Hendon, where ATF had worked earlier in his career. Mr Froggatt later went to Hall, Lewis who at that time were still deeply involved in luxury car manufacture and in due course comes back into the story as a major player (in particular see page 58).

Later in 1928 the former Crayford men arrived, spearheaded by the forthright and outspoken but likeable Bill Black who now took over from Mr Walker as General Manager. With Mr Black, amongst others, came Moss Nelson who with Harold Cook became a lynch-pin in Weymann's drawing office. Mr Walker now went out to Indianapolis to take charge of the car building plant there, but it was a lost cause and as previously mentioned closed in 1931. It was another venture in which CT Weymann was involved with London bankers Bernhard Scholle, but a very long way away from Station Road, Addlestone.

Clearly from now onwards, with all the changes in market and economic forces, and the change of personnel with their different attributes which had taken place, car building was not going to be a priority on the Weymann organisation's Addlestone agenda. Soon it would be off the agenda completely.

This advertisement from the February 1931 issue of *The Motor* magazine demonstrates only too clearly what Weymann's were up against in the car building market. Pressed Steel had opened in 1927, initially supplying only Morris Motors with their body pressings but by 1930 they were trading on the open market and supplying all and sundry. 'Lightweight and free from rattles', mentioned in the advert, were of course two of Weymann's own key selling points. By this time Morris were producing their £100 family car, a far cry from the expensive and bespoke Weymann limousines.

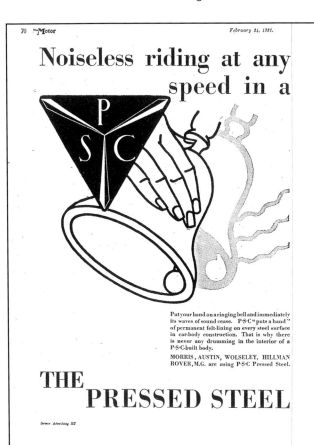

THE CHANGES BEGIN

The task facing the new General Manager was daunting. The market for the firm's basic product was evaporating, there was a Bank to satisfy in addition to the shareholders, and the depression and slump were approaching. Orders were hard to obtain and even though many competitors were going out of business there was still not enough work to go round.

It cannot have helped that the shareholders – and the Bank's Directors – were mainly from that part of the Company's background which was becoming irrelevant. One immediate problem on the car side was addressed, the difficulty of obtaining an acceptable paint finish. Different materials were tried and eventually a compromise was struck whereby the lower part of the cars was panelled in aluminium, which could of course be painted, whilst only the top was finished in the Zapon leathercloth type material. One of the last cars to be built at Addlestone has survived, an Austin carrying body number 5750 completed in 1931, and illustrated below. Now under restoration by its owner Gareth Jones it features the 50/50 construction.

These measures gave a breathing space whilst the serious business of addressing a change of product took place. The temporarily stunted market for buses, and other vehicles, was clearly going to recover sooner or later, and although the Road Traffic Act of 1930 would change the rules Weymann's were in on the ground floor as it were.

There must have been some fairly fast moving for, in January 1929, some six months after Bill Black arrived from Crayford, the inaugural buses were launched. The first, appropriately in view of the Company's antecedents, was on a Renault R1 chassis. The second was a demonstrator on an example of the new Leyland Tiger chassis. Both bodies were based on the same flexible system of construction as was used on the cars, and both were covered with

The Austin car referred to in the text, photographed when purchased by its present owner in 1966. It is undergoing a full restoration. *Courtesy Gareth Jones*

the infamous fabric. The Renault, lettered along its waistrail as a Weymann Coach, was purchased by S&E Crawley of Barnby Dun, near Doncaster. The Leyland later went to the Irish operator HMS Catherwood, the initials representing the Christian names of the operator, not indicating a naval connection.

Further orders quickly followed, the smooth riding characteristics and quiet running being welcomed for long-distance travel by several customers. Early orders included Giltords, Maudslays and Thornycrofts in small numbers.

Alongside the flexible bodies work now began on producing conventional timber-framed bodies, known at Addlestone as 'Coachbuilt' and carrying a **C** prefix in the firm's body lists as opposed to the **W** prefix of the Weymann Patent bodies. Delivery of these would begin in January 1931. The first order for coachbuilt bodies was actually for 59 AEC lorry cabs, and by far the greatest number of chassis now came from the AEC company, which had recently moved to Southall, reflecting the developing association between the two companies.

The very first C series coachbuilt bus bodies were built to the order of Green Line, being based on AEC Regals and forming part of the Green Line T class. The design had been prepared by the Chiswick LGOC staff, working under Eric Ottaway, with Philip Lunghi as the brilliant designer and chief draughtsman. Lunghi originated from Naples, though no-one would have guessed this from his speech or demeanour. This was the start of an association with London's transport which lasted until the end of production at Weymann's.

Right: The new era beginneth: the bonneted Renault, seen at the rear of the Addlestone factory grounds in 1929 before delivery to the customer.
Courtesy :
National Motor Museum.

Below: The Leyland Tiger TS2 demonstrator which went to HMS Catherwood, and whose correct registration Is AZ 2355. Its arrival in March 1929 coincided with the opening of the operator's then-new coachbuilding plant where similar looking bodies, most likely using Weymann-machined framing from Addlestone, were assembled. Although both vehicles on this page were fabric-covered on Flexible Patent frames metal panelling would soon be introduced below the waist.
(See also page 94.)

EVENTS AWAY FROM ADDLESTONE

It will already have become apparent that Weymann's existence was being continually affected by circumstances beyond its control. Not surprisingly then, during 1929, a whole raft of apparently unconnected events gradually came together in a way which would shape the Company's long-term future.

We saw in Chapter One how the Metropolitan Cammell Carriage, Wagon and Finance Company Ltd was formed (MCCW & F), and, with the expertise and resources available from the various companies in the combine, it would have a major contribution to make in the production of rolling stock for home and overseas. During the First World War combine members had been the major producers of military tanks. The new company was registered in January 1929.

A much more important event later that year was The Wall Street Crash on the American Stock Exchange, on Black Tuesday 29/09/29, which sent shock waves throughout the world and marked the start of the Great Depression. Trading in over-valued shares eventually collapsed and two-and-a-half million people became unemployed in the USA. Since American banks were financing banking and industry in other countries the global effect was catastrophic.

Many companies in Britain which had been struggling throughout the slump of the late 'twenties now saw themselves forced into liquidation. Some survived financial reconstruction; most did not. In 1926 *Commercial Motor* listed 30 'prominent' commercial bodybuilders in London and south-east England. By 1933 there were just six left: Beadle; Duple; Park Royal; Shorts; Strachans and Weymann's. Before the end of 1937 Shorts came out of bus building.

Some of those who fell by the wayside had little direct impact on Weymann's. Others, such as Hoyals at Weybridge, had been building large numbers of Weymann patent flexible bodies on vans and light cars, thus providing steady income from royalty payments. Hoyals had expanded in 1924 and were bodying large numbers of Morris chassis. They and many others, including Vickers, fell victim to the output of the new Pressed Steel plant (see page 21).

Another company to run into financial trouble, in 1930, was Hall, Lewis. A builder of bespoke limousines, charabancs and buses, its Head Office was in Cardiff and it was part of an empire based on railway wagon manufacture and hire, mainly for coal traffic. The slump crippled the core business as well as reducing the demand for the north London factory's road transport products. Purchased from the liquidator by the principal creditor, H Yager (the timber supplier to the company), it was reconstituted as Park Royal Coachworks, the name reflecting the (unchanged) location of the coachbuilding company. The Directors of the new company included, amongst others, Yager, Homfray-Davies and Arthur Froggatt. Links between Park Royal and Weymann's will crop up time and again from now onwards, even though they were arch rivals.

Despite this decimation of the industry's manufacturers, and the fact that some 22,000 buses would be scrapped prematurely between 1931 and 1933 as non-compliant with the requirements of the 1930 Road Traffic Act (although operators would have varying time limits in which to fully comply with its regulations), there was still nowhere near enough business to go round. All firms were forced to lay off large sections of their workforce at frequent intervals.

One problem was still the seasonal nature of the charabanc/coach business where customers wanted their vehicles delivered for the start of the season at Easter, and then often bought nothing else until the following Easter. By switching the emphasis to buses the more farsighted companies were able to even out these peaks and troughs to some extent.

One factor in the busmen's favour was becoming apparent. The great tramway boom had passed and many tramcar operators were facing up to the prospect of renewing their worn out tracks and replacing their ageing rolling stock. The cost of relaying tramtrack was considerable and became a justification in many towns for scrapping the tramway systems. Some operators

An early example of Rackham's ground breaking Leyland Titan TD1. The combination of lower chassis and the modern body, way ahead of its time in 1927, ensured its popularity. Although Black had built examples for Leyland under sub-contract whilst at Vickers, the model was a rarity at Addlestone, and Weymann's bodied only two TD1 chassis, for Redcar of Tunbridge Wells. They were to the Leyland standard design, but of the 'hybridge' variety as opposed to the lowbridge version seen here. One is illustrated on page 101.

Lancashire United, owner of the Titan, placed small orders with MCW during the 'thirties but it was not until 1939 that the first of these came to the Addlestone factory. After the war the company, which multi-sourced both chassis and bodies, obtained many of its vehicles from Weymann's.
Leyland, Courtesy BCVM

chose to replace their trams with trolleybuses, thus enabling them to retain the overhead infrastructure, and also to continue to use their locally-produced power – before the nationalisation of the electricity industry in 1948 many operators had their own generating stations. A Royal Commission on Transport which sat between 1928 and 1931 eventually decided that the tramcar should be regarded as obsolete and over the coming decade Weymann's, and others, built many buses and trolleybuses to replace those which were withdrawn.

An unexpected move took place in July 1928, about the time Bill Black moved to Addlestone, when GJ Rackham left Leyland, where he had designed and launched the new range of passenger models including the hugely successful and all-pervading Titan, and joined AEC where he designed the similar and equally successful Regent. Rackham had very definite ideas on body design as would become apparent in due course, particularly with his 'Q' double- and single-deckers. A factor in AEC's decision to prise him out of Leyland's empire, reputedly engineered by the mastermind Lord Ashfield, may have been connected to the fact that AEC was at that time considering creating a bodybuilding plant on its Windmill Lane site in west London. It would have known of Vickers' impending pull-out from Crayford and also recognised that a large measure of Leyland's success was its ability to supply complete vehicles.

Among the major chassis manufacturers Leyland stood out in having substantial in-house body making facilities, dating back to the beginning of its charabanc business before the First World War. Such was the demand for its products that even a capacity for building some 1,200 bodies per year was sometimes insufficient, and in addition to Vickers, already mentioned, Shorts also produced Leyland look-alike bodies under sub-contract. AEC offered to help and to join the sub-contractors if it went into bodybuilding, but apparently received a very less-than-enthusiastic response from the Lancashire company. For whatever various reasons the idea was dropped and Rackham proceeded to put his stamp onto his models through collaboration with the various coachbuilders. Being party to the imminent setting up of the new MCCW&F company in Birmingham through its Director Percy Wheeler (page 16) AEC probably thought it better to invest in other areas of its production facilities at such a difficult time.

Hardly had Rackham settled in at AEC than more trouble surfaced at Park Royal, as it now was. Hymie Yager was, by all accounts, somewhat of a rough diamond. In the difficult period following the 1929 Wall Street Crash when orders were next to non-existent he became even rougher and Homfray-Davies decided that it was time to make a move. Orders were just as thin at Weymann's and he was welcomed there with open arms – and appointed Sales Director. Such was his standing that he was very shortly to be promoted to higher places.

Photograph taken in May 1929 showing the finished but unpanelled appearance of a full-size bus body using the flexible construction. This may be compared to the drawing reproduced on page 12 which shows more clearly the metal brackets joining the frame sections. This was a Daimler CF6, with body number W588, and believed to have been supplied in 1932 to Lewis in Manchester, perhaps after being with Daimler as a demonstrator.

EARLY DAYS AT ADDLESTONE

It was normal practice in the late 'twenties and early 'thirties for most operators to order their complete vehicles from the chassis manufacturer, or the manufacturer's agent, such as Oswald Tillotson who represented first Leyland and then later AEC, leaving them to make the choice of bodybuilder. One of the main reasons was the manufacturers' ability to offer extended payment terms (hire-purchase) to their customers

The first two Weymann's bus bodies produced were, as already recorded, demonstrators in 1929. Orders soon came in, but in ones and twos and mainly for small operators, usually independents. In June 1930 an AEC Regal demonstrator with the new metal panelled finish was shown to delegates at the Tramways, Light Railways and Transport Congress held in Hastings, whilst in December that year the Company announced that "it had decided to extend its business into the omnibus and coach section of the trade" and invited representatives of the industry to inspect its facilities. *Tramway & Railway World* reported that they were impressed with the extent of the shops and their suitability for single- and double-deck construction.

Be that as it may it took the arrival of Baden Rhys Aubrey Homfray-Davies from Park Royal in 1931 to get things into a different gear. Homfray-Davies, as he was always known, was a bus salesman *par excellence*, and a Welshman. His success when visiting the 'home teams' in the valleys can be seen in the list of customers in the appendices, but it was his work in establishing Weymann's as a supplier to the BET companies that was to be the making of the Addlestone order book over the years. His efforts did not go unnoticed.

Whilst Weymann's were enjoying the first fruits of Homfray-Davies' labours events elsewhere were less encouraging. During the summer of 1931 Britain found itself in the middle of another financial crisis – but this time of such magnitude that the country was on the verge of bankruptcy. The Government resigned and a National Government was formed under Ramsay MacDonald. Drastic measures including the stopping of borrowing and imposition of strict economy measures were applied in an attempt to balance the budget. World conditions, in addition to British problems, made this very difficult to achieve and, following a run on the pound by speculators, at this time Sterling came off the Gold Standard, followed by a devaluation of 30%. This measure was to have repercussions for the Central Mining and Investment Corporation in South

An early production example of the flexible vehicles, one of four AEC Regal coaches supplied in 1929 to Orange Bros. for their London to Scotland service using the Great North Road. Orange Bros. remained a regular customer until 1933, taking small batches of flexible bodies each year, but were taken over by United Automobile Services in 1935. United had had their own bodybuilding plant in Lowestoft, by then part of Eastern Counties, and consequently no further orders went to the Addlestone factory.

An Orange Bros. Maudslay flexible bodied saloon was displayed at the 1931 Commercial Motor Show, making Weymann's fourth body on display. The dull, sombre appearance of the vehicle, would have reflected to some measure the depressed times of the period . . .

... whereas in contrast the bright glossy paintwork on the AEC demonstrator, below, as exhibited at the November 1931 Olympia Commercial Motor Show, could not have failed to catch AJ Boyd's eye when he came down from Birmingham (see page 29). If he had ever thought that Weymann's were just small time builders of wooden-framed single-deckers for independent operators this would have quickly convinced him otherwise. Painted in the dark blue livery of Sheffield Corporation it was the Addlestone factory's first double-decker motor bus and after a period of demonstration was purchased by Sheffield's transport department. It gave around 14 years service, being withdrawn in 1945.

The rather rakish frontal styling on this Regent made the vehicle obviously different from the other Weymann's double-decker bus body at the Motor Show, on a Daimler chassis. Built to low height specification it seated 22 passengers upstairs, with twin gangways to avoid infringing Leyland's patents. Just visible through the front upper windows is the faint outline of the ladder which hinged out to provide the means of emergency escape from the upper-deck in the event of an accident. (See also page 100).

Africa which were to affect Weymann's as described on page 19. During this crucial period many British companies and even municipal operators were obliged to implement severe wage cuts to even the most senior of their staff in order to remain solvent.

In addition to financial uncertainties and difficulties there were other constraints on customers preparing to place orders for new vehicles. Although Herbert Morrison's 1930 Road Trafffic Act was now in force, some of the requirements were still not fully defined due to their being introduced in parts over a period of some months. The Act was designed to regulate the industry, to cut out wasteful and often dangerous competition through the licensing of services, and to enforce uniform and often improved standards for vehicle specifications, especially in matters such as braking and emergency exits.

Although there would shortly be a set of national standards to which all vehicles would have to comply, through the Construction and Use Regulations, local watch committees and others could still impose restrictions which might not be met by vehicles built to the very latest manufacturer's specification. Not until these Construction and Use Regulations came into force in January 1931 was this area clarified, allowing customers to go ahead and place orders knowing that their vehicles would be able to operate countrywide without restrictions being imposed at the whim of local authorities or watch committees.

Two examples will illustrate the dilemma. Bolton Corporation wished in 1930 to order two enclosed double-deckers but, mindful of the uncertainty of the forthcoming but as yet undefined requirement for upper-deck emergency exit arrangements, and the additional cost of an arrangement which might subsequently be rejected locally, chose instead to take a backward step and order two further open staircase models. Potteries Electric Traction, later, as PMT, to become a significant Weymann's customer, took two single-deckers whose chassis were standard and in service with other operators. The local Watch Committee refused licences for them to be operated because 'the petrol tank was within the passenger area' (instead of being under the driver's seat as

was the arrangement in the 'twenties!). The petrol tanks were, of course, underslung, but such tactics were commonly used to restrict unwanted competition or favour another operator. The 1930 Act put a stop to this.

The C & U Regulations affected not only dimensions and weights, overhangs, doorway layouts and emergency exit arrangements, but also such matters as provision of mirrors, compulsory from 1st January 1932, and the clear marking of unladen weight and speed, mandatory from 1st April 1932. Yet another complication was arising concerning the use of safety glass, not mandatory except for windscreens and front windows, but becoming increasingly desirable and kept in the public eye by publicity given in the transport press to accidents where the only major injuries arose from flying glass. Derby took a leading role here, specifying safety glass throughout for its trolleybuses and buses from 1931. Commendable as it was this measure meant that another standard stores-consumable would henceforth have to be replaced by a bought-in specialist item, increasing costs at a time when everyone was looking for savings. Safety glass manufacture had become a profitable growth industry.

It seems strange that in this era of so much transport-based legislation it was still not necessary to take any form of test before being allowed to drive a car. Transport Minister Percy J Pybus, Morrison's successor after the change of Government in 1931, was quoted as saying in November 1932 that there was no need since research had shown 'that most accidents were not caused by novice drivers'. Perhaps he was placing great store in the newly created first issue of the Highway Code but whether or not, tests finally became obligatory in 1935. One law which was to be scrapped at this time would henceforth allow parked cars to be left locked – previously they had to be left open!

Development of the first six-wheel double-deck trolleybus by the local vehicle maker, Guy Motors Ltd, in 1926, encouraged by C Owen Silvers, General Manager of Wolverhampton Corporation's transport department, led to the latter's operation of a fleet of such vehicles. By 1928 there were enough to complete tramway abandonment and by 1931 the Wolverhampton undertaking was the largest trolleybus operator in Britain, with 70 vehicles, including 38 six-wheelers. The Sunbeam concern, also based in the town, decided to enter the trolleybus market and the choice of Weymann's to body its prototype trolleybus, type MS1, completed in May 1931, was hardly a surprise with Louis Coatalen on its Board as well as that of Weymann's. It was also quite a bold venture for Weymann's as its first double-deck body. In 1933 three of an improved MS2 model, again with Weymann's bodywork, were purchased along with the prototype, JW 526, nearest the camera in this view of all four outside the depot.
Courtesy Geoff Lumb

A 1931 advert subtly drawing attention to the fact that the fabric body was no more. Note the Weymann trade mark within the knight – this had appeared on a metal plate carried by the patent flexible cars. It was a clever adaptation of the initials CTW and the theme would later be continued when the MCW trademark was prepared (see page 41).

An overall problem facing all builders was the constant need to work within weight limits, now 10 tons for a fully-laden two-axle double-decker. As vehicles became more sophisticated and passengers looked for greater comfort, weights increased and chassis manufacturers and body builders were obliged to work very closely to keep weight down. The increasing popularity of the (heavier) diesel engine added to the problem, but although fuel economy was the prime motivation, as with safety glass passenger safety was also a major consideration.

Chassis manufacturers had to play their part and AEC reduced the weight of its Regent chassis such that Park Royal, who used aluminium quite extensively in their bodies, managed to build a 60-seat body upon it in 1931, stated by the makers to be an improvement of nine passengers over their previous product. Weymann's bodywork was heavier, and although they managed to build 56-seat vehicles in both composite and metal framed versions in 1932/3 these were exceptional and 48-52 was more usual until around 1935. They did not exceed 56 seats in a two-axle motor bus for the period covered by this first Volume. Throughout the 'thirties there was constant lobbying by operators and manufacturers for increased weight limits, and the popularity of six-wheeled vehicles (three-axled) was a means of getting round the problem. Operators replacing bogie trams, which typically carried between 70 and 80 seated passengers, had a particular problem here.

Against this complex background work continued in the factory in preparation for the forthcoming 1931 Commercial Motor Show at which the firm's first double-deckers would be exhibited: the very first Sunbeam trolleybus – a demonstrator in Wolverhampton's colours; a full-height Daimler CH6 demonstrator in Ashton-under-Lyne's colours; and a lowbridge AEC Regent demonstrator in Sheffield's colours. Quite a presence for this re-directed former car company, though a flexible patent bodied Maudslay single-decker retained the link. By now, of course, all Weymann's vehicles were metal panelled and coach painted and this would be the first showing of coachbuilt vehicles. The Sheffield vehicle incorporated a hinged panel at the front offside of the upper-deck which swung out to allow a ladder to drop down as a means of emergency escape.

At the Show, held at Olympia in November 1931, AJ Boyd, a Director of the recently-formed Metropolitan Cammell Carriage, Wagon & Finance Company, was clearly impressed by the three double-deck coachbuilt Weymann's bodies to be seen, two in impressive dark blue liveries for very differing operators, and the other in Wolverhampton's green and cream, on the Sunbeam stand, in addition to the single-decker for Orange Bros. An apparently chance meeting took place between Boyd and Messrs Izod and Homfray-Davies and introductions were made. The Weymann's men were already keenly aware of the advantages that metal-framed bodies would offer and now had met the man who held the key to their next move.

The outcome of this initial meeting was the suggestion that there might well be advantage and mutual benefit by a pooling of resources. The Addlestone Company had wide experience of building a variety of types of wooden-framed vehicles, and already had an impressive sales organisation. The Birmingham Company had developed a metal-framed body which would turn out to be a world-beater but, with its railway background, had little experience of selling into the bus industry. From this encounter, and largely at the instigation of Homfray-Davies, more discussions followed so that by late spring of 1932 it had been agreed that a joint sales organisation should be created, funded by the two companies, and having its office in central London.

Prior to the Motor Show, during 1931, as mentioned in the previous chapter the decisions had been made concerning Weymann's policy in relation to car building. On 5th January 1932 the Board agreed to withdraw completely from this market, and also accepted Charles Weymann's resignation. CTW was paid the sum of £55,000 for his shareholding, and this included reimbursement for money he had spent in purchasing the Cunard Company and a consideration for loss of future royalties. With the increasing decline in demand for his flexible bodies he was probably wise to take the money. He played no further part in the Company and nothing more appears to have been heard of him at Addlestone though he remained an active, even prolific, inventor, registering many patents during the late 'thirties and beyond. When Mrs Margaret Colman, the former receptionist, was interviewed, she was surprised to hear that there actually was a man called Weymann and was quite sure that, between the end of 1927 when she joined the organisation, and 1942 when she left to start a family, CTW had never visited the Addlestone factory.

In those early days Board Meetings were believed to have been held at the Registered Office at Austin Friars in the City, but it came as a surprise to the writer to find that Weymann had apparently never even visited the bus plant. This appears to confirm that as cars diminished in importance from 1928 his interest declined and he played no part in the Company's new activities.

Weymann's departure marked the end of an era. Central Mining now appointed a new Chairman, AW Rogers, and financial and manufacturing arrangements came under intense scrutiny. The change in direction had not taken off until coachbuilt metal panelled vehicles were offered in 1931 – output for the years 1930 and 1931 had been 22 and 212 buses respectively – but there was a long way to go and the accounts for the year ended 31st December 1931 showed a loss of over £12,000.

Despite this and the overall gloomy picture described earlier there was clearly confidence that things were going to improve. Accordingly capital was expended on improvements in the factory, and in late January 1932 the trade press were again invited to Addlestone, this time to inspect a brand new paintshop facility which had just been put into use, again reflecting the change of direction and the requirements of the bus industry for coach-painted vehicles.

This was a necessary move, but a brave one when seen against the general economic situation and the fact that many customers had undoubtedly held back from placing orders. Karrier Motors' Chairman, commenting on his Company's problems at the same time, revealed that many customers whose orders had been accepted and completed were then unable to take delivery because their financial situation had deteriorated.

As if there were not enough obstacles to progress the Royal Commission on Transport had thrown another large spanner in the works when it set up the Conference on Rail and Road Transport, consisting of four railway General Managers and four representatives of transport of goods by road, under the chairmanship of Sir Arthur Salter – a man who was in his day to be the equivalent of the infamous Dr Beeching of the 1960s – to consider the apportionment of charges for road usage in the freight transport industry and, inter-alia, to find ways of reducing the Treasury's burden for the ever-increasing cost of road building and repair through new or increased taxation. The pages of the transport press were full of letters condemning the proposals: no representatives from the passenger transport industry, the lack of adequate consultation, insufficient provision for representation, enormous proposed increases in road tax – from around £370 to £555 for a 60-seat double-decker bus, an increase of some 50% – and a host of other objections. Tramway operators who had, in some cases, been stung by the Royal Commission's recent edict that tramways should be regarded as obsolete, and that money should not be invested in new projects, suddenly realised that with such proposals for greatly increased taxation on buses their trams would be more economic to operate.

Whilst the big guns of the day, including Richard Howley, the Deputy Chairman of British Electric Traction, and Manchester's Transport Manager R Stuart Pilcher, waded into the fray to attempt to force the Government to heed the industry's warnings, and to make speedy decisions, rather than as the Report proposed wait until the 1933 budget, the saga dragged on and yet more orders for new buses were put on hold. Then, to make matters worse, in

Green Line Coaches Ltd was created as an LGOC subsidiary in July 1930, its new services connecting London with surrounding towns proving popular. A new fleet of 150 AEC Regal coaches was soon in use but a fresh factor adding to the haste to expand further was the introduction of the new road service licence system in the Road Traffic Act, 1930. It came into effect on 9th February 1931, after which only services already running counted as 'established'. Bodies to LGOC design for a further 100 Regals were thus required quickly, and Weymann's did remarkably well to win and execute a contract for 25 of these as its first order for bodies of conventional composite construction – at that stage no order even for its patented flexible coach bodies had gone beyond seven examples for any one customer. Fortunately Black and his team from Vickers were experienced in such work. The coaches were duly delivered in January-February 1931. The illustration shows one, by then in London Transport's version of Green Line livery, still looking very smart in August 1937. *G H F Atkins*

Below is a vehicle from the first big order for Flexible bodies, and in fact one of the biggest ever received for the Weymann patent type. The order was for twenty 20-seater Flexible bodies mounted on the newly-introduced Leyland Cub chassis built at Kingston-on-Thames. According to the records it took some 5-6 months – November 1931 to May 1932 – to construct these vehicles, suggesting a rate of about one per week alongside the by-then more numerous coachbuilt vehicles. The customer was Crosville Motor Services, a Tilling/BAT company based in Chester and requiring lightweight vehicles for its services across Telford's suspension bridge over the Menai Straits into Anglesey where a severe weight restriction was in force. The lightweight construction of the Flexible body – W877 being shown – was ideally suited to this requirement. The petrol-engined Cubs gave good service but Crosville took no more Weymann's bodies until it received a diverted order from the Midland General Company in 1950.

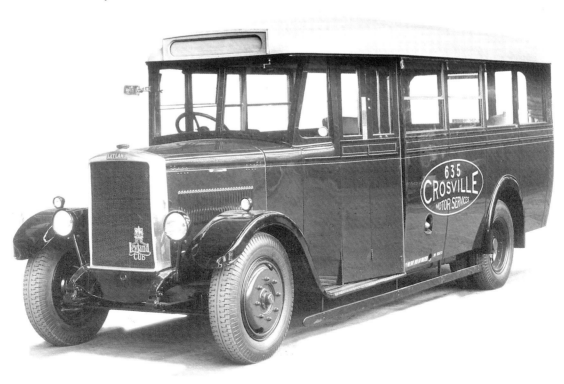

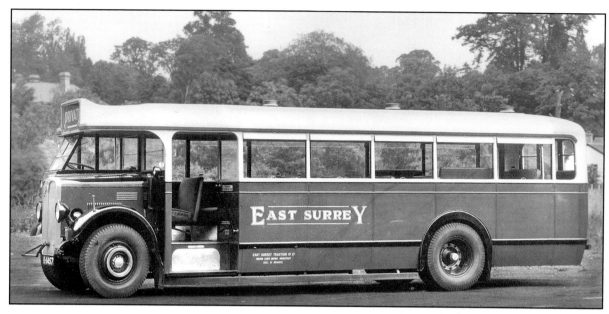

The East Surrey Traction Co Ltd, of Reigate, was controlled by LGOC but the body design of three 30-seat AEC Regal buses of May-June 1931 was unusual within that empire in being of the 27ft length then optional for the Regal. The bodies departed from LGOC practice in other respects, save for the deep destination box and wide entrance, devoid of door, both similar to those of the LGOC LT-class six-wheel single-deckers of that year. Note the Weymann bodybuilder's plate, of the type usual on the firm's products of the 1930s, on the entrance step. Also supplied at the same time were six 20-seat buses on Morris-Commercial Viceroy chassis. ESTC became London General Country Services Ltd from January 1932, passing to the London Passenger Transport Board (LPTB) from 1st July 1933. The vehicle shown, PL 6457, with body C147, became T381 in the LPTB fleet, though this did not occur until the country area fleet received fleet numbers in 1935.

No uniformity of outline was discernible among Weymann's earliest double-deckers. This was the fifth (body C169), the first on a Daimler chassis and one of the three at the November 1931 Commercial Motor Show, being in the blue and white with red waistbands of Ashton-under-Lyne Corporation, with whom it was to run as a demonstrator, registered KV 64. Although the Addlestone design team did not repeat this style, there were some hints of what was to follow. The sloping profile was there at the upper front of the upper deck and the slight rounding of the cab front below the windscreen was later to become more voluptuous. Ashton returned the CP6 to Daimler after a year, preferring to support nearby maker Crossley for its next buses, but their bodywork had much the same odd-looking concave profile. Daimler KV 64 next went to Coventry, see page 101. *Courtesy WGS Hyde*

The formal announcement in the Municipal Tramways & Transport Association's *Journal* in July 1932 following the setting up of the new company.

September 1932 an increase in the price of petrol from about 1s 4d per gallon to about 1s 8d (around 7p to around 8½p) literally added fuel to the flames. Not until May 1933, some three months after the not-too-popular PJ Pybus resigned as Minister of Transport and returned to English Electric, was the situation resolved but by then it was too late for some – this unsettled period was the time that London Lorries, Hoyal and Dodson, amongst others of Weymann's contemporaries, ran into the difficulties which caused them to cease trading.

Meanwhile, following the agreement to collaborate, Weymann's and Metropolitan Cammell prepared to formalise matters and on 5th July 1932 the new jointly-owned company – Metropolitan-Cammell-Weymann Motor Bodies Limited – was registered. Announcements appeared in the trade press and the new name appeared thereafter in all advertising of the two companies' products. The popularity of metal-framed bodywork in the industry was already apparent, and, as mentioned, some alterations had already been made at Addlestone in the paint shop area. If the potential they believed existed was to be capitalised upon, more expansion of facilities would be soon be required.

It was announced in November 1932 that an additional Director had been appointed, Sir Joseph L Napier, Bart., a 37 year old veteran of the First World War, a member of the Napier car family and a Lloyds Underwriter, whilst in December a financial reconstruction was undertaken. Weymann's capital was written down from £66,000 to £23,100 by cancelling 12 shillings (60p) in respect of each Preference Share and 10s 8d (53p) on each Ordinary Share. There were also now £50,000 worth of debentures. Subsequently all shares were to be consolidated into one class of 5 shilling (25p) shares and the Nominal Capital was increased to £100,000 by the creation of 307,600 new 5 shilling (25p) shares.

Weymann's were fortunate that their bank was able, and willing, to continue to support them. It doubtless helped that their owners also owned half that bank.

By 1932, and gaining in confidence, the company was evolving its own body designs. By the middle of that year, this style of double-decker was becoming identifiable on sight as a Weymann's product. Although its roots lay in AEC's 1931 Show sloping-front style with projecting cab cowl, Weymann's tended to favour a more upright profile and the use of six- rather than five-bay construction. This one, with body number C424, was one of five 50-seat examples dating from July 1932 on TSM D60A6 chassis for Notts & Derby Traction, of Langley Mill, Derbyshire. This was one of the Balfour Beatty companies, strong in that area and soon to be among Weymann's most loyal cutomers. The use of TSM as a marque name had been adopted by the former Tilling-Stevens concern, for a time retitled T. S. Motors Ltd, evidently to emphasise that it was no longer an associate of Thomas Tilling Ltd. The D60A6 was TSM's six-cylinder double-deck model, but these were the only examples bodied at Addlestone.

Below: The British Electrical Federation (later called BET Federation) acted as purchasing agent for some of the BET and TBAT companies where BET influence was strong. It provided complete body designs to a distinctive series of styles, Weymann's being one of several bodybuilders successful in obtaining contracts, for which there was fierce competition. Yorkshire Traction, based at Barnsley, was an early customer and the vehicle shown was one of six (C365-70) on Leyland Tiger TS4 chassis supplied in May-June 1932. At that date, several operators used the same BEF exterior for both bus and coach duties, and as seen here, these vehicles were used by the Yorkshire Services pool of operators on their London services. In this case, the interior, with comfortable seats and curtains in typical contemporary style, was sub-contracted by Weymann's to H V Burlingham of Blackpool, specialists in coach manufacturer, perhaps at that time able to do this work more cheaply than could be accomplished at Addlestone. Simple board-type destination indicators were still favoured by several operators of such services, in this case lit by a roof-mounted lamp as shown.
Both photographs by GHF Atkins

Above: Mansfield District, also a Balfour Beatty subsidiary, took 30 similar bodies to the Notts & Derby example opposite, but on AEC Regent chassis and seating 54, when it replaced its tramway system, also in 1932 – four more Regents also supplied had Short Bros. 56-seat bodies. The petrol-engined chassis had the 16ft 3in wheelbase, by then standard. Manufacturers were now making much use of tram replacement pictures, this one of No. 64 (VO 8564) with body number C500 appearing in AEC publicity of the time.

Below: Devon General was to become a good customer for Weymann's, taking its first order in March 1932 and continuing buying, except when wartime stopped the normal supply, until 1962.
The Leyland Lion LT5 seen below was one of 21 supplied in two batches during 1932, actually the first of the second batch, and carries composite body C357. The position of the destination box, dropped to avoid breaking the roof line, would recur time and again. Note that a sunshine head is fitted, allowing the centre of the roof to be rolled back. An early Patent Flexible body supplied to this operator around this time survives, just, in a west of England bus museum. It represents perhaps one of the few remaining opportunities to recreate an example of this unique type of body construction.

CHAPTER THREE: 1933 – 1937

THE TEMPO INCREASES

The difficult financial period from 1929 was beginning to ease somewhat by 1933 and orders were coming through for new vehicles. Devaluation of the pound in 1932 had also opened up an export market for Weymann's in South Africa, though it was significant that the first orders were for customers in whom Central Mining had invested in the mid-'twenties, namely Cape Town, Port Elizabeth and Charabancs of Johannesburg.

The arrival of Homfray-Davies in 1931 had set in motion the improvement in Weymann's order book. Now the link with Metropolitan-Cammell (MCCW&F) through the new sales organisation (MCW) was about to give a welcome boost to the factory. The demand throughout the bus industry for metal-framed bodies was increasing and Weymann's would now be able to share in this market. After the kerfuffle of the previous few months the opportunity to capitalise on the changing situation must have come as something of a relief in the new Sales Office in Vickers House, Westminster, and also in the Addlestone factory.

The economy was picking up slowly, with various measures including Bank Rate, eventually down to 2½%, all playing their part. The Road Traffic Act was seen to be having positive benefits; many of the Salter Report's damaging proposals in respect of the bus industry had been quietly put aside, after being described by new Transport Minister, the Hon. Oliver Stanley MC MP and younger son of Lord Derby, as 'arising from unfortunate ambiguities'; customers were placing orders and, most importantly, the demand for the newly-available (to Addlestone) metal-framed bodies was encouraging.

During 1932, some 200 bus bodies had been built of the two wooden-framed varieties. In 1933 the comparable figure would be only 66 with an additional 44 metal-framed bodies. But then a glance below will reveal that the total 1934 output was more than double that of 1933 and the figures would increase steadily until 1939. The table shows the respective numbers of orders gained in the period covered by this chapter. Profitability increased in line with output and the late 'thirties were very successful for the Company. There was also non-psv production, not accounted for in these figures.

Chart showing numbers of flexible, coachbuilt and metal-framed bus bodies built in the period 1933-40, that year marking the end of normal peacetime production rates.

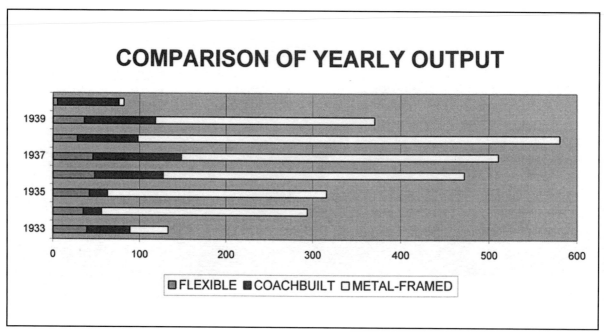

METAL-FRAMED BODIES

As the fight for survival in the industry had intensified, innovation in manufacture and design had become vital. Reduction in costs, material and manufacturing, and reduction in unladen weights were all becoming more and more important.

Onc major development was the change from wooden to metal framing, introduced by Shorts and using their aircraft expertise. Brush had actually pioneered the metal-framed body in 1907 but it was Max Meltz's work with aluminium at Short Bros. Rochester which really made the industry take notice from 1927. The resultant frame could be lighter, stronger, could carry more passengers, and was more easily suited to batch manufacture. Vickers and the other steel manufacturers were also looking into metal framing as an outlet for their steel production but it was work in Birmingham which was to influence the whole industry, and especially Weymann's. It is therefore appropriate to take a look at the history of the MCW body.

Freddy Rayer

Joint designer of the MCW patent metal-framed body.

During the difficult times of the late 'twenties some of the railway companies were looking to becoming bus operators in their own right, and MCWF (the predecessor to MCCW) was looking to diversify from railway rolling stock into bodywork for the growing bus industry in an attempt to keep its workshops busy. The Chief Designer at the Metropolitan Railway Carriage and Wagon Company was Freddy Rayer. He had come to Birmingham from Leeds Forge, another company in the group, where he had also been Chief Designer. He had served his time in the Great Western Railway's Swindon workshops, following his father who, amongst other achievements, had designed the pumps

Leyland Titan TD3 with body M22, Weymann's first metal-framed front-entrance double-deck body, seen at Leyland in February 1934, shortly before it was registered TJ 4511 by Leyland Motors. The registration plate still showing "MCW 1934" suggests it may have been an MCW exhibit for the November 1933 Olympia Show. It was in Thames Valley livery but was a highbridge bus and that concern used lowbridge double-deckers exclusively. No doubt Leyland's body engineers had a good look at its construction, but its registration at that date suggests that active demonstration duty was planned, perhaps aiming at fleets favouring its body layout – it was not until May 1934 that troubles with Leyland's own metal body began to appear, the upshot being the head-hunting of Colin Bailey from MCCW to run Leyland's body department. Sold in 1935 to Northern General it went to its Tyneside subsidiary in 1936.

which keep water out of the Severn Tunnel. Over 70 years later his nephew, Joe Allen, explained to the writer that Rayer, working with Philip Brunton, had been the designer of what became the MCW patented metal-frame body. During 1929 he developed a frame using a special section drawn from a rolled tube which had enormous strength without great weight (see illustration).

The design work on the metal framing was considered successful and two prototype vehicles were produced, one built in steel for London General and the second in Duralumin for Birmingham Corporation. Both were well received and the decision was taken to go into full scale production.

At this stage the project was passed to the Assistant Works Manager to prepare jigs and set up an assembly line. The AWM was Colin Bailey who had been apprenticed at Cammell Laird's shipyard at Birkenhead in 1919. In 1922 he was transferred to Cammell Laird's wagon works in Common Lane, Nottingham where he was assistant to the Works Manager, Lewis Ord, a Canadian. The Managing Director at Common Lane was AS Bailey, Colin's father. Bailey Snr. decided his son was better suited to rolling stock than shipping and Colin was tasked with designing a ventilation system for a contract for London Underground stock. After a spell with Newlay Railway Carriage, and then with Leeds Forge, both members of the group and both involved in the railway contract, he was transferred in 1923 to Cammell Laird's factory in Ward End, Birmingham, working with Mr Cheesley who had been AWM at Leeds Forge.

By 1924/5 Colin Bailey had become Chief Engineer at the Midland works where amongst other foremen was W Shirley, in charge of the gas producer plant. His son, Bill Shirley Jnr., was apprenticed there under his father. The millwright foreman was affectionately known as 'tear-arse' Needs, better known as Ted in his days at Weymann's. Needs became foreman of the bus project in Birmingham and helped design the various jigs necessary for assembly. Thus we have here the embryo team who designed and produced the MCW patent metal-framed body honing their skills within the MCW&F group.

AS Bailey later became Joint MD of MCCW and one of the first Directors of Metropolitan-Cammell-Weymann Motor Bodies Ltd (see below). Colin Bailey was later personally head-hunted from Birmingham in 1935 by Henry Spurrier of Leyland Motors to sort out that company's disastrous entrée into metal-framing. Leyland had started work on metal framing in 1932, produced a prototype by 1933, gone into production in 1934 and found themselves in very serious trouble by 1935. CC Bailey joined the Lancashire company and redesigned the Leyland-MetSec structure, using a pillar section similar to the MCW one but without infringing the Birmingham patents. His 1936 body served Leyland well – in fact until the end of its bodybuilding activities in 1954.

A major difference between the MCCW body construction and all others so far encountered in this series of bodybuilder histories is that the body pillars and sections were joined together by hot rivetting, using the same methods employed in the railway and shipbuilding industries to which the MCCW constituent companies' backgrounds belonged. Bailey did not take this particular routine with him to Leyland, though it gave enormous strength and rigidity and was a major factor in the success and long-life of Rayer's bodies.

By 1932 when the tie up with Weymann's took place MCCW&F had built around 150 bus bodies, and their competitors would soon start making moves to combat the headstart they had gained.

The metal framing specialists were all to be in demand. Needs later went to Park Royal where their first metal framed body, for Reading, had been completed in September 1933. Rayer went to Brush to develop their metal-framed bodies whilst Max Meltz, the man responsible for Short's success, moved to Strachans, also in 1933.

An advertisement placed by MCW in the AEC Gazette in July 1936 showing the patented pillar section. This was one of several patents – others covering the flexible mounting to the chassis are illustrated in the Appendices. All were taken out by the company to protect its structure from copying by other bodybuilders. From mid-1932 all advertising was placed by MCW using the London address and neither Weymann's (page 29) nor MCCW&F adverts (page 40) appeared from then onwards.

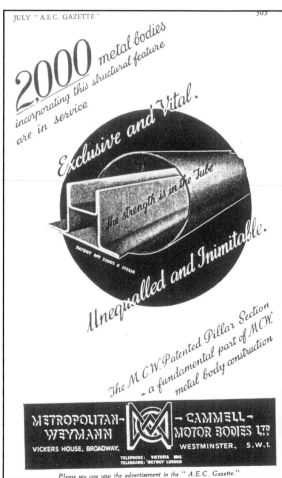

JULY "A.E.C. GAZETTE"

2000 metal bodies incorporating this structural feature are in service

Exclusive and Vital.

The strength is in the Tube

PATENT Nº 350613 & 355630

Unequalled and Inimitable.

The M.C.W. Patented Pillar Section – a fundamental part of M.C.W. metal body construction

METROPOLITAN-WEYMANN
VICKERS HOUSE, BROADWAY.
TELEPHONE: VICTORIA 8846
TELEGRAMS: 'METWEY' LONDON

CAMMELL MOTOR BODIES LTD
WESTMINSTER, S.W.1.

Please say you saw the advertisement in the "A.E.C. Gazette."

METROPOLITAN-CAMMELL-WEYMANN MOTOR BODIES LTD

Colin C Bailey was born in India in 1902 whilst his father was Chief Mechanical Engineer of the Bengal Nagpur Railway, based at the works in Khargpur. Sent back to England in 1908 he was educated at Marlborough College. In 1919 he became a Pupil Apprentice with Cammell Laird, the company his father was then working for. After working his way up the ladder following a transfer to Laird's Nottingham rolling stock factory he became a lynch pin in the MCW metal-framed body project.

Head hunted by Spurrier to join Leyland Motors in 1935 he was appointed Body Shop Superintendent in September 1935, and designed the famous Bailey body which remained essentially unchanged to the end of Leyland's bus production.

During the Second World War he was moved to take charge of the BX tank factory at Leyland. He became Group Production Controller for tanks, co-ordinating teams from Leyland's Kingston works; English Electric Stafford; Fowlers in Leeds; Beyer, Peacock Manchester; North British Loco Works Glasgow; Metropolitan Cammell Carriage Birmingham; Birmingham Waggon Works; also the Nuffield Group.

After the return to peacetime conditions he was again in charge of Leyland's South Works bus factory. When Spurrier decided to run down bus bodies in favour of lorry cabs CCB moved to Duple as Director and General Manager, and introduced metal framing into that organisation. His first such design was the Duple Roadmaster. After leaving Duple he moved into the commercial manufacturing industry, joining Birmetals, and responsible for design and production of their aluminium sections.

Colin Bailey died in October 1991.

There appears to be a widespread belief by enthusiasts and even many in the bus industry that Metropolitan-Cammell-Weymann, or MCW as most people refer to it, was the manufacturer of bus bodies which were seen throughout the land, and which had been built either in Birmingham or Addlestone. It was not.

The jointly-owned company, whose Registered Office and Sales Administration was in Westminster, London SW1, close to London Transport's Head Office, was set up in July 1932 specifically as a sales organisation which would also enable a pooling of technical information between the two companies who owned it – Weymann's Motor Bodies (1925) Ltd of Addlestone and the Metropolitan Cammell Carriage, Wagon & Finance Company of Birmingham, to whom the orders were sub-contracted in the ratio of the capital introduced by the two companies. For further details see the relevant appendix.

Intended to be non-profit making, MCW, during the period covered by this volume and until 1966, built no vehicles and had no assets. It rented office space from MCCW&F's parent company Vickers, and was the tool which Homfray-Davies had proposed should be created to allow the two companies to make use of each other's strengths whilst opening up a vast market for both in patented metal-framed bus bodywork once they had agreed to work together.

By this means it enabled the Birmingham factory to increase its output by using the sales skill and contacts of Homfray-Davies and his team, whilst, in return and in parallel, allowing Weymann's access to the patents, technology and know-how through training from the Birmingham designers and technicians to allow them to construct metal-framed bodies to a tried and proven design.

In 1933 ND Bruce joined the organisation as Sales Manager. He had previously been with Shell, but before that and doubtless of greater interest to MCW, he had been the manager at Dartford with the Balfour Beatty Group, an organisation for whom Weymann's would build a great many bodies. He had trained with Brush Electrical Engineering Company Ltd. Unfortunately he suffered ill-health and left in March 1937, being followed in October of that year by RM (Bon) Cole, also from Brush, who joined WCS Chatfield at Vickers House to complete the sales team.

The effect of the tie-up on the Addlestone portion of the MCW order book can be seen at a glance when the comparative yearly outputs are examined in the diagram on page 36, and it is obvious that without the ability to produce and sell metal-framed bodywork Weymann's output would have been constrained to the extent where it is unlikely that the Company could have survived.

Homfray-Davies was indeed entitled to be congratulated on his far-sightedness.

Extract from the Memorandum and Articles of Association of the joint Sales Company.

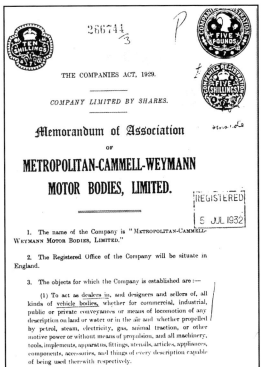

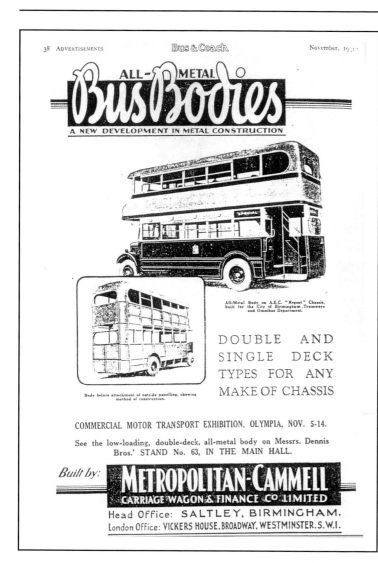

This Metropolitan-Cammell advertisement in Bus & Coach for November 1931 shows the original prototype metal-framed body designed and developed by Messrs Brunton and Reyer and built by that firm on an AEC Regent chassis in 1930 and supplied to Birmingham Corporation, its number 209 (OG 209). It broadly conformed to that undertaking's standard style of the period, as was also the case with a second Regent for London General (LGOC), numbered ST211. Birmingham found 209 entirely satisfactory and 20 further bodies of similar style on Regent chassis, plus ten single-deckers on Morris chassis, were delivered in 1931, followed by further substantial orders built by Metro-Cammell in 1933 and every year up to the war. In London, the Metro-Cammell body, transferred to other ST chassis in the normal process of overhauls, remained in service until 1948. A further 25 double-deck bodies very like the ST style were ordered via LGOC for Overground Ltd, but these were on Dennis Lance chassis, some being seen (below) before delivery in 1931. The advertisement also draws attention to "a low-loading, double-deck, all-metal body" on the Dennis stand at the 1931 Show and this is thought to be another Lance with body of what would later be called lowbridge form placed in service by the major independent company, Lancashire United Transport and Power Co. Ltd, of Atherton, Lancashire, in 1932. They later became a regular MCW customer, initially being supplied from Birmingham but from 1939 taking regular orders from Addlestone.

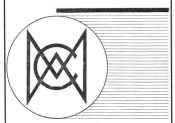
Right: In the difficult period of the early 'thirties when orders for bus bodies were thin on the ground Weymann's built considerable numbers of AEC lorry cabs, and also produced these lightweight steel bodies for carrying gravel for the Ham River Grit Company. They featured regularly in adverts of the time by virtue of enhanced carrying capacity at lower tax levels through a lower gvw. All manufacturers, operators and trade associations were continually pressing the Government to allow the weight limits to be increased throughout the 'thirties. Yet, from 1934, the Government actually increased the need to reduce goods vehicle weights by a change in the taxation system.

Below: More familiar through Dinky models, perhaps, were the Commer lorries for Shell Mex of which six were built in 1933.

CHANGES IN THE FACTORY

Two people who joined Weymann's during the changeover from cars to buses were Cyril Smith and Don Dixon. Cyril worked in the bodyshop and remembers quite clearly the fiddly job of fixing the zapon leathercloth onto the framework of the early W series buses. He spent the whole of his working life in the factory, leaving when the plant closed. Don also started in 1931, and, when interviewed in May 2001 was the oldest survivor, being 93 at the time. He recalled, as an eight year old, watching the factory being built in 1916 and later watching the completed Blériot Spad fighter planes being partly dismantled to allow them to be taken away by road, there being no possibility of flying them from the factory grounds. Less than three miles away, unseen by Don, even as we talked the bulldozers were at work demolishing that same factory.

Don had worked for a local building firm and was a qualified tradesman when he joined Weymann's and began working in the saw mill under Tom Bradbury, eventually himself becoming foreman in that department. He also stayed to the end. One of his early recollections was of the cutting and machining of components for Weymann Patent construction Riley cars, though the actual assembly was carried out by Riley personnel in Coventry. It is believed that these would have been for the popular Kestrel model.

He was one of the few to enjoy the perk of going with the timber suppliers' representatives to select the wood to be used in the factory and recalls that there were always golf clubs in the rep's car on those trips to the yards.

Another octogenarian interviewed is Frank Hooker. Frank also started in the mill, in March 1931, as a 'learner', but unlike Don who was a tradesman, when the demand for cars dried up the young lad found himself laid off 'until after the Motor Show'. Frank decided to go elsewhere and didn't return until 1945 when he was put to work on intermediate floors for London Transport RTs in the separate factory on the Weybridge Trading Estate. Some lay off! In 1976, some ten years after the factory closure, his daughter Val married Dave Humphrey and she joined Vic Smith and husband Dave in the darts team.

In pre-war days, and particularly the early 'thirties, it was quite common to finish a job, go to the foreman for another, and to be told instead to collect your cards from the front office. Instant layoffs were a fact of life and not necessarily any reflection of the person's ability or character. Most people interviewed were soon able to find another job, usually at Vickers 'just down the road' or at Hoyals before their demise. When orders picked up at Weymann's they went

The very first metal-framed body went to City of Oxford, and they were to be a regular customer for metal-framed double-deckers until the end of Addlestone production. London Transport took the second metal-framed body, M2, a single-decker used to replace an earlier, damaged, body and seen here when photographed by Geoff Atkins shortly after Green Line became part of London Transport in 1933. Note the stepped waistrail, then in fashion. See also page 110 for further illustrations of this vehicle. *Alan Townsin collection*

The standard outline for most Weymann's metal-framed double-deck bodies in the mid-1930s may have been set by a batch of three AEC Regent buses for Morecambe & Heysham Corporation, the first municipality to take them, of which M17 is seen below in August 1933. The profile was generally similar to that of six coachbuilt Regents supplied in March 1932, but the contours were slightly more rounded, notably that of the rear dome, where a very distinctive outline, with the rain guttering gracefully falling in an elongated 'S' shape, was to remain a characteristic until interrupted by the war. Note how the shape of the front-end dictates that the windscreen was angled quite strongly in two planes, this, too, often being a 'Weymannism' until the later 1930s. Both these early batches of Morecambe buses were 56-seaters, a capacity obtained only with difficulty at that time of tight weight limits. Homfray-Davies of Weymann's remarked on that fact at the handing-over ceremony of the 1932 batch which had travelled north in convoy, complete with posters proclaiming their builder and the fact that they were being delivered for the start of the 1932 holiday season.

back and apparently picked up where they had left off without any bad feeling. The foremen had orders to protect the married men with homes and families and so the younger men, living at home with their parents, went first.

Unusually, in 1932, Izod had found it necessary to read the riot act about quality. In a letter "to the tradesmen" he warned that the standard of workmanship was not good enough. Weymann's had, he said "a first class sales organisation, but needed to improve its quality if men were not to end up on the dole". The necessary improvements must have been made but one can envisage that there must have been hard words all the way down the line including to General Manager Bill Black and General Foreman George Biggs. Whether there is any connection between this apparent dissatisfaction with quality and the departure of Bill Black a few months later has to be a matter of conjecture.

One can, however, be certain that Joint Managing Director Homfray-Davies would also have been at the sharp end of this exchange between Izod and the shop floor since poor craftsmanship was the last thing he and his team needed when firms were cutting their prices to the bone to get orders. The message seems to have got through, for there were apparently no more such letters from Izod to his workforce and Weymann's name for quality of build and elegance of design became widely known and respected.

We have now seen how in the short space of four years the new factory had been used for the construction of motor cars, then motor coaches based on that method of manufacture, then metal-panelled coaches and buses on the flexible frames, followed by 'traditional' coachbuilt buses, and now, in 1932, a completely new product was to be introduced – metal framing with hot rivetting. The three different methods of construction and assembly (flexible, coachbuilt, metal) were to run in parallel and yet even in the early days the factory was sufficiently large that men working on one type could be unaware of what was happening elsewhere. As mentioned earlier a new paintshop was opened in 1932, catering for the extra work involved in coach painting vehicles much

bigger than the former motor cars, but also correctly anticipating the increase in business that the tie-up with Metropolitan-Cammell would bring.

The workforce numbered some 200 prior to the increases to accommodate the orders received for the metal bodies. As mentioned earlier, nearby Hoyals, who had also built buses for AEC, had fallen victim to the depressed times, going into liquidation in August 1931. They had been located on what became the Weybridge Trading Estate and some of their people were eventually able to get employment at Weymann's as the expansion started there.

Amongst the 1933 intake two names will be familiar to most Weymann's employees, and both have helped enormously with this book. Joe Allen, already mentioned, joined first in the spring. He was a qualified tradesman, and worked in the Body Shop before being moved to the Drawing Office. After Bill Black left he found himself working under his old boss from Midland Red's Carlyle Works' days, Hugh Wootton. Joe's colleague Norman (Bunny) Beaver also joined in 1933, but at the end of the summer after leaving school.

The two were part of the influx of new employees, along with Cecil Fleming who returned after a three year spell back at Vickers where he had served his time. All three would shortly come together in the Drawing Office, where Chief Draughtsman Harold Cook, who had joined Weymann's in 1931, was in charge, and form part of the team which remained in control of design until the end of production at Addlestone in 1966, and then continue to work together in the Phoenix Drawing Office at Frimley. Fleming apparently worked on the AEC 'Q's which Weymann's bodied for London Transport in 1933, and soon came to the attention of both AEC and LPTB when in successive years he won Bronze and then Silver medals awarded by the Society of Motor Manufacturers and Traders, The Coachmakers Company, and the Institute of British Carriage and Automobile Manufacturers for his design work. The Silver, awarded in 1935 together with a cheque for £20, was for a front entrance double-decker for London Transport. Perhaps his father's influence was coming through for Fleming senior worked for Dennis Bros. in Guildford. The family line continued, as children Gillian and Robert both followed him into Weymann's.

Bunny Beaver started as a drill boy in September 1933 and by Christmas Ted Needs had put him in the Setting-Out Department, below the Drawing Office. He spent five years there although he had soon worked out (at 15) that he wanted to be 'upstairs' where he could see that promotion lay. Jumping forward slightly in our story he gave Wootton's successor no peace until finally, through a piece of good fortune, he was moved into the Drawing Office. As

Although metal-framed bodies were to account for the majority of 1934's output, wooden framing continued to be popular. Some customers, including South Wales Transport Company of Swansea, took examples of all three types including both Flexible Patent and, as seen below, coachbuilt single-deckers in small batches from 1933. British Electrical Federation design bodies, always of 'coachbuilt' construction, were built by Weymann's from time to time, and this view of one of ten built for South Wales in 1933 (C550-9) shows the distinctive rear-end styling very effectively – in later years the outline became progressively less upright but the rear and rearmost side window shape, well rounded at the top but square-cut at the bottom, remained characteristic. Usually the three-window rear implied that there was an emergency door in the centre rear, but here it was at the offside front, just behind the driver's door, these being rear-entrance vehicles. They were also coaches, with very comfortable seating for 28 passengers. They were Weymann's first bodies for South Wales, which was to prove one of Addlestone's most regular customers. Of greater significance, however, South Wales became a major customer for metal-framed double-deckers, taking batches in most years from 1934 until the war, including orders for 50 and then a further 12 in 1937 when the Swansea Improvements Company was replacing the town's trams. Weymann's would continue to supply South Wales almost to the end of Addlestone production.

Above: The twelve composite-bodied trolleybuses for Derby Corporation in July 1933 were already old-fashioned looking when built, but this was not due to the Addlestone design team. The bodies were built largely to the customer's specification to match existing vehicles designed by Brush; Dodson and Ransomes also supplied bodies to this outline, all very much in the style of the late 'twenties though Weymann's incorporated their then standard coachbuilt rear. Built on Guy BTX chassis they served the town well, most remaining in service until c1952.

Below: By contrast the appearance of this Weymann's metal-framed bodywork on the AEC 'Q' chassis was ahead of its time, but again this was not wholly attributable to Weymann's. In this instance the design had been specified by AEC where Chief Engineer GJ Rackham had, as mentioned, put his stamp on body design when he arrived at Southall in 1928. The AEC 'Q' chassis with its side-mounted engine behind the driver was an advanced design of Rackham's and he wanted the bodywork to complement it. Accordingly bodywork on the double-deck versions was built to his registered designs by English Electric, Metropolitan Cammell, Park Royal, Roe and Weymann's, though there were detail differences between the different makers in the finishing of the product. The smooth lines of this body were in great contrast to most other double-deckers built at the time and give a hint of what AEC might have produced if its in-house bodybuilding plant had come to fruition.

Above: The origin of the forward entrance design is interesting for it is one which became popular with several operators. One such design was registered by Midland Red, the Birmingham based operator which designed and built its own chassis and bodies. Bodies to this design, known as FEDD by the operator, but of normal height, were first supplied to Midland Red by Short Bros. in 1934, with 100 from Metro-Cammell in Birmingham in 1936, all on Midland Red's own SOS chassis. Here an early Addlestone example carrying the 'General' fleetname before the adoption of 'London Transport', on an AEC Regent chassis, is seen when new in 1934, the time when Weymann's General Manager was Hugh Wootton – previously in charge of Midland Red's Carlyle workshops in Birmingham. Of low height configuration, with side gangway in the upper-deck, the class became known as the Godstone STLs after their designation and allocation to Godstone garage. London Transport later took full-height versions as also did Trent Motor Traction, Mansfield District, Midland General Omnibus Co., Northern General Transport, Tynemouth and District and South Shields Corporation.

AEC-design bodies, built to distinctive and stylish outlines approved by Rackham, were built by Weymann's to its Patented Flexible construction on seven Q-type single-deckers, beginning with one for the 1933 Show and continuing with other demonstrators or examples purchased as 'one-offs' until 1935. Edinburgh Corporation took delivery of WS 1508, an oil-engined example with 39-seat body W996 in October 1934, this view clearly showing the engine cover on the offside. A more conventional Daimler COG5 with coachbuilt Weymann's 34-seat body, C602, which had been at the 1933 Show, had been purchased in March 1934 and the city decided to standardise on Daimler chassis with MCW metal bodies until 1939, the single-deck bodies being built at Addlestone.

mentioned he stayed there until the very end, being part of the Frimley office. His very first task was working on M22, the Leyland demonstrator shown on page 37.

The factory was laid out on parallel production flow lines, with work beginning at the Station Road end and moving towards the old dope and paint store before exiting through the large hangar doors. The Directors, management and other offices were located on the balcony, also at the Station Road end, with the Pattern Making, Setting-Out, Seat Making and Drawing Office also on the upper level. Seats were sometimes produced for other customers as with two large contracts in 1933 for 820 sets of double 'bucket' seats for the LNER tourist stock, some supplied direct and the others to Birmingham Railway Carriage & Wagon Co. who were building stock for the railway company.

Directly below the balcony, with little or no insulation or protection from the considerable noise they generated, were the fitters, blacksmiths, panel beaters and other metal workers. Working in the offices could be a noisy occupation and there was no peace for the designers or Drawing Office personnel. The fumes from the coke braziers also filtered up to the higher echelons, as did the smell of the acetylene welding and other delights. Homfray-Davies may just have given this some thought when he elected to have his office in Westminster.

Meanwhile, on the shop floor where the raw materials were converted into finished buses, the situation was much worse as the new rivetting procedure brought not only the clatter of hammers but also a long-lasting irritation, and long-running bone of contention, when metal frame assembly began – the coke braziers that were needed to get the rivets red hot with their attendant pungent and unpleasant fumes as they simmered lasted until Huck Bolts replaced them in the early 'sixties. In later years shop floor opinion was divided between the demerits of the braziers and the exhaust emission from the ancient paraffin - fired Fordson tractor used to move the part-built vehicles around the factory – both were considered equally obnoxious.

One immediate effect of the introduction of the patented metal-framed structure into Addlestone had been the despatch of a team from Birmingham,

Leyland took another metal-framed demonstrator in 1934 – it was Weymann's number M169 – but this one was soon out on the road where it belonged, unlike its earlier stablemate (page 37). It spent time demonstrating to Exeter before being purchased by the undertaking. Photographed at Leyland in May 1934 the body design is now more clearly recognisable as an Addlestone product, particularly in the area under the driver's windscreen, but the upper deck front was very similar to the Park Royal design of the day. Indeed many Weymann's designs of this period had much in common with Park Royal and even the earlier Hall, Lewis designs of the later 'twenties. The classic Weymann's design with outswept skirts, convex frontal outline and central slotted vent above the front windows was still in the future.
Leyland, Courtesy BCVM

including, amongst others, Needs and Shirley, to the Surrey factory to assist with training and to start production. Some of these men remained at Addlestone whilst others returned to Birmingham when their task was completed.

Some major reorganisation and re-equipping was also necessary at Addlestone to allow the metal-framed bodies to be built. The frame sections, manufactured and supplied from Accles and Pollock in Birmingham were cut to length as required, individually marked in the Setting-Out Department for subsequent drilling and punching (there being no facility in the factory for batch drilling in those days), and then bent to the correct profile.

This whole area was under the jurisdiction of the aforementioned and very talented engineer Ted Needs, moved as noted into Weymann's as part of the agreement in the setting up of MCW, and famous for his trilby hat, whilst the actual frame bending was carried out by the young Jack Guarnori, who, many years later, would take charge of RT production on the Trading Estate. The department joker at this time, with a sometimes cruel streak, was none other than Bill Shirley Jnr., and on one occasion two of the young lads thought he needed to be brought to book. They duly nailed his smock to the bench, and, knowing they could out-run him, waited to see the result. Some 35 years later when Shirley, by then Managing Director of Park Royal Vehicles, was recruiting staff from Weymann's former Drawing Office after final closure of the Frimley (near Camberley) facility, perpetrator Bunny Beaver reminded him of the occasion. Beaver had already decided he didn't want a job at Park Royal anyway, preferring to go to work for London Transport at Chiswick where he remained until he retired. (The Frimley DO was created as a sub-office of Met-Cam when Addlestone closed in 1966, thereby retaining the essential skills of those who were not prepared to move to Birmingham. In the event only three people were transferred from Addlestone to Birmingham: Jack Guarnori as Erection Shop Foreman until he retired; Maurice Bullivant as Buyer until he left 6 months later; Keith Barkham offered a position in Sales but then after secondment back to Addlestone found the position had changed and took redundancy.)

The pattern of busy spells and lay-offs was gradually becoming less acute now and to cope with the increase in orders plans were made to extend the factory; a planning application had been lodged in anticipation in 1931 and this work was carried out in January 1932 when the space between the original building and the old paint store was filled in, and again in 1935 when a completely new paint shop was built alongside but not connected to the original building.

Plans of the factory site as it was in 1917 and was still when Weymann's moved in during the early part of 1928; and then subsequently. These are taken from 'Air, Road and Sea', an excellent booklet describing all the owners and use of the factory over the years up to final closure. Reproduced by kind permission of J and B Barker, publishers, Addlestone.

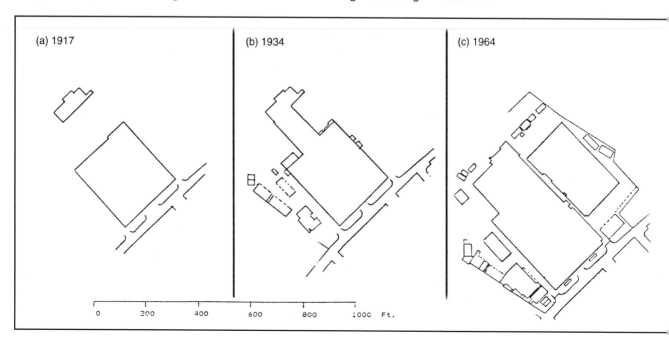

(a) 1917   (b) 1934   (c) 1964

0   200   400   600   800   1000   Ft.

Above: An identity crisis for one of Weymann's trolleybus bodies on a Ransomes chassis in Cape Town during 1936, photographed soon after entering service to begin replacing the former tram system. They were popular and very successful, with 80hp electric motors and regenerative braking to make them suitable for work on the steeply graded routes. The metal-framed bodies – M351-400 – included special insulation between the outer and inner panelling to assist in keeping the interiors cool, and also to prevent corrosion. Weymann's owners, Central Mining and Investment Corporation, had invested in Cape Electric Tramways some ten years earlier. Note the deep louvres to keep the sun out and the all-over advertising, twenty years or more before it became common in the UK. The bodies were despatched from Addlestone in all-over grey primer and painted in the Cape Electric company's workshops by its own staff.
University of Reading. Rural Life Unit

Right: Liverpool Corporation began purchasing Weymann's metal-framed bodies in 1935 and became a major customer. AEC were pleased to be able to announce their success, almost on arch-rival Leyland's doorstep. They were featured in the AEC house magazine as can be seen. By 1942 when peacetime construction ceased Liverpool had taken 215 Addlestone bodies, many delivered to them as frames on chassis, to then be completed in the department's Edge Lane workshops where hundreds of the city's trams were built. Moves to allow such undertakings to use their overhaul/repair facilities for the construction of complete bus or trolleybus bodies had been blocked by Government as far back as 1932, despite intense lobbying by Glasgow to be allowed to use its workshops for this purpose to safeguard local jobs as its construction of trams was scaled down. Glasgow took eight frames for bodies, to a style usually built by Weymann's for this fleet, but these were supplied by MCCW and completed at the Corporation's Larkfield Bus Works in 1942.

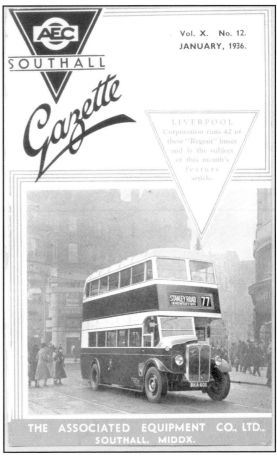

During the summer of 1933, as work was under way on the exhibits for the Motor Show in November of that year, Bill Black left Weymann's and went to work for JC Beadle at Dartford; Hugh Wootton now became Manager. He was in post only until the arrival of Arthur Froggatt the following year and memories of him are not too clear though Joe Allen had worked with Wootton at Midland Red where the latter was in charge of that company's coachworks. Wootton's colleague Spencer worked in the Addlestone paint shop.

The exhibits at the 1933 Show included two Flexible Patent single-deckers, one on an AEC 'Q' and the other on a Dennis Lancet, confirming that the Company still regarded this type of construction as one of its key products. The Dennis was for South Wales Transport, soon to become a regular customer. There was also a single-deck Daimler coachbuilt body in Edinburgh's colours whilst a Sunbeam trolleybus, to be demonstrated to Bournemouth (who later purchased it) carried Weymann's bodywork to a more modern style than its earlier trolleybuses and in great contrast to the two English Electric-bodied AECs with their pseudo bonnets and radiators also demonstrated to Bournemouth where the transport department was preparing to replace its trams. Homfray-Davies must have been very disappointed when, after a satisfactory period of demonstration of 'his' vehicle in Bournemouth, Park Royal bodywork was chosen, and of a style more like the Weymann's design! It would be some years before any further Weymann's bodies were supplied to Bournemouth who then became a regular customer.

Other new customers in 1933 included South Wales, Western Welsh, Westcliff on Sea and Norwich Electric Tramways, whilst Derby and Walsall Corporations took trolleybuses – once again the demise of life-expired tramway systems helped to provide orders. AEC continued to take lorry cabs but the big order in 1934, however, was for 30 double- and 20 single-deck Ransomes trolleybuses for Cape Electric Tramways where that South African operator was starting to replace its complete tramway system with trolleybuses. This was Weymann's first major export order and the vehicles were shipped from London in grey primer and with interior fittings and paint stowed inside the saloons for completion in Cape Town. Repeat orders, always a good indicator of satisfaction, came from City of Oxford, Mansfield District, Rhondda and Yorkshire Woollen District.

In mid-1934 came the big upheaval. The overall atmosphere at Park Royal had not improved (page 25), relationships between Yager and the rest of the

The Metropolitan Police took some small batches of Leyland Cub chassis onto which it had Weymann's fit prison van bodies. Leyland Journal's editor wryly commented that passengers in these conveyances travelled free, but were charged later. One is seen here before being handed over.

One of the most interesting and unusual vehicles to pass down the assemby lines in 1935 was this three-axle AEC Renown demonstrator hired between August 1935 and July 1936 by Cumberland Motor Services of Whitehaven. This flexible body seated 43 passengers, the highest number in any pre-war Weymann's single-decker, and this was the only three-axled chassis to carry a patent flexible body. Reseated as a coach the vehicle was later sold by AEC to Valliant of Ealing, an operator who had taken flexible bodies in the early days. Note the large roof mounted luggage carrier.

In 1936 Tynemouth and District, based in Cullercoats, Whitley Bay, borrowed the prototype forward entrance bodied Leyland demonstrator (page 37) and clearly liked the body configuration, but decided to take AEC chassis for the three metal-framed vehicles it ordered in 1937, body numbers M1223-5. These seated 52, but when it took a further eight examples in 1938, 55 seats were fitted into the bodies on Leyland TD5 chassis. This body design was popular in the midlands and north-east and similiar vehicles went to nearby Northern General, another BET subsidiary and Tynemouth's parent.

management were worsening, and so this time the General Manager and a good proportion of his key men upped sticks and headed south for Addlestone. It created a major crisis at Park Royal which was only resolved when Bill Black moved from Beadle's at Dartford and went in to take charge. Subsequently engineer Ted Needs left Addlestone to join his former boss in north London.

The new General Manager at Weymann's was to be Arthur Froggatt (ATF), who had, of course, worked with Homfray-Davies at Hall, Lewis and, briefly, Park Royal. Wootton disappeared from the scene and a new attitude began to pervade the firm. Perhaps the increase in orders and growing profits gave ATF scope to relax the pressure on the reins a little, whilst the Park Royal situation was clearly in his mind; he put his stamp on affairs at Addlestone very clearly.

Izod was joint Managing Director with Homfray-Davies, but ATF was the man running the factory through his foremen. His arrival marked a significant milestone and the Company expanded and prospered through the combined efforts of the talented trio of Izod, Homfray-Davies and Arthur Froggatt.

The increasing levels of business now required greater manufacturing capacity and during 1935, in addition to the provision of degreasing and rustproofing facilities for the metal framework, a major development took place with the creation of a new finishing and paint shop, parallel to and alongside the existing building but separate from it. Part completed vehicles now passed through the hangar doors of the original building into the yard before turning through 180 degrees to enter the new complex and head through it in parallel and in the opposite direction towards Station Road.

At the 1935 Olympia Show MCW's stand had three exhibits: the by-now usual flexible example, again on a Dennis Lancet for South Wales Transport, together with two metal-framed double-deckers from the Birmingham factory, one on a Daimler for Edinburgh and the other on a trolleybus chassis for Newcastle. Other Addlestone vehicles at the show included a three-axle double-decker trolleybus for Capetown on the Ransomes stand, a single-decker flexible body on an AEC Regal for Rhondda, together with a full-fronted Regent for Leeds Corporation, both on the AEC stand, whilst on the Daimler stand was another flexible body, this time for Potteries Motor Traction, along with a metal-framed double-decker for Bradford. There was yet another metal-framed double-decker Daimler in the demonstration park. Another Daimler for Birmingham Corporation carried bodywork from the MCCW factory. One can visualise the midnight oil being burned to get all those vehicles up to show condition alongside the normal every-day orders.

Meanwhile, another member of the Drawing Office team had arrived in 1935 when Gordon Whindle, destined to be another long-serving stalwart, joined the Company. Gordon's sister Margaret was still in charge of the front office and telephones, and was now becoming aware of a rather smart young man from London Transport who was part of the Chiswick Inspection team. Henry Colman gradually became more than a visitor and he and Margaret would marry a little later in our story. In 2000 they celebrated their Diamond Wedding Anniversary, having regaled the writer with many memories of the early days at Station Road.

Whilst all this activity was taking place, unbeknown to all but a very select few, the Company's bankers were gradually going under and whilst there was no immediate sign of this in the factory, events were leading up to another major financial shake up.

Orders continued to increase, however, and although the international situation was worsening, notably between Japan and China and with the rise of Hitler in Nazi Germany, output was still exclusively for the domestic market until, in 1936, recognising the marked change in the outlook the British Government bowed to the inevitable and prepared to re-arm. From now onwards Ministry of Supply orders would begin to appear in virtually all bodybuilders' output figures, and although MCW received orders from the MoS for

William Rushton Black was born in January 1893 in Barrow in Furness. He was apprenticed at Vickers Barrow shipbuilding factory in 1908. His career took him to Vickers Head Office in 1920, then to America where he studied their mass production methods, and eventually to the Crayford (Kent) works where, as General Manager of the Vickers body-building plant, he put his experience of mass production techniques into practice. In 1928 Black was head-hunted by Weymann's, joining them that year as General Manager.

He left Weymann's in the summer of 1933, moving to JC Beadle of Dartford and in June the following year joined Park Royal Coachworks, where, with his engineer Ted Needs, he expanded metal framing in that company. Appointed initially as General Manager, he joined the Board in March 1935, but by 1939 he had become Managing Director and also a Director of ACV.

As President of the National Federation of Vehicle Builders he was in charge of the wartime Utility bus body design concept.

He became Managing Director of ACV in 1957, Chairman of ACV Sales in 1963, whilst remaining a Director of Park Royal, CH Roe and BUT (British United Traction, the Leyland-AEC trolleybus and later railcar manufacturer). He maintained his office at the Park Royal factory until Leyland closed the plant.

A Freeman of the City of London and also a Liveryman of the Worshipful Company of Coachmakers and Coach Harness Makers he was President of the SMMT Ltd in 1953, and created a Knight Bachelor – Sir William – in 1958. Between 1965 and 1972 he was a member of the Queen's Award to Industry Advisory Committee. Elevated to become a life peer – Lord Black – in 1968, he died in December 1984.

ambulances for the RAF in 1936, '37 and '38, which MCCW built in Birmingham, it was actually 1940 before any MoS orders passed through Weymann's factory – from then on there was to be no respite until the conflict was over.

Back in 1936 another significant move took place when Norman Froggatt, son of ATF, left Duple and joined the Drawing Office. He later became Estimator and as he worked his way up the ladder, eventually becoming Assistant and then General Manager, promotional opportunities arose for those in the DO. It was this train of events that led to young Beaver being moved 'upstairs'.

The increased output was now impressive and, as stated earlier, profits increased accordingly. Thus it was that when the ailing Bank had finally gone into liquidation in 1935, the Liquidator had on his hands a growing and successful company at Addlestone – profits for the year ended 31st December 1936 were a healthy £43,248. In December 1937 he sold Weymann's to the Prudential Assurance Company for £174,124.

The Prudential then introduced more capital, and the issued figure rose from the £23,100 at which it had stood since the 1932 reorganisation to £99,613, representing 398,452 of the authorised 400,000 shares being issued. Some of the debentures were also starting to be cleared at this time. RA MacQueen and AW Rogers, the Mining Company's men, left and Izod now became Chairman and Joint Managing Director, alternating with Homfray-Davies. The Registered Office was moved to Station Road, Addlestone and FC Webb became Company Secretary, and soon afterwards a Director. No other Directors were appointed and thus it is clear that the Prudential was not involved in the day-to-day running of the business in the same manner that the previous owners had been.

In the factory life continued much as before, and since it was an 'odd' year work was in hand for the London Motor Show. Once again in 1937 the exhibits featured the Flexible body, again on a Daimler COG5 single-decker for Potteries Motor Traction, a confirmed Flexible user and regular customer who would take batches again in 1938 and 1939 and, almost inevitably, an AEC Regal, again for Rhondda. When the time came for these vehicles to be driven up to London the drivers found that they had a new venue – Earl's Court. The new building had been under construction for 18 months and was described as then being Britain's biggest building. Capable of seating 20,000 people, it weighed 200,000 tons, spanned six railway lines and was designed by C Howard Crane, the architect of some of New York's skyscrapers. The nine acre site was noted in *The Leyland Journal* as being the graveyard of some 31 previously unsuccessful attempts to develop the plot and, with war looming and exhibitions

This Flexible Patent body – W7554 – was displayed at the 1937 Motor Show, the first to be held at Earls Court. Rhondda was another good Weymann's customer, taking some 136 vehicles before peacetime production ceased. It was another devotee of the Flexible bodies, finding them ideally suited to the poor roads in its territory. The company's headquarters were located at Porth, south Wales.

The Caledonian Omnibus Co of Dumfries took four Leyland coachbuilt single-deckers in 1935, having them fitted out for express services with deep high-backed seats and roof-mounted luggage carriers as seen. Note the rear ladder giving access to the roof. The batch was numbered C760-3 in Weymann's coachbuilt series, the final numbers before the new numerical series began at C5000.

Kingston-upon-Hull had been taking coachbuilt double-decker bus bodies from Addlestone since 1934, having 45 Daimlers in service when, on 23rd July 1937, it inaugurated its new trolleybus system, two days before the new vehicles entered revenue service and it started to replace the former trams. The chassis were Leylands, Daimler not then having started to produce trolleybuses, and the batch of 26 carried Weymann's coachbuilt bodywork finished in Hull's blue and white livery. They incorporated a new type of MCW concealed gantry for the trolley gear, neatening the roof outline, and for which patents had been applied. Note the unusual destination blinds with black lettering on white ground, the reverse of normal practice. *GHF Atkins*

being cancelled, unfortunately it also turned out to be financially unsuccessful, with a Receiver being appointed in 1940. Weymann's buses were more successful however, and orders continued to flow in.

New customers in 1936/7 included Trent Motor Traction, and Glasgow Corporation with an opening order for 37 metal-framed double-deckers and a further 65 in 1938. These buses were part of the increased public transport infrastructure for the Empire Exhibition held in the city in that year. There was also a new fleet of 100 'Coronation' tramcars, built by the corporation in its own workshops where, before long, some of Weymann's framed chassis would be completed by the same craftsmen. Investment on this scale was a massive endorsement of the role public transport could, should and did play in a big city. Much smaller orders came from Llanelly & District, Rochdale and Great Yarmouth. A massive order from London Transport in 1936 as its trolleybuses-for-trams replacement got into its stride was the biggest pre-war contract ever received, whilst orders from Port Elizabeth Tramways – a subsidiary of Cape Electric Tramways – for buses to replace trams continued the South African export business with links to Central Mining. A Leader in *Transport World* at this time commented that year 1937 looked set to be a good one as the problems of the recent past were receding, and re-armament orders would help the motor industry. So it was, and Weymann's enjoyed it to the full.

As the increase in business could be seen translating into profit, new owners Prudential must have been pleased with the latest addition to their portfolio.

Bradford was a progressive undertaking, buying AEC and Daimler motor buses alongside its trolleybus orders. Here one of its metal-framed Regent double-deckers is seen at AEC in September 1936, before delivery to the operator. Bradford's General Manager, CR Tattam, made news in the trade press when, shortly after the introduction of the 30 mph speed limit, he was fined 10s for causing one of his drivers to be in charge of a vehicle which did not have an operational speedometer – such items then only recently being legally required. Tattam immediately gave notice of his intention to appeal on the grounds that "if the conviction was upheld not only would the undertaking have to fit speedometers, it would have to maintain them in working order". Clearly he was having none of that!

CHAPTER FOUR: 1937– 1941

THE PRUDENTIAL YEARS

The purchase of the company in 1937 by the Prudential was a recognition that it was doing well, and its new owners appear to have assisted it to continue to expand. Unfortunately the depressing world situation became steadily more worrying as 1938 progressed and no-one could really be in any doubt as to how things were going to end. Nonetheless orders continued to pour in and this was to be the best year the firm had yet had, either in terms of output – a grand total of 596 vehicles of all types – or gross profit at £59,740.

Communication within the factory between management and workforce, and within the various departments at shop floor level, was becoming ever more important. With such a large workforce Izod's speeches from the balcony were no longer sufficient, especially when there were now subversive elements at work. The move came from the shop floor with the launch of a house magazine – **THE WEYMAG** – to keep people up-to-date, principally in regards to sports and social matters. Since there were so many sporting activities it did indeed reach a very high proportion of the workers. It was not an official company publication but its pages also give a good insight into contemporary attitudes and events in the factory.

Mr Izod, as Chairman and Joint Managing Director, put a letter into the third number, in June 1938, congratulating the Editor and then making what today would be classed as a mission statement. Because it sums up the feelings of so many people who have tried to explain to me what it was like to work at Weymann's I have included the second paragraph verbatim –

> " I think that most of our "boys" know that my colleagues and I are very anxious to do all we can to make life with us a truly happy and contented one, and the development of the team spirit in work and play is definitely helped by your little Magazine.
>
> Yours truly, EG Izod"

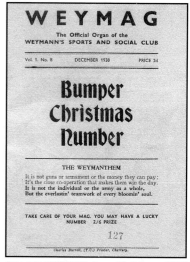

WEYMAG

The Official Organ of the
WEYMANN'S SPORTS AND SOCIAL CLUB

Vol. 1. No. 8   DECEMBER 1938   PRICE 2d

Bumper
Christmas
Number

THE WEYMANTHEM

It is not guns or armament or the money they can pay:
It's the close co-operation that makes them win the day.
It is not the individual or the army as a whole,
But the everlastin' teamwork of every bloomin' soul.

TAKE CARE OF YOUR MAG. YOU MAY HAVE A LUCKY
NUMBER 2/6 PRIZE

127

Charles Burrell, (T.U.) Printer, Chertsey.

An early WEYMAG, from Christmas 1938. The first issues were printed locally by a different printer and the Editor was challenged, in a letter he printed, for using a non-union house. Whilst he defended his actions by saying, rightly, that the magazine was non-political, the agitators won the day and the printer was changed. A sign of worse things to come . . .

Below:- Midland General took a variety of types of vehicles in the later '30s, based on Leyland and AEC chassis. Double- and single-deck buses were accompanied by bus shells fitted out for express work – dual-purpose in the terminology of later times – and coaches. This attractive AEC Regal is clearly intended for this latter type of work, with its roof mounted luggage carrier. *GHF Atkins*

But those sentiments hid a concern which the Magazine carried on its front page, where the **Weymanthem,** as it was called, clearly tells us what was happening on the production lines –

> It is not guns or armament or the money they pay;
> It's the close co-operation that makes them win the day.
> It is not the individual or the army as a whole,
> But the everlastin' teamwork of every bloomin' soul.

Those lines, or later just the last two of them, appeared on all issues and 'the everlastin' teamwork of every bloomin' soul' became the company's motto.

WORKING AT WEYMANN'S

Weymann's factory in Addlestone's Station Road was situated in what its one-time employees describe as a comfortable and respectable part of Surrey, good Tory country as they put it, where 'most people had shoes on their feet and food in their stomachs'.

Whilst it was generally conceded that no one ever got rich working at Weymann's it was, on the whole, considered to be better than down the road at Vickers 'where you could be fired for laughing'. Albert Cox confided that he had been laid off, been re-employed, made redundant, re-joined and been made redundant again three or four times over. A company that attracts people back in those conditions must have had plenty going for it and the loyalty of that type of workforce undoubtedly helped make Weymann's what it was.

From the relatively small beginnings at Addlestone in 1928 the firm grew to be the employer, at its post-war peak, of some 1,500 persons. Most of these were men and boys, though there were some women employed in the factory in addition to those working in the more usual (for those days) office positions. During the war the number of women employed rose to several hundred.

London Transport, wishing to replace its private hire and sightseeing coach fleet for the Coronation year, 1937, chose AEC Renown three-axle chassis for the 24 vehicles, giving the class the designation LTC. They were of the same short wheelbase as used on the LGOC LT-class double-deckers of 1929-32, the choice of model being made purely on the dubious claim of superior ride comfort, whilst the resulting length of 27ft 6in was no more than an equivalent two-axle Regal. For this new class, the Chiswick Drawing Office designed bodywork of generally similar style to that on 50 metal-framed bodied Regals that had been built by Weymann's in 1936, these being for the Green Line services and usually known by the design code 9T9. The LTC bodies, which had Weymann's numbers M1274-97, were fitted with luxurious seats for 30 passengers, a sliding roof and radio (then still quite rare on coaches), and had six-cylinder petrol engines in the interests of quiet running – the unladen weight of 8tons 5cwt, was more than most LPTB double-deckers.

From the start the factory worked a normal five-and-a-half day week of 48 hours, with overtime when required but no shift working. The working week reduced to 44, then 42½ and finally 40 hours over the years, and Saturday mornings ceased to be a part of the normal week in the autumn of 1951.

Piece rates were fixed for work and the men were left to get on with the job, supervised where necessary and the work inspected when completed. Joe Allen recalls that soon after he began working at Weymann's in 1933 he was put onto the construction and installation of the intermediate floors in double-deckers. This was a one-man job, and it took him roughly two days to complete the floor in each vehicle. It was made of two thicknesses of pine tongue-and-groove boarding, laid longitudinally one over the other with oilskin between. He also painted the timber with a protective red lead coating – no demarcation lines here. He was paid 30 shillings for that work – £1.50 in today's money.

There was a canteen alongside the factory and lads from each department would be sent to get the cups of tea for breaks. They would also go across the road for cigarettes or other items which the canteen did not sell. At midday those staying for lunch were catered for in the works canteen. Because the factory was part of a close-knit community many would walk or cycle home, having ample time within the hour to have their meal, return and clock in again.

Amongst the 'perks' for the shop floor, the local barber came into the factory each day and employees could book an appointment through their foreman and have a haircut in their section at the appointed time. They were also allowed to purchase materials, scrap or otherwise, for 'home jobs'. The relevant foreman would sign a chit which was presented to the gateman at knocking-off time as authorisation to take the items out of the factory. There was an understanding that good measure was always given, and apparently fitted bedrooms and kitchens were commonplace in Addlestone long before MFI came on the scene.

In 1934 when Arthur Froggatt (ATF) joined Weymann's from Park Royal he brought with him several men who became foremen and who are still remembered in Addlestone 65 years later. This caused some understandable resentment at the time and one of those who came with him, George Page, and who later became Chief Inspector, confided to his daughter when she went to work in the factory that it took some years before the atmosphere cleared. Nonetheless ATF became a father figure in the firm, taking a very close interest in the men and would walk round the factory each morning, knew everyone by name, and would enquire after their families.

Some examples of ATF's good heartedness came across during interviews. On one occasion one of the few employees who had a car at the time was stopped by the police and found to have a boot load of ready cut timber for which he could not account. Taken to court and fined, he had his fine repaid outside by ATF with the admonishment "let that be a lesson, don't do it again, and get back to work". On another occasion one of the old retainers, a labourer of advanced years and one (very slow) rate of progress was marked down for dismissal and sent to ATF for the axe to be wielded. ATF, trying to pave the way, asked the man how he was feeling. "Never better guv'nor, except I need some new boots" was the reply. He came downstairs with money for a new pair and resumed his leisurely progress along the shop floor with his broom!

Whilst Izod was every inch 'a ladies man', and not above strolling through the factory with his African sjambok tucked under his arm to impress the girls and generally cut a dash, ATF was a different kind of man altogether. He regarded the welfare of the workforce as a principal concern, and also engineered with Homfray-Davies some sort of *quid pro quo* whereby orders from Welsh customers were linked to the movement of unemployed young men from out-of-work coalmining families in the depressed valleys; they were then trained to become part of the Addlestone workforce. There are those who believe he paid a high price for this benevolent attitude when some of the Welshmen later began to sow the seeds of 'organising' the labour force, with

Arthur Thomas Froggatt was widely seen as the father figure at Weymann's. Born in 1881 in Wellingborough he started his coachbuilding career in that area with Mulliners, also spending time with Dennis Bros. He returned to Mulliners as a draughtsman and in 1905 opened their London showroom as Works Manager. In 1913 he moved to the Cunard Motor & Carriage Co., leaving them in 1923 to become Works Manager at Windover's new factory in Colindale. Next, in 1927, he went to Hall, Lewis (later becoming Park Royal) as Works Manager before joining Weymann's as General Manager in 1934.

In March 1940 he was elected a Fellow of the Institute of British Carriage and Automobile Manufacturers in recognition of his work in the industry and in acting as a Judge for them.

Awarded the MBE in 1945 for his work during the war he became Chairman and Managing Director in 1947 following the death of EG Izod. Amongst his many other positions he was a Liveryman of the Worshipful Company of Coach Makers and Coach Harness Makers of London.

A kind and compassionate man who was always interested in the welfare of the workforce, and knew everyone by name, ATF supported many local charities, particularly the Gordon Boys School at Woking. He loved children and his daughter-in-law Beryl recalls that his suit pockets were always bulging out of shape with sweets for them.

Arthur Froggatt was respected throughout the company – and the industry – and his sudden death which occured whilst he was waiting for a Green Line coach to take him home from an evening function at the Grosvenor Hotel in London to honour Henry Ford only a month after enforced retirement – having reached the age of seventy – came as a great shock in July 1951.

His work had been his life and, like Lord Ashfield (page 18) his death so soon after leaving the environment which had meant so much to him reflected the blow that retirement had brought about. Such was his standing that his funeral was attended by virtually everyone from the Company. In 1954 the Council of the National Federation of Vehicle Trades assisted in establishing a permanent memorial to him by the creation of a five-bedded ward – The Arthur Froggatt Memorial Ward – in the Epiphany Convalescent and Rest Home in Truro, where his daughter, Sister Anne, a Nun, was in charge.

ATF was later to be succeeded at Weymann's factory by his son Norman, who had been working with him at Addlestone since 1936, and whose career we shall trace in Volume 2 along with further details of his father.

results which ultimately bade ill for everyone's job when the agitators gained the upper hand.

The sons of the coal miners had long memories, especially regarding the treatment of their forbears in the 'twenties and the events leading up to the General Strike of 1926. If this gave them a somewhat jaundiced and suspicious outlook on life it was perhaps understandable, but, if true, was unfortunate when ATF was attempting to make some recompense.

Nearer home ATF continued his support for the Gordon Boys. The Gordon Boys Schools had been founded by General Gordon and catered for under-privileged boys, orphans and potential tearaways. They were well looked after whilst being given the opportunity to learn a trade, and, if need be, also learning to toe the line. Frank Higgs spoke of his time there when interviewed in 1999, and recalled that the West End, Woking, Gordon Boys were already proficient in the use of tools and handling of timber when they went out looking for employment. ATF saw the advantage of this in the days before indentured apprenticeships and supported the home financially through factory open days and in other ways, something Frank was readily able to confirm.

An interesting fact emerged as Cyril Smith (who started in 1931) and Frank Higgs (1936) reminisced with the author about their time with the Company in the 'thirties. Cyril recalled that when lay offs occurred the foremen would check as to who lived at home and who was in digs (and therefore having a commitment to pay rent). Those living 'rent-free' as the foremen saw it went first. Frank was surprised to hear from Cyril that the Gordon Boys also got special treatment here and laughed until his eyes watered to hear how Cyril had been laid off whilst he had been kept on. It had taken 60 years for this gem to reach him.

The family aspect was reflected in the large numbers of people in the factory and offices who were related to each other. This tended to encourage co-operation, and, in days before the 'Closed Shop', helped keep production running smoothly; this, naturally, was the name of the game. Factory open days were another regular event, providing an opportunity for families to see where the

Customer's special destination boxes must sometimes have caused despair in the drawing office when designers were working to create the graceful flowing lines for which Weymann's were rightly known. Few could have been uglier than those fitted to Glasgow's double-deckers before the war and a typical example, metal-framed body M1578 of 1938, demonstrates the point. More importantly, however, Glasgow was a good customer and its requirements kept the factory busy. In the period between 1937 and 1943, 206 bodies were supplied to the Scottish operator by the MCW organisation. Interior finish was to a high standard with Almabriminal decorative panels used for the ceilings and matching the contemporary Coronation tramcars being built in the operator's own Coplawhill works.
Courtesy Alan Townsin

men worked and how the buses were built. Employees were encouraged to go to the Commercial Motor Shows and to assess their products against the competition. Given this sort of background, and many other aspects of fair treatment, the company was seen as a good one in which to work and boys joined fathers, uncles – and grandfathers – in the works. It seems to be generally agreed that Weymann's was a good firm to work for, and that they never needed to advertise – word of mouth through families was always sufficient.

Another way of encouraging this family spirit was through sports and other social activities. The Directors and Managers, actively encouraged by Izod who was a keen sportsman, played a full part in ensuring the success of the sports events. In addition to the Tennis Courts by the factory, football, hockey, tennis, tug of war and cricket were all played on the sports ground in School Lane, Addlestone, with Weymann's teams competing against other company's teams including Leyland, Metro-Cammell, AEC, Park Royal, Duple and other coachbuilders. Matches against teams from Buckingham Palace Mews perhaps reflected the connection with nobility in Weymann's earlier bespoke car days. The first Sports Day, held in 1938, attracted over 1,200 people and, continuing its support, tea was provided by the Company. By this time a full-time Sports Organiser had been appointed, in addition to the groundsman (and his goat). Management next presented the sports and social club with a Billiard Hall, in July 1939, with Sports Club President EG Izod expressing the hope that it would help maintain the happy atmosphere which existed in the firm. Boxing, tug-of-war, darts, dancing and use of the allotments were also popular whilst the Ten-Bar-Two darts team, founded in 1941 after the call-up of many of the pre-war players, still meets every week 60 years later.

Works outings were another feature of the social life, with a special train (later a fleet of motor coaches) for the annual trip to London, and then down river. These steamer trips to Southend from London were remembered with great affection when former employees were interviewed, some reflecting that once aboard on these trips often they never saw the water until they left the boat, such were the liquid attractions below decks. There were also outings to

Trent Motor Traction, another BET subsidiary, first came to Weymann's for bodywork in 1937. Between then and the end of peacetime construction they took four batches of the 54-seat front-entrance body but, unlike other customers, specified coachbuilt construction; all Weymann's other front-entrance double-deckers were metal-framed. Recollections that heavy braking caused the heavy open door to slam shut with some considerable force may explain why the bodies did not last as long as their metal contemporaries but whether this accounted for the early demise of the Trent examples is uncertain; most were rebodied soon after the war ended. C5262, RC6004 is seen here, being one of the second batch comprising 15 vehicles delivered in 1938. Delivery of the fourth and final batch was completed in February 1941. *GHF Atkins*

Brighton and elsewhere, and it had been the custom to visit one of Weymann's customer's home towns where the whole ensemble of up to 400 people would be treated to a slap up tea and then given a pep talk over the beer, often with a guest from the local transport authority as he was a Weymann's customer! It gave the management the opportunity to address the men in a relaxed attitude, and to talk about progress – and perhaps problems – whilst future prospects could also be announced.

Pocket money would be provided to allow everyone to enjoy the event, reflecting the fact that money would be tight in those pre-war days with many people having little opportunity to save. The very first such outing, in 1929 soon after Izod had arrived, had been to Portsmouth and in 1938 the annual outing was once again to Portsmouth whilst for two shillings (10p) participants enjoyed transport and time to look around, but for the first time there was no 'beano'. Although 'The Firm' had contributed £50 towards the cost of the day out there was no doubt that the sit down tea was missed. Since Portsmouth was not one of Weymann's customers perhaps the local council saw no reason to go overboard with the hospitality. In 1939 THE WEYMAG carried a notice advising members of a forthcoming trip to Dieppe – daring stuff at a time when everyone feared that war was only just around the corner. The following issue recorded how successful the outing had been so their confidence was not misplaced.

Another form of social life took place in Edith Cottage where Mr Izod entertained customers, members of the Trade Press, friends and suppliers, in addition to the legendary lunchtime hospitality at the Woburn Park Hotel. For the rest of the workforce, each year the whole of the factory would be taken for the Annual Dinner Dance at the Grosvenor Hotel, London, a high profile, formal and undoubtedly most enjoyable event for all concerned.

The sports facilities and Christmas parties, annual dinners and works outings, appreciated as they were, were no substitute, however, for the guaranteed employment everyone so desperately sought. Whilst management also wanted continuity of orders, it was not always possible to find them, and indeed Weymann's may be judged fortunate to have survived the 'thirties when compared with many others in the London area who had gone out of business. A measure of how wages had improved, however, was the fact that men were earning four times as much in 1939 as they had in 1933, well ahead of increases in the cost of living.

With a certain inevitability all good nature will be put to the test, and taken advantage of. So it was that gradually the emphasis switched from a situation of mutual trust to one where an ever-increasing number took far more than they ever gave. The culture changed and paved the way for agitators to press for unrealistic claims in wages, piece rates and other conditions. The forthcoming war would not help the situation.

Although taken in post-war days this view illustrates the 52-seat forward entrance bodies supplied to the Midland General Omnibus Company of Langley Mill, Nottinghamshire. The rear is of one of the 25 from the 1937 batch, DNU 971 being M1007, whilst facing the photographer is FNU173, M1655 from the 1938 batch of 10. These vehicles gave some 20 and 18 year's service respectively. They were among the earliest examples of what was perhaps Weymann's best-remembered front-end design. The new treatment of the corner pillars and gently curving unbroken profile from cab front to roof gave a look to remain characteristic until the mid-'fifties. The rear styling of the upper-deck shown by No. 58 had been typical of Weymann's metal-framed double-deckers from 1933 and was to remain so until generally displaced by the Orion style in the 'fifties. Midland General was another good customer for Weymann's as the illustrated section of this book will show, and the company's allegiance to Addlestone continued unabated after the war. *GHF Atkins*

THE ORGANISATION OF THE COMPANY

Little information has survived about the management structure at Putney, but when the move was made to Addlestone as recorded earlier Mr Walker was in charge as Manager. Bill Black replaced Walker as General Manager in 1928. Of the Directors only Izod appears to have been resident until Homfray-Davies joined him, as Joint MD in 1931. ATF came as General Manager in 1934.

Below this level of top management was the Works Manager, his assistant, the General Foreman and the Works Foreman. There were then foremen in each department, some seventeen of them, with deputies and clerks in the bigger departments, and then chargehands and, finally, at maximum, approaching 1,400 shop floor workers. The company was the major employer in Addlestone and in addition to those employed in the factory itself there were clearly many more whose livelihoods depended on the well-being of Messrs Weymann's.

Some of the various departments are represented by the management portrait which Izod had taken in 1938 and which is reproduced below.

The different unions representing their members's interests included The National Union of Vehicle Builders (NUVB); The Electrical Trades Union (ETU) and The Transport & General Workers Union (TGWU).

Below:- A Management line up of 1938 in the garden of Edith Cottage.
Front row left to right: -
FRED OSBORNE - Foreman Panel Shop; CYRIL COLLINS - Foreman Body Shop; ALF COUSINS - General Foreman; FREDERICK C WEBB - Company Secretary; EDWIN G IZOD - Chairman & Managing Director; ARTHUR T FROGGATT - General Manager (later Managing Director); JACK DAVIES - Contracts Manager (later Managing Director); HAROLD COOK - Chief Draughtsman (Later Chief Engineer, then Joint General Manager, finally Chairman & Managing Director); WALTER DODSWORTH - Chief Estimator/Buyer (Later Works Director, then Joint General Manager); RH MORTER - Assistant General Manager (In 1946 joined Bus Bodies (S.A.) Ltd Port Elizabeth S.A.)
Back row left to right:-
JIMMY LYNDEN - Foreman Trimming Shop/Seat Makers; JIM KNIGHT - Foreman Finishing Shop; GEORGE BANNAN - Foreman Polishing Shop; CYRIL HUTCHINS - Foreman Paint Shop; TOM BRADBURY - Foreman Mill Shop; HARRY WEBSTER - Foreman Mounters Shop; CYRIL WARD - Assistant Buyer (Later Chief Buyer); BEN CARNE - Chief Inspector; GEORGE HOXLEY - Foreman Electricians/Maintenance; POP DAVIES - Stock Buyer (Timber/Paint); GEORGE BIGGS - Foreman Engineering (Later Development Engineer).

The aerial view above was well-known, being sold locally as a postcard, and shows the factory as it was c1955 after shop 5 had been completed alongside number 4, the one with the Company name painted on the roof. The size of the complex can be judged by the buses standing in the yard.

The site plan reproduced below shows the 1939 position. Shops 1 and 3 dated back to Bleriot's days, two was the infill from 1932 whilst 4 had been built in 1935, all as mentioned in the text.

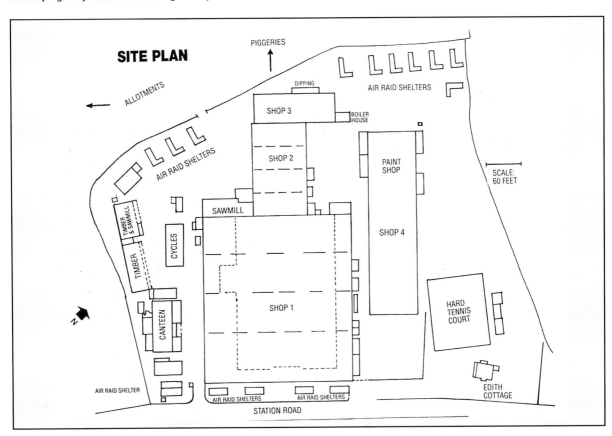

THE CUSTOMER BASE

Reference has been made to the fact that in the early years of flexible bodies, most of which were coaches, orders usually came to Weymann's from the chassis manufacturer. From 1931, with the introduction of the coachbuilt bodywork and the arrival of Homfray-Davies from Park Royal, Weymann's was to be a **bus** building plant, and as such Homfray-Davies went out for fleet orders from large operators, the initial London contract being a good example. A breakdown of customers for the period covered by this volume shows orders for Balfour Beatty and the so-called Territorial Companies such as the TBAT/BET subsidiaries accounting for 33% of production, whilst various Municipalities accounted for a further 22% of production. Although the opening order for London had augured well in fact less than 8% of the pre-war output went to the capital, a situation that would change dramatically after the War of course with the huge RT contract which features in Volume 2 covering the story to closure. Supplies to Independent operators accounted for less than 3% of the total and several of those were supplied before Homfray- Davies joined the organisation. Undoubtedly a major factor in this strategy was his recent unhappy experience at Hall, Lewis/Park Royal where he had experienced at first-hand the unpleasantness of liquidation, and it is noteworthy that orders were obtained from customers whose ability to pay for their buses would be a primary consideration.

By contrast Duple, Burlingham and Harrington, for example, were building luxury coaches for small operators throughout the land, with only small numbers of buses for the big fleets. A bewildering number of body designs and chassis makes was involved but those companies were structured to deal with that type of business and in pre-war days were very successful. Obtaining payment could be difficult however, and repossessions were commonplace where instalments to the chassis manufacturers, or dealers such as Yeates, could not be kept up.

Weymann's were only just getting into their stride in this new field when the tie-up with MCCW&F came into being. Homfray-Davies was the instigator and his strategy continued – indeed the main reason MCCW&F needed his expertise was that their own background as railway manufacturers meant that they had little or no knowledge of the bus industry. Up until the formation of Metropolitan-Cammell-Weymann as the joint sales organisation the Birmingham factory had built less than 150 bodies since it began production in 1930.

The new arrangements required a definite policy on customer allocations since the ratio of 60:40 in Birmingham's favour had to be maintained in line with the capital structure of the sales organisation and the joint sales agreement between the two companies. Birmingham's methods of construction and production routines made greater use of templates and patterns than did Weymann's, and they also had the floor capacity to deal with very large orders. This clearly influenced matters and the allocation of orders was quickly established. Since Birmingham built only metal-framed bodies all orders for wooden-framed (Patent Flexible) and Coachbuilt (Composite) bodies automatically went to Addlestone. Thus, with a few exceptions, the following breakdown will be found to hold good from 1933 until the cessation of peacetime build.

Both factories built highbridge and lowbridge double-deckers, though with less than 3% of the Birmingham production being of lowbridge configuration, and then only for seven customers, clearly Met-Cam was intent on producing a standard vehicle of full-height specification. Both factories built trolleybuses, but whereas, thanks to LPTB orders, 26% of the Birmingham output was for such vehicles only 9% of Addlestone's vehicles were electrically propelled. Both factories built overseas contracts, including motor buses and trolleybuses whilst Met-Cam was also heavily involved in railway contracts.

Birmingham built over eight times as many double-deckers as single-deckers, whereas at Addlestone the ratio was just over two to one in favour of double-

The 'thirties were the growth years for trolleybus systems, reflecting the demise or decline of many of the defunct tramway systems, and thus Weymann's built a variety of bodies for the Bournemouth, Bradford, Brighton, Brighton Hove & District Co., CapeTown, Hastings Tramways, Llanelli, London, Notts & Derby, South Shields and Wolverhampton fleets. Board of Trade Regulations required metal-framed trolleybus bodies to have low-voltage lighting circuits, to avoid the possibility of potentially-lethal high voltage electricity leaking through the metal framework, and generators or dynamos were incorporated for this purpose. They were not needed on coachbuilt bodies where the lighting was taken from the traction supply, with groups of bulbs being arranged 'in series' for the purpose, hence Osram's advert. Brighton took its first trolleybuses in 1939, a batch of 44 metal-framed vehicles being supplied to the Corporation and the first is seen on test in 1939. Similar bodies were fitted to ten motor buses, as seen below; there were also eleven coachbuilt bodies which had originally been ordered from Harringtons at Hove but then transferred to Weymann's. By a happy co-incidence two examples survive in preservation: motor bus FUF63 is privately owned and in full working order whilst trolleybus CPM61, an identical model from the Brighton, Hove and District fleet, is kept in restored condition in the Science Museum's collection at Wroughton, near Swindon.

deckers. This is partly explained by the larger numbers of 'Company' orders passing through Weymann's, with big Municipal orders for double-deckers keeping the Met-Cam figures up. With the exception of one Leyland Tiger for Yorkshire Traction, and the original Balfour Beatty trolleybuses, apart from orders for BMMO (Midland Red), or for Trent when taking BMMO chassis, orders from BET/TBAT, Tilling, Balfour Beatty and Red & White Group usually went to Addlestone. London orders were split between the two factories, roughly two to one in favour of Birmingham thanks to the large trolleybus contracts.

Municipal orders for small and some medium sized undertakings usually went to Addlestone, in addition to Glasgow and Liverpool where all orders were also handled by Addlestone. Large municipal orders such as those for Birmingham, Manchester, Nottingham and some other medium sized undertakings went to Birmingham though some municipal orders went to both factories. The very few orders for independents went mainly to Addlestone but until 1939 the very small numbers of vehicles ordered from Lancashire United, then the country's largest Independent (or Non-Combine) company, were built in Birmingham when it might have been expected that they would have been built in Addlestone. There will be other exceptions to the above but it will hopefully assist in understanding the relationship between the two factories.

In 1936, with the deterioration in the international situation, particularly in relation to Japan, China and Germany, the British Government bowed to the inevitable and began to prepare for the possibility of another war. The MCW organisation received an order for 204 ambulances for the RAF, a contract carried out in Birmingham during 1936/7/8, whilst Addlestone's first MoS contract, for 125 composite-bodied military vehicles, was received in June or July 1939. Both organisations were, of course, involved in the production of thousands of military vehicles during the war. Many of these would be similar in construction to commercial vans or lorries, others would be very different with armour plate and specialist fittings exclusively for war work.

In October 1937 it was announced that following the resignation of Mr Bruce through ill health in March, the sales company had a new Sales Manager, RM Cole, who had been assistant chief engineer in the engineering and inspection

Western Welsh, the largest of the BET subsidiaries in south Wales, had taken modest numbers of AEC buses with Weymann's bodies in 1933-4 but in 1935-40 the Leyland Tiger, generally with bodywork to British Electrical Federation design, became the standard single-decker, Weymann's being among the main suppliers. The example shown, with body C5239, was one of 20 on TS8 chassis and dated from December 1937 – by that date, the Federation design had been updated somewhat, including outswept skirt panels. The vehicle shown was one with reversed livery for use on express services – note the sliding roof and company logo on the corner of the canopy. Weymann's had bodied a previous batch of 20, on TS7 chassis, in 1936, and in 1938-9, a further 30 TS8 followed – other suppliers of similar bodies to this fleet included Brush, Eastern Coach Works, and Roe.

department of the British Electrical Federation – BEF, the organisation which handled BET orders and contracts for Weymann's and the rest of the industry. Cole, always known as Bon Cole, had been with BEF since 1925, gradually working his way up, and since 1931 had been chiefly involved in negotiations with manufacturers. He was to be a most useful addition to the sales team.

The formation of the Joint Sales Organisation in 1932 had resulted in a rather unusual situation. Customers would deal with Homfray-Davies or his subordinates, and specifications would be drawn up for the preparation of quotes. The factory would then work out a price for the job and MCW (not Weymann's) would quote for the work. Some contracts were split between two suppliers, and if so it would be a racing certainty that the other supplier would be Park Royal. Prices were therefore very tightly controlled by the customers.

Before the MCW price was submitted it was necessary to decide which factory would build the vehicles if the quote was accepted. Some customers decreed that their vehicles should always be built in Birmingham, such as Manchester Corporation for whom Addlestone never built a single vehicle. Others were only supplied from Addlestone, including most BET and Balfour Beatty group companies. Many customers were supplied by both. But underlying all this was the need to maintain the 60:40 ratio of production as laid down in the 1932 Agreement. The twist in the tail is that as MCCW in Birmingham became more efficient, whilst the agitators at Weymann's became more powerful, and as prices became more and more competitive, the situation developed where one factory could handle a particular contract profitably whilst the other could not. In the final years an Addlestone product was 15% more expensive to produce than its Birmingham counterpart due to higher wage rates increasing the man-hour content.

Those who did not understand why Addlestone could not survive should consider this very carefully.

When peacetime production of buses came to an end and Ministry of War Transport allocations became the order of the day the situation changed to reflect the production of standard wartime utility buses for customers who, in many cases, were new to the MCW organisation. Prior to this the balancing of the values of the orders, whilst maintaining an even flow of work between the factories, must have been quite a task.

Meanwhile Northern General Transport continued to take single-deck AECs, and in 1939 also purchased a batch of 20 and with coachbuilt bodywork. A special chassis design allowed 38 seats to be fitted into these bodies for NGT, ramping the floor as can be seen to avoid losing space over the wheel arches. The vehicle is seen outside the factory on a wet day prior to a long journey north. The small label attached to the radiator front carries the body number and was used for identification in the works.

There was no lack of variety in the factory in 1939 for, in addition to full-sized single- and double-deck buses, and double-deck trolleybuses, a pair of 20-seat Leyland Cub buses were built for Devon General – among the last examples of this type of chassis in passenger form to be built. The KPZ4 chassis was normally intended as a 24-seater but in this case space was left at the rear for luggage. The body was of simple design but the seats were of a comfortable type often fitted to Federation design bodies. The Cubs operated largely in the Tiverton area, that shown being the operator's M452 (DDV 542) with body C5419.

1939 – WAR DECLARED

We have seen how the increased pace of orders had brought prosperity to the Company, its shareholders and employees as the 'thirties progressed. In 1939 this began to change and orders were not as fulsome as they had been, many operators wanting to 'wait and see' before placing orders. Others, more far sighted or more confident perhaps, took as many new vehicles as they could, knowing full well that if the worst came to the worst it could be a long time before they would be able to replace their older vehicles.

The crisis in Europe was now putting all the hard work and its rewards at risk and no-one could really believe that war could be averted. Hitler's invasion of Poland was, of course, the last straw though many in the factory were unable to grasp the full implications, 'appeasement' still being the operative word in 1938. As the situation deteriorated EG Izod was asked to contribute a piece for THE WEYMAG explaining just what the circumstances were. He pointed out that he, and hopefully everyone else, recognised their duty to support the oppressed and persecuted. Patriotic words which were not wasted on some of his men who volunteered to join up when the opportunity came, not waiting to be 'called up'. Although many of the workforce would be put into what was classed as a 'Reserved Occupation' – meaning they were too valuable to be called away for war service – many had already gone. These men had found themselves torn as to their loyalties. The company had treated its operation like that of a large family concern, but some of the family now felt that their duty lay elsewhere. Clearly the good times, and they had been good times, were coming to an end.

On Friday 1st September 1939 many people in the factory must have been listening to the BBC Home Service at mid-day in the work's canteen, or in their homes, to keep up-to-date. They finished their afternoon's work, clocked off and went home for the weekend – and came back on Monday morning knowing they were at war. Neville Chamberlain's announcement, broadcast by the BBC at 11 o'clock on Sunday September 3rd, that "this country was therefore at war with Germany" had finally put an end to all the uncertainty. Underground air-raid shelters had already been created around the factory some months previously and so most people had already been resigned to the inevitable. On 16th September it was announced that the Sales Office had been moved from Westminster to the Addlestone factory.

Many of the men were now called up, and gradually lots of the familiar faces disappeared. New employees joined but as soon as they were old enough they too were drafted into the forces. Hence one of the first changes which became apparent was the replacement of those men by women in the factory. Over the next few years hundreds of women would take over the men's jobs at Addlestone and one of those who worked in the Paint Shop, with a team of around 50 other girls painting the timbers for wartime trucks, was Olive Straker – daughter of Finishing Foreman Jim Knight. Olive recalled those days when interviewed in 2001, confirming that her group were fully employed painting components for military vehicles in the area above the Paint Shop and hardly came into contact with the hundreds of other girls working elsewhere in the factory.

Another change was the conversion of some of the spare land around the factory into allotments – 'Dig For Victory' would soon be the message in Addlestone and throughout Britain.

Amongst those who joined at that time and have assisted with the book, Wally Healy, Maurice Bullivant, Reg Allen, Margaret and Bill Playford and Vic Smith have each contributed many different memories of those dark days in Weymann's factory and in the Addlestone area itself.

Lisbon Electric Tramways Ltd was a British-owned company in which Central Mining had invested. By the time Weymann's started to supply vehicles, however, the link had been lost as the Addlestone Company by then belonged to United Molasses. Portugal celebrated its Centenary in June 1940 and purchased its first buses, six AEC Regents with single-deck bodywork, to help carry the crowds expected to attend the celebrations. One is shown below, illustrating the hybrid arrangement whereby both driver's cab and entrance/exit doors were situated on the same side of the bus. Double-deckers to the same configuration would later also be supplied. Lisbon was to become a major Addlestone customer in post-war years and it was fortunate that the outbreak of war had not prevented these first batches from being shipped.

For several months there was a 'phoney war', where very little enemy action was seen, but in the spring of 1940 the reality came home when, following the invasion of Denmark and Norway in April, Axis forces overran the Netherlands, Luxembourg, Belgium and France in May and the British Expeditionary Force had to be rescued from the beaches of Dunkirk.

Meanwhile, back home, as virtually all factories switched to production for the war effort, most bus building had almost been brought to a stop, only to restart when 'unfrozen' chassis and other components were released to allow vehicles required for transporting war workers to be built or completed. A variety of chassis then came to Weymann's, some having been fitted with frames in Birmingham to be completed at Addlestone as mentioned in the next chapter.

THE END OF PEACETIME PRODUCTION

Passenger vehicle production of 'normal' buses actually dragged on until 1942, records revealing that the last to be built to virtually full peacetime specification were delivered in April of that year. An early casualty, however, was the Patent Flexible range, with the final examples – a batch of five for City of Oxford delivered in March 1940 – marking the end of this link with the very beginnings of the Company. Since production of buses had taken over from cars exactly 400 examples had been built between 1929 and 1940, an average of some 34 per year if 1940 is taken out of the equation, with a peak of 53 in 1932.

Although clearly production figures had never been high, the marque had a strong following with certain operators. Potteries Motor Traction, Rhondda, South Wales and City of Oxford, amongst others, would miss their flexible friends, for after the war production was not resumed.

Coachbuilt orders seem to have come to a halt in June 1939 with a delivery of three AEC double-deckers to Oxford being followed by the first MoS contract. Bus production resumed later that year with the next deliveries, to Devon General, in January 1940. The order was not completed until July and in that time further single-deckers had been built for Red & White, Lincolnshire and Oxford. The last pre-war coachbuilt trolleybuses were delivered to Hastings in July. There then seems to have been a gap before the final single-deckers were built and delivered to East Yorkshire Motor Services. These were on Leyland's TS11 chassis, the only ones bodied at Addlestone, but of the 27 ordered only three were produced, together with the final batch of Trent's forward-entrance double-deckers. East Yorkshire's Leylands were delivered in November 1940, along with some of the Trent Daimlers. It was at this time that Chief Draughtsman Harold Cook was promoted to become Chief Engineer and shortly afterwards the final 'peacetime-ordered' coachbuilt bus appears to have been the last of Trent's Daimlers delivered in February 1941.

Metal-framed production continued throughout 1939, and at a slower rate through 1940. Sheffield, Potteries, Lancashire United, Glasgow, Northern General, Rhondda and Maidstone & District all took new vehicles, whilst Liverpool took 35 AEC Regents with frames for completion in their own workshops. Exports to Lisbon and Durban would be the last overseas orders supplied 'for the duration'. Orders were being cancelled by August 1940 and all deliveries had stopped by October 1940. Some orders were stopped part way through production, others were later diverted to other customers, perhaps the best example being eight single-decker Daimler chassis intended for Southern Rhodesia seven of which were instead delivered to Potteries and the eighth to West Monmouthshire as shown on page 73.

Production of coachbuilt and metal-framed bodywork resumed at the end of 1941 as will be seen in the next chapter, with Chesterfield Corporation taking seven double-decker motor buses and Notts & Derby ten double-decker trolleybuses, all of pre-war design but through Ministry of War Transport allocations whereby operators had to apply for permission to acquire new vehicles, permission being given only where special needs could be demonstrated.

ANOTHER CHANGE OF OWNERSHIP

A surprise change of ownership occurred in 1941/2, although once again most people in the factory would have been unaware of the change at the time.

The Prudential had found Weymann's to be a good investment, unlike some of the others in its portfolio. One in particular had caused it great problems when it tried to support the ailing British cinema industry through the purchase of London Films Ltd, and later the creation of Denham Studios in 1935/6. The original management was left intact to run Denham, but Prudential's own history records that escalating huge losses caused its Directors to take drastic action when its investment totalled £3m and London's deficit was over £1.8m and clearly quite out of control. In a move to raise cash, Weymann's was one of the companies sold on.

Whilst the 'Pru was seeking a buyer, quite separately another company was looking to purchase an engineering company with a transport background. That company was United Molasses, a company within the Tate & Lyle group.

United Molasses (UM) were shippers and processors of molasses and had a large fleet of ocean going tankers. In the dark days of 1941 many of these fell victim to the German U-boats as Hitler tried to cut off vital supplies to Britain. UM, like Weymann's, was at this time under the control of the MoS. UM Board Minutes and extracts from the company's history reveal that although they were compensated for the lost shipping it was not then possible to replace the vessels such was the load on British shipyards at the time. Thus a considerable cash mountain was accumulating as revealed in the balance sheets.

The Government, meanwhile, were desperate to find ways of reducing dependence on crucial oil imports and made available grants for research into, and development of, suitable alternatives. Someone from the MoS, aware of the huge resources UM already had, and the steady increase due to insurance payments on lost tankers, suggested to UM that they might with advantage investigate one particular grant, for the development of an electric car. In addition to a substantial cash grant other attractions included British Empire and World Selling Rights after the war and transfer of relevant Patents. A new type of electric motor, and the all-important lightweight battery, were apparently in development.

UM's Board discussed the matter at its meeting of 27th July 1942 and decided to go ahead. Accordingly a new company, The Q Vehicle Company Ltd – Company number 735555 – was registered by UM on 14th August 1942 to develop the electric car. Adverts were then placed in the national press in an attempt to find a suitable engineering company with which to progress matters.

Shortly afterwards, at an evening function at the Bank of England, UM's Chairman, FK Keilberg was approached by K Hoare, a broker, and informed of the Prudential's wish to sell Weymann's. He was introduced to PC Crump, Joint Secretary of the 'Pru and before the evening was over a deal had been struck. Next day, 30th August 1942, UM's Board ratified its Chairman's action and by the next UM Board Meeting on 28th September Weymann's had passed into UM's hands. They paid £272,945 17s 6d (£272,945.87½p) for the 360,323 shares, (15s (75p) for each 5s (25p) share plus the broker's fee) and roughly the value of one its medium sized tankers at that time. Weymann's nett assets were currently quoted at £166,000.

United Molasses then appointed its JM Don to prepare new agreements with the Weymann's management and its new owners, and Messrs Izod, Homfray-Davies and Arthur Froggatt were given contracts to run from New Year's Day 1943 until 30th December 1947.

Meanwhile work continued unabated in the Addlestone factory, but events back at UM were less uneventful as we shall see in the next chapter.

Production of complete buses appears to have stopped in Birmingham around December 1940; remaining orders were supplied to customers or other builders as frames on chassis for completion. All Utility vehicles were built at Addlestone.

Amongst the last Addlestone vehicles built before construction of utility buses began (see next chapter) were ten Notts & Derby AEC trolleybuses delivered from November 1941 through to March 1942. Although finished to full peacetime specification the vehicles were delivered to the operator in wartime grey paint. This was common practice by this time in the war, supplies of pigments for some colours, notably red, being reputedly difficult to obtain. Notts & Derby varnished these vehicles as soon as they were able. Body number M2408 is seen here in post-war days in normal blue and ivory livery. *GHF Atkins*

By 1940, the curved-profile double-deck body had very nearly reached the form to become so familiar post-war. Seen above, M2290, was one of a pair of AEC Regents for Tynemouth, and that concern's parent, Northern General, received eight similar buses. They marked a return to rear-entrance layout for double-deckers in these fleets, where it seems that the flared skirt was not favoured and the windscreen outline was squared-up.

As the risk of loss through enemy action to allied shipping increased, some export orders were cancelled whilst others were diverted to the home market. A batch of Daimler chassis intended for Salisbury, Southern Rhodesia, were completed as shown below, and of the eight all bar one then went to Potteries Motor Traction, the odd one, M2523, going to West Monmouthshire Omnibus Board. The vehicles were significant in being to South African dimensions, 30ft long and 8ft wide, requiring special dispensation before they could be certified for use in the UK.

CHAPTER FIVE: 1942 – 1945

The change of ownership to United Molasses had taken place in September 1942 and the new owners had made the various arrangements necessary for continuation of employment for Messrs Izod, Homfray-Davies and AT Froggatt. The next moves came in January 1943 when Mr James Don was appointed to the Board of Weymann's as the UM nominee. Don became an active member of the Addlestone team and is spoken of highly by those who remember him. Later in our story the Company name was changed to Weymann's Ltd – the name most people used anyway – this being formalised on 5th January 1945.

Having settled Weymann's affairs, as it were, UM now turned its attentions to the Q Vehicle Company where, it soon transpired, matters were not so straightforward. Briefly, Crompton Parkinson and Messrs Steel Bros. were the other companies involved in the project, along with the inventor Mr Kay.

Unfortunately it very soon became apparent that they had been sorely misled by this member of the 'partnership' in the new company, the inventor of the motor and developer of the lightweight battery, neither of which now seemed actually to exist. On 27th April 1943 UM's Chairman reported to his Board that to his chagrin the project was clearly going nowhere and it was agreed that the whole matter be shelved 'until after the cessation of hostilities'. UM had actually transferred the ownership of the Q Company to its subsidiary Athel Line who, with UM behind them, were big enough to stand the financial loss involved but, more importantly for this story, UM stood by Weymann's in a determined way.

Whilst clearly their newly acquired bus manufacturer was of little interest to them now the car project had been shelved, and they tried on more than one occasion to sell it, firstly to Park Royal in 1945 and later to Metro-Cammell, they nevertheless provided financial and management back-up from the date of purchase until, reluctantly, in 1964 they conceded that Weymann's apparently had no further future and they sold the company to Metro-Cammell – whose only reason for a change of heart in finally agreeing to the purchase was to remove some excess capacity from the industry by closing it down.

This Mansfield Regent, body number M2109, had one of the last pair of metal-framed front-entrance bodies of the pre-war type built at Addlestone, and delivered in December 1939. Now, a couple of years later, it sports its wartime additions: anti-blast netting on the windows; masked headlamps and white edges to its body extremities to make it easier to see in the blackout. A surprising feature at this late date was the half cab door, clearly visible in this picture. Bus photography during wartime was likely to invite trouble, always assuming that there was any film available. We are fortunate to have such excellent material available from veteran photographer Geoffrey Atkins who had already been recording the local transport scene for some 14 years when gems such as this were recorded. He was presumably sufficiently well-known in the area to avoid the risk of 'being taken in for questioning'.
GHF Atkins

Chesterfield Corporation took seven metal-framed lowbridge Leyland TD7s, in January to April 1942. They were finished in all-over wartime green as shown. Note the rear bumper, now a useful precaution against rear end black-out collisions. The interior view of the same vehicle reveals the spartan finish, though the seats are still upholstered and not wooden slatted as would soon become standard on the Utility buses built later in 1942. The side gangway of the lowbridge bus will be noticed as will the shades on the lamps, reducing the lighting to a trickle to prevent the bus becoming a target for enemy aircraft in the days when raids would be carried out at fairly low level. On the bulkhead, clearly visible on the original print above the Clayton Dewandre heater, the Weymann's transfer as also normally applied to the exterior panel behind the front nearside wheel is prominently displayed. Above it, almost apologetically, or perhaps defiantly, is another single line transfer proclaiming 'WAR FINISH'. Note that sliding windows have now made their appearance in this fleet.

The Mansfield area was strategically vital to the war effort through its proximity to various coal mines. Allocation of war transport, through the Ministry of War Transport, depended on need – to replace vehicles absolutely beyond further use or to expand services for war workers involved in production of munitions and raw materials or other essential wartime activities. In addition to deliveries of 'diverted' buses, as seen below, and then Utilities as shown overleaf, there was another solution proposed by the powers-that-be, and one which received a very lukewarm reception from the industry. The idea was to use trailers of the type shown, manufactured by the British Trailer Company and theoretically capable of carrying some 56 passengers, when coupled to a Bedford or, as here, Commer Superpoise Q4 tractor unit. In fact it was found that seating complying with regulations for public use would accommodate only 38 passengers, despite the vehicles being much longer and more unwieldy than a conventional single-decker. After strong criticism from operator representatives, no more to this specification were built, though somewhat similar Bedford-hauled artics bodied elsewhere were used as transport within Royal Ordnance Factories. The man charged with looking into the whole wartime bus concept was none other than Bill Black and we can imagine his forthright and absolute condemnation of this idea. This one, body C7336, and another went to Mansfield District, two with bodywork by CH Roe of Cross Gates, Leeds, to Liverpool Corporation whilst one with a shortened AEC chassis seems never to have gone into operation (see page 78). *Alan Townsin collection*

A more productive move was the use of parts of chassis or bodywork still in stock from contracts that were in hand when bus production had stopped. Metro-Cammell had one for body frames to Manchester Corporation's 'streamline' outline in hand in 1940, some being intended for Daimler chassis not built as the result of the bombing of the Daimler factory in Coventry, and then set aside when the general cessation of bus work took effect. When it was decided to make use of them, Metro-Cammell was fully engaged on tank and other war production, so it was decided that they should be taken to Addlestone for completion – they thus became rare examples of true MCW manufacture, in the sense of having been made at both the partner companies' premises. By the time that could be done, the 'unfrozen' chassis of other makes had been bodied and thus these bodies were mounted on examples of the new Guy Arab utility bus chassis. The example shown, M2631, was one of the first such buses completed in December 1942, being supplied to Midland General as its 188, HRA 815. *GHF Atkins*

However, back in 1943 there was a war on as Weymann's employees were only too well aware. Despite being only 25 miles from central London and the docks, and notwithstanding the many choice targets in the area including Vickers and the Airscrew Propeller Company, fortunately the factory escaped the bomb damage which was to beset many organisations though a V1 'doodlebug' did explode very near to Norman Froggatt's house, causing considerable damage. Thankfully no harm came to Norman, his wife Beryl or their two children, all of whom were in the garden when the flying bomb's motor cut out above their heads. The family moved into Fieldhurst, one of the firm's houses in Addlestone; the Wages Department was similarly moved from the factory – to create more working space presumably – as Walter Healy recalls.

Work in the factory in 1943 included the Utility buses and odd contracts for bus companies with great need for vehicles to move war workers, but the main emphasis was on military production. Bodies for Bedford trucks by the hundred were turned out, along with armoured personnel carriers and armoured cars, photographic vans for survey work and decompression chambers for the RAF for training pilots. The work force remained at a high level of activity, and as mentioned, hundreds of women came in to replace the men who were away fighting the war. There was considerable variety in the greatly reduced bus building activity, with war damaged London trolleybuses being rebuilt, many semi-utility variants, bodying of trolleybuses whose export had been blocked, two articulated trailer buses and the finishing of the part-completed Manchester buses. The number of Utility bus bodies built was 687, 527 on Guy Arab chassis, 30 on Daimler and 35 trolleybuses. This variety is shown here and in the photographic survey in the second part of this book. Maurice Bullivant recalls after the war Weymann's won a contract for a further 500 radar vans, for which 70 other firms also quoted, such was the competition.

In 1942 Vic Smith, a Lowestoft man with relatives in the Addlestone area but who had previously worked at Eastern Coach Works, joined the firm, and soon began to make his mark in the sports and social areas. He had joined the reserves in 1938, had been seriously ill on camp and then been declared unfit for the army. Vic had heard there were vacancies in the factory, rang to ask for an employment form and was told, instead, to report for duty at 8 o'clock next morning! His skills as a bodymaker were invaluable but in addition his background and enthusiasm for sport were welcomed by Izod who saw him as the means of keeping the company's sports interest alive. With encouragement from the management and materials provided by the company, and with some assistance, Vic later extended the sports pavilion to create a scoring hut. Darts were a favourite pastime of his and 57 years later he was still secretary of the Ten-Bar-Two darts team, and still playing with the team every Friday night, when interviewed for this book. His many reminiscences and memorabilia have been invaluable. In later years he was a familiar figure in the factory with his sledge hammer, and his assistant Dave Humphrey, as he squared up and aligned the body framing before the part completed buses went down the line.

More or less as Vic joined, receptionist Margaret Colman, the former Margaret Whindle, left to start a family. Her connection dated back to 1927 and there was, literally, no-one who had been at Addlestone longer than she had.

Margaret's place was to be taken by Marcelle Prenton and her sisters, and the young Walter Healy soon became friendly with Marcelle. They married in 1958 and they too have become good friends of the author during the production of this book – whilst Marcelle still acts as prompter for the Annual Reunions. Her father Harry worked under George Biggs in the fitting shop.

THE WEYMAG allowed those away in the forces to keep in touch, and amongst the items recorded was a note that Sales Manager Bon Cole was missing, and then had turned up as a POW in Libya during the north African campaign. He was by that time a Major in the Tank Regiment. Later there was a reference to Weymann's armoured cars and trucks having being spotted in French Indo-China – did the military vehicles also carry Weymann's markings then? One of the youngest of the conscripts was Reg Allen, called up in 1941 and who recalled being the youngest on his ship – a Royal Navy destroyer – at two successive Christmastides. It was a naval tradition that the youngest boy took command of the ship for the day on Christmas Day and Reg thus had this honour twice. He remembered the terrible time that the people of Malta had endured, having seen it first hand when they were in Valetta dockyard, and was pleasantly surprised when I sent him a post card from the island showing a cruise liner standing in the harbour exactly where his destroyer had been photographed during the war, a picture he showed me when we first met.

Despite the deprivations of war there were lighter moments. 'Workers Playtime', the radio show designed to lift the spirits of those at work on the war effort and at home came twice from Weymann's canteen, being broadcast on the BBC Radio, with popular singers Anne Ziegler and Webster Booth on one occasion and comedian Cardew (the cad) Robinson on the other. In 1942 the Works Brass Band was formed and went from strength to strength in the years to come. The canteen also came into its own during the war when rationing and non-availability of many foods made provision of meals very difficult. The canteen management were able to obtain a better selection of food than individuals on their own account could secure.

An idea of the shift in the balance of production can be gained by the following statistics: in 1938 the factory built 483 buses and trolleybuses; in 1939 the total was 447; in 1940–301; 1941–17; 1942–91; 1943–175; 1944–185. The rest of the output which kept the huge workforce fully occupied was of vehicles for the military. The MCW Silver Jubilee Brochure recorded that Weymann's had built over 9,000 special steel bodies for service vehicles, including over 3,000 artillery tractors, 2,000 radio vans for the RAF and many vehicles for special duties. Then, in 1944, there was another attempt to persuade the domestic transport industry of the merits of the articulated trailer bus, this time using a cut-down old bus as the prime mover, as seen in the extract reproduced below. The response was even more tart than that in 1942 and the idea was dropped.

On a happier note the annual children's Christmas party was reinstated for 1944, anticipating the end of the war, and some 500 of the employees' children sat down to Christmas fare, with presents handed out by Father Christmas – Arthur Froggatt as ever was. The huge canteen which could seat over 1,000 people really came to life for this event.

The gradual increase in the number of buses passing though the factory, and the return to painting in full liveries as supplies of paint became available again, heralded better times on the way. The end of the war would bring huge changes, however, and for many years shortages of materials and the need to give priority to exports would dominate post-war production. Weymann's would not be alone in experiencing great changes, and many who longed for the good old days would become unhappy at the way things were going – not least the management.

Early in 1944, the Ministry of Supply had another go at the trailer bus concept, ordering a prototype without any consultation with the industry, for which Weymann's was required to build the 55-seat body (given the number Q17). The tractor unit was cut down from a 1939 AEC Regal coach (ex-Timpson's, FLM 386) with wheelbase reduced by 6ft to 11ft 6in. The trailer underframe was made by the British Trailer Co., was over 33ft long and weighed over 8 tons, heavier than a utility double-decker. The Public Transport Association, representing big operators, bluntly described it as "quite unsuitable", with particular criticisms on safety. It released its comments to the trade press – an unheard-of step, especially in wartime, pointing out that the seating layout did not comply with existing regulations, the seating capacity dropping to 44 if this was rectified. Steps leading to the high front part of the trailer were condemned as "extremely dangerous", with a risk of passengers falling from this level and out through the front doorway. Nothing more was heard of the vehicle, and no more of the type were produced.
Courtesy Geoff Lumb

The Utility buses and trolleybuses were intended to be rugged, no-frills, reliable and economical vehicles which could be produced with minimum recourse to scarce resources or commodities. As such they were an undoubted success, many giving 15 or more years service, though in many cases having been rebodied after around 7-10 years due to the poor quality of the original timber. Part of the success was the simplicity of the chassis and the inclusion in most, but not all of the buses, of the legendary Gardner engine. The specification included steel replacing aluminium, the elimination of normal domes to avoid the need for skilled panel-beaters, only one half-drop window per side on each deck, and the replacement of upholstered seats by wooden slatted ones. One single-line indicator was fitted as standard. Despite this basic concept the vehicles were rugged and reliable and it is true to say that many post-war customers for Guy were introduced and converted to the marque by these vehicles. Similarly, many post-war MCW customers first encountered the bodywork from that organisation during the war. Above is an example from Colchester, seen c 1943 with soldiers mingling with the civilians.

Right: A Utility trolleybus on the standard wartime W4 chassis, built in Wolverhampton and badged as Sunbeam or Karrier according to the customer's normal preference is seen here. This example was for South Lancashire Transport of Atherton, Lancashire, parent company to Lancashire United which was an old MCW customer, having taken bodies from either Addlestone or Birmingham since 1932. SLT had previously taken only Guy and Leyland trolleybuses but they preferred the locally-produced Metro-Vick equipment to whose factory they ran many workman's services and with which these vehicles were fitted – the Karrier badge can just be discerned at the base of the windscreen. They were the first trolleybus bodies supplied to SLT by MCW, and the link remained for after the war the Company took many Weymann's bodies including its final batch of Karrier trolleybuses. These had actually been ordered during the war but the MoWT would not sanction production of three-axled vehicles until the return to peace.

The change of Government in 1945 with Labour coming in with a landslide paved the way for the militant unionists to put in claims which could never be supported, but strikes and other pressures forced changes which the company could not prevent. United Molasses must also have longed for the days when the Prudential had seen steady production and rising profits. There was one bright cloud ahead, however. London Transport needed thousands of new buses and Weymann's were to secure a contract so large they would need an additional factory to cope with it. All that and more will form the basis of the second volume of the history of Addlestone's best remembered company.

At their annual reunion in 2001 (the last the writer attended before finalising the manuscript for publication) thirty-six years after the closure of Weymann's factory, its former employees, almost without exception, still remembered with pride and affection their time at Addlestone. They spoke of the family atmosphere which pervaded the factory, partly from the large number of employees related to each other — as many as eight or ten from a family group being not uncommon — and partly from the attitude of the management to its workforce. Those who had started when the company moved from Putney to Addlestone recalled that Addlestone was just a quiet village at that time.

They remembered the good times and the bad, but believed that the good far outweighed the bad. They recalled that when orders were not forthcoming they were laid off, or paid off, often at only an hour's notice. They accepted this for, in its day, it was commonplace and other employers treated their workforces similarly. They confirmed that before and after the war into the 'fifties they could expect to come back when times improved, which might be only a matter of months later, but there was no animosity on either side. Local companies where they could expect to find employment without difficulty included Vickers and Airscrew, both in Weybridge, and many people moved backwards and forwards between these factories over a period of years.

Their pride in their time at Weymann's made writing this book both a privilege and a pleasure. I hope they will feel I have done them justice. There may well be many who I have been unable to contact, particularly surviving former Directors or their families, and who have reminiscences they feel would be of interest for the next volume, or who can fill in some of the gaps or correct errors in this volume. If so do please make contact with me via the publishers in Pikes Lane, Glossop, Derbyshire SK13 8EH. Thank you.

A reminder - from an original folded in someone's wallet for many years - of a byegone age – a view of one of the firm's Annual Dinners, held at the Grosvenor Hotel in London's Park Lane.

APPENDIX 1 : OWNERSHIP & FINANCE

THE FIRST COMPANY: Weymann's Motor Body Ltd
Company Number 191815, Registered 8th August 1923

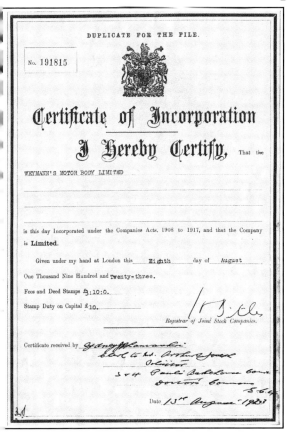

Charles Weymann was a prolific and extremely successful inventor who made himself a considerable fortune. He already had business interests in France manufacturing components for, and licensing construction of, his patented motor cars and in 1926 opened a factory in America, but it is his English activities which relate to this narrative.

Weymann is on record as speaking little English and to establish his British company he entered into partnership with the brothers Aron who already had a London based company: the British company was registered on August 8th 1923 with the name Weymann's Motor Body Limited. The Directors of this company were shown on the return dated August 3rd as being CT Weymann (French); Eugen Aron (British of German origin); Hermann Aron (British of German origin); and Maurice Tabuteau (French). Weymann is listed as an Engineer, the Aron brothers as Directors of Rotax (Motor Accessories) Ltd, and Tabuteau as a Sales Manager. Weymann and Tabuteau both gave their address as 20 Rue Troyan, Paris. Declaration of nationality was required in the light of anti-German feeling after the First World War.

The Registered Office was situated at Rotax Works, Victoria Road, Willesden London NW10. The connection between Weymann and Rotax was that Rotax, as manufacturers of motor accessories, were one of Weymann's sources of supply for his patented components for motor car construction. Two shares were issued, one each to the Arons.

The share return dated 17th September 1923 shows the Arons as holding 501 (Eugen) and 249 (Hermann) but by 16th December 1924 the holdings had been revised to Eugen Aron 625, Hermann Aron 125 and CT Weymann 250. Weymann still gave his Paris address on the official Annual Returns but Monsieur Tabuteau no longer appears in the list of Directors by this date. Eugen Aron was the Company Chairman.

In 1925, as described in Chapter 1, to enable it to expand and to begin manufacture as opposed to licensing of other manufacturing companies, Weymann's Motor Body Ltd purchased from the liquidator for £3,500 cash the assets of the Cunard Motor and Carriage Company Ltd, with its premises in Putney, south west London. Additional finance was required for this purpose and, accordingly, the Weymann company was re-structured. The new money came from the Company's bankers – Bernhard Scholle and Company Ltd of London – and the association with the Aron brothers and Rotax appears to have come to an end.

The 1923 Company's Certificate of Incorporation, dated 13th August 1923. The Company's function was the manufacture and procurement of components, and the issue of licences for others to build complete Weymann patented cars. An advertisement, below, for Weymann components. Note the inclusion of the Rotax Works address, this being the Registered Office of the 1923 Company.

At an Extraordinary General Meeting held at the RAC Club in Pall Mall on 25th November 1925 members of the Company confirmed an Agreement prepared between the Company, CT Weymann and the Bernhard Scholle Bank for the sale of Weymann's Motor Body Ltd, and also confirmed that the Company should be wound up voluntarily to enable this. The 1923 company had assets and monies owing of some £23,675 according to the liquidator's statement. Finally, because all debts were to be cleared in full, the liquidator was authorised to consent to the registration of a new company with the same or a similar name.

Accordingly a new Company was duly registered on that same day, 25th November 1925, paving the way for a new and very different future.

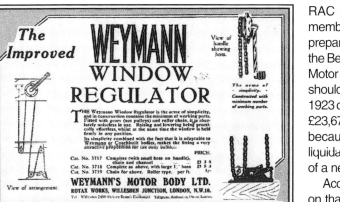

THE SECOND COMPANY

Weymann's Motor Bodies (1925) Ltd.
Company No. 209936, Registered 25th November 1925

Following confirmation from Companies House, Cardiff, that all documents relating to the above Company were destroyed, in 1990, we have been left to look elsewhere for details of the Company structure, shareholders and Directors.

It is clear that the Bernhard Scholle Bank now becomes very important in the story, and that a substantial amount of the opening capital for the 1925 Company came from the Bank. The Bank itself is not without interest, seemingly catering largely, though doubtless not exclusively, for the finance of companies or projects with a transport connection.

The Bernhard Scholle bank was set up by the Central Mining and Investment Corporation, a subsidiary of Rand Mines of South Africa, during the early 'twenties at a time when gold mining was going through a difficult period. Having large cash reserves available Rand Mines decided to invest in new areas, transport and banking being two which relate directly to our story. The bank was registered in December 1922 in London and its Directors included Sir Sothern Holland and Felix Heim, respectively Chairman and London Manager of Central Mining, representing the CM&IC and holding the 2,000 'A' shares, together with Jesse Frank, Herbert Rothbarth, Lawrence Tweedy, BJ Montford Bebb and The Lord Dunsmore who collectively held the 2,000 'B' shares. The Registered Office was at 22, Austin Friars London EC2, later moved to 1, London Wall Buildings EC2, this being the headquarters of Central Mining in London. 22, Austin Friars then became Weymann's Head Office also.

The choice of the Bernhard Scholle bank to finance Weymann's expansion apparently came through CT Weymann's influential motor racing and manufacturing friends, one of whom – Maurice Dollfus – was a Director of the bank. Dollfus was also the head of the Ford Motor Company in France.

Thus appropriately financed, and having taken over the Cunard Motor and Carriage Company's assets, the new Company was able to prepare for expansion into the manufacture of motor cars to Weymann's patented construction. As recorded in Chapter 1 fashions changed, and then in the increasingly difficult times of the late 'twenties Weymann's Motor Bodies (1925) Ltd was obliged to change direction, and to accommodate this change to acquire even larger premises. Since the market for its cars had hardly been impressive it is reasonable to conjecture that it would have built up little additional capital and that the bank would have been required to provide the additional finance required for the move to Addlestone and to equip the 'new' factory there.

At this time, EG Izod was appointed as Managing Director. Izod had been a Consultant Engineer and later a Mine Manager with Central Mining, half owners of the Bank, and specialised in the assessment of plant and machinery requirements for new or expanding companies. His position in Weymann's would thus be both as a professional engineer and as a watchdog for the Bank and its investors.

The entry in Motor Transport Year Book for 1929 shows the Directors as :-

Charles T Weymann [Chairman]; Edwin G Izod [Managing]; Lt Col Llewelyn Evans; Jesse Frank; Louis Coatalen; Maurice Dollfus. Since we know who Weymann was it will be useful to look at the other Directors' backgrounds –

As stated Izod had previously been a consultant engineer to the Central Mining and Investment Corporation in South Africa. Born c1883 he is pictured in an illustration of senior officials of the Corner House Group in 1914 in South Africa included in "Golden Age", the official history of Corner House, owners of CM&IC. (See page 19 for a Biography of Izod.)

Lt Col Llewelyn Evans, who had been in charge at Cunard [post 1925] appears to be a representative of Bernhard Scholle; Jesse Frank was an American citizen

Bernhard Scholle letterhead
showing the London and Paris
addresses. There was also an
American office.

BERNHARD, SCHOLLE & CO., LIMITED

TELEGRAMS "BERNSCHOL LONDON"

DIRECTORS
HERBERT ROTHBARTH
BASIL J. M. BESS
FELIX HEIM (GERMAN ORIGIN) BRITISH
THE EARL OF DUNMORE
V.C., M.V.O., D.S.O.
LAWRENCE I. TWEEDY
JESSE FRANK U.S.A.

WARNFORD COURT
THROGMORTON STREET
LONDON E.C.2.

TELEPHONE
7854 LONDON WALL
6 LINES

PARIS
15 BOULEVARD DES ITALIENS

THE GOLDEN CONNECTION

The concept of a British bus building company in Surrey being owned by a South African gold and diamond mining corporation with its headquarters in the City of London must, surely, arouse the curiosity of even the most diehard nuts-and-bolts bus enthusiast. But then, perhaps, the curiosity gives way to the common fall-back of "So what?"

So this! Because of its unusual ownership between 1925 and 1937 Weymann's survived when many of its contemporaries, lacking a parent company with cash reserves of over £13m, went to the wall. In addition, some of its substantial and impressive overseas orders turn out to be effectively in-house contracts within the group. Its resident hands-on Chairman, Izod, was a former South African Mining Manager and Engineer, born in Rugby. It was virtually wholly-owned by a bank whose funds came from South Africa and America. These facts will already have came out in the pre-war history in Chapters 1 and 2. And so the more important question is, how did it all come about?

The Central Mining and Investment Corporation was formed to look after the interests of Rand Mines, a major mining conglomerate in what after 1910 became the Union of South Africa. Central Mining was a British company, registered in 1895 and located in the City of London.

After the First World War the cost of mining rose to the extent that some mines could no longer be viable and the whole industry faced an uncertain and possibly very short future. In the face of this potential calamity Central Mining decided to extend its policy of investing outside the gold and diamond industries, and chose banking and transport as two key areas for continuing and future investment. It already had experience of the profits to be made from transport, having invested in Lisbon tramways, Port Elizabeth tramways, Cape Town tramways, Birmingham tramways (SA) and others. It decided also to invest in a huge but potentially very lucrative Spanish railway project.

It created a bank to finance these and other transport projects, Bernhard Scholle and Company Ltd, also registered in the City of London. Through personal connections with the Bank mentioned in the text it financed the growing and potentially attractive international motor car building company which Charles Weymann was developing, with its factories in Paris, London and Indianapolis.

The 1929 Wall Street Crash, and the ensuing Depression, created world-wide financial chaos and led to great difficulties for British industry. In September 1931 Sterling was devalued and many companies either collapsed or drastically wrote down their capital. South Africa was obliged to follow suit, reluctantly, 15 months later after it found it could not export to Britain because its products were too expensive. The South African devaluation, however, meant that the value of the previously non-viable gold mines rocketed and huge profits once again flowed into the company.

Weymann's then became a dispensable minority interest which was sold on in 1937.

and a Bernhard Scholle Director holding just under 50% of the £4,000 opening capital of the Bank; Louis Coatalan was the joint Managing Director of the Sunbeam Motor Company which built motor cars using Weymann's patents; Maurice Dolslfus as stated was the head of Ford in France.

Weymann's Motor Bodies (1925) Ltd's opening capital was £66,000: 55,000 £1 Cumulative Preference Shares and 220,000 Ordinary 1/- (5p) Shares, this figure being some three times the liquidated value of the 1923 Company. It sold all its shares, Preference and Ordinary, to Bernhard Scholle except for 88,000 Ordinary 1/- (5p) shares (value £4,400) which were recorded as 'Credited as Paid Up and allocated to CT Weymann'. This allocation was to reflect CT Weymann's financial interest in the former Cunard Company and also to recompense him for the loss of future royalties or licence payments in respect of his Patented Motor Car Construction, these monies in future becoming the property of the Company rather than, as previously, of CTW himself.

A major function of the Bank was financing the Mining Company's £2m plus involvement with the construction of a 270 mile long broad gauge railway in Spain between Santander and Burgos, in which the Bank, Central Mining and the Anglo-Spanish Construction Company became partners. The huge contract was completed satisfactorily and ahead of time but then as the political situation exploded and the Spanish Government fell the new Government blocked payment. Bernhard Scholle was caught up in a situation whereby the stage payments for a contract whose eventual total value was over £3million were being withheld purely due to Spain's internal problems after the uprising and in no way reflecting any unsatisfactory aspect of the handling of the actual contract or the quality of the finished railway built by the Central Mining Company and the Anglo-Spanish Construction Company.

It appears that Weymann's unsuccessful American company must also have caused difficulties for Bernhard Scholle, though not on the scale of the Spanish problems. Nevertheless as matters dragged on the Bank's position became untenable and on 26th August 1935 it went into liquidation. The liquidation was a long-drawn-out affair, complicated by claims from overseas against a Director who was indemnified by the Bank. The Second World War further protracted matters and not until 1954 was the Bernhard Scholle affair finally settled. Unfortunately by that time many of its subscribers were deceased.

Of direct relevance to this narrative, however, was the fact that from 1935 the Bank's liquidator was seeking to sell the shares in the Weymann's Company, including those held by the Bank and its nominees. In November 1937 the Prudential Assurance Company purchased 360,023 Weymann shares from the liquidator and took control. The Pru appears not to have appointed a representative on the Weymann's Board, and day-to-day running of the Company remained in the hands of Messrs Izod, Homfray-Davies and Froggatt as previously.

The purchase reflected the Prudential Company's policy, then as now, of investing in what appeared to be sound and profitable companies whose profits would go towards increasing the value of the Prudential portfolio for the benefit of its investors. It was an endorsement of Weymann's standing but reflected a significant change inasmuch as the new owners were not in the transport business whereas since 1923 the shareholders had always included a majority of people with direct connections to the industry. In the eyes of its new owner the Company would merely be a tool for making money for its shareholders.

Weymann's remained with the Prudential until after the outbreak of the Second World War. A change of ownership then followed in rather strange circumstances. The catalysts for the change were the Ministry of Supply, with whom Weymann's were involved through war work, and United Molasses who were at this time an Agent of the MoS, and the reason was the urgent desire by the MoS to progress the development, construction and marketing of a battery-powered electric motor car at a time when Germany's U-boats were sinking many British tankers with tragic loss of life and catastrophic losses of vital oil supplies. Many of the tankers lost were those belonging to United Molasses.

It was intimated to United Molasses that a new and potentially ground-breaking electric motor was on the point of becoming available, and that substantial Government grants and post-war British Empire and World patents and selling rights were available to a company which would take on the development, manufacture and marketing of such an electric motor car. UM was a very large company – its share capital as far back as 1926 had been £1million – and was a potentially willing partner with huge cash reserves. Ironically it was building up further large reserves from the insurance payments for the loss of its tankers which it could not at that time replace. It had, however, no suitable vehicle development/manufacturing capacity and placed advertisements in the national press seeking to acquire a company which would meet this requirement.

The UM Board, having discussed the matter further, agreed to proceed, and whilst awaiting responses to its advertisements, formed the 'Q Vehicle Company Ltd' – Number 375555 – which was registered on 14th August 1942, ready to take on this project and in order to progress matters.

Shortly afterwards United Molasses' Chairman MK Keilberg came into conversation with Hoar & Co., Merchant Bankers, who informed him that the Pru would be interested in selling their shares in Weymann's. Here was the manufacturing company they had been seeking. UM offered 15/- (75p) per 5/- (25p) Share for the 90% of the shares which the Pru held and the deal was struck.

The Pru were keen to dispose of their holding for, although Weymann performed quite well for them, turning in profits of £27,260 (1937), £59,740 (1938), £32,050 (1939), £33,900 (1940), and an expected £65,000 (reflecting increased output in wartime) for 1941, the Prudential at this time had potential cash problems brought about by over-stretching itself in aiding the British cinema industry through the purchase of London Films and the creation of Denham Studios. When an opportunity arose to sell Weymann's shares it moved quickly.

Weymann's total authorised capital at this time was £100,000 of which £99,613.5s 0d had been issued. After the initial approach in Threadneedle Street the purchase was agreed and the matter was formally ratified by UM's Board at its meeting on 28th September 1942, confirming the purchase of 360,323 shares (90% of those issued) for a total price of £272,945 17s 6d.

The improved financial performance in the later thirties meant that the shareholders were starting to feel the benefits by this time. After years of seeing no return, a dividend of 15%, had been declared in 1937. This was followed by 25% in 1938, 15% in 1939 and in 1940, 25% in 1941 and 20% in 1942, the year of the changeover.

Following the purchase Keilberg wrote to Izod, informing him that UM now had control of Weymanns, and arranging for new Service Contracts and Pension arrangements to be prepared. Izod and Froggatt were expected to retire in 1948, presumably at the age of 65. Izod died before reaching retirement but Mr Froggatt was later to have a battle with UM when he attempted to stay on past retirement age. As part of the new arrangements Mr James Don, UM's Secretary, was appointed as the UM representative on Weymann's Board but once again day-to-day running

Copy of the telegram from Hoar, the Broker, to Crump, Secretary of the Prudential, confirming that Keilberg of UM had "decided to purchase Motor Bodies" (Weymann's).

Archives of Prudential plc.

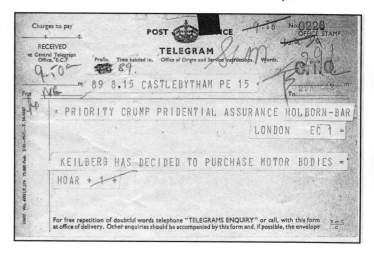

of the Company remained with Messrs Izod, Homfray-Davies and Froggatt, each of whose contracts was to run from New Year's Day 1943 for five years. Some time after completing the purchase UM changed the name to the shorter (and already generally used) Weymann's Ltd., this being formalised in January 1945.

United Molasses now had the Q Vehicle Company Ltd, Weymann's Motor Bodies (1925) Ltd, large amounts of ready cash, Government grants and the encouragement of the MoS, all backing the electric motor car project.

In the event, and much to his chagrin, UM's Chairman Keilberg, at a Board Meeting on 27th April 1943 had to report to his colleagues that in respect of the Inventor and Partner in the electric car development "his opinion of Mr Kay's integrity, reliability and general capabilities had undergone a complete change during the last year". Since the project had depended on Kay these words were to be a major blow to the scheme. In the light of this the UM Board agreed to "put the matter into cold storage for the duration of the war". Precisely what happened to the Q Company's electric car is not clear since the Official Papers have not survived but UM certainly took no further part in its activities and after his death in September 1948 Mr Kay's estate was reported to the Board as being "hopelessly insolvent".

UM, sadder and wiser, therefore sought on several occasions to divest itself of Weymann's (which it now no longer needed) though around this time it had also purchased, amongst other companies, Eric Bemrose, the cheque and security printers. In another slightly embarrassing though more amusing admission to the Board, it was in due course revealed that United Molasses could not afford to use Bemrose for the production of UM's Annual Report and Accounts, such were the security printer's charges for its work! These were but minor blips, however, for UM was and continues to be a very successful Company.

In 1945, as part of the first attempt to sell Weymann's, James Don entered negotiations on behalf of UM with William Black, who many at Weymann's would still remember as the one-time General Manager at Addlestone, but who was by that time Managing Director at Park Royal Coachworks, Weymann's main rival. Black declined the approach but the opportunity to assess Weymann's standing whilst the joint RT project for LTE was being finalised must have been useful to the Park Royal Board.

In 1946 the UM Board was advised that Weymanns were considering investing £60,000 in additional plant and improvements, and whilst they expected to be able to meet this from their own resources they wished to able to call on UM should the need arise. UM were pleased to confirm their agreement. This was almost certainly preparatory to the massive RT contract for London Transport..

Whether there were further attempts to sell Weymann's other than to Metropolitan Cammell, the partner in MCW, in January 1948 is unclear but the company was destined to remain in the ownership of United Molasses, and though profits became ever slimmer in the final years, sliding frequently into the red, the Addlestone management and workforce were supported by their parent company.

Finally, in 1963, after previous overtures had been consistently rejected, the Metropolitan Cammell Carriage and Wagon Company of Birmingham at last agreed to purchase the Addlestone company, but for the sole purpose of closing it to reduce excess capacity within the industry.

Last ditch attempts by the Surrey work force to purchase the company came to nothing. They were doomed to failure since the last thing Metropolitan Cammell now wanted was a continuation of coachbuilding activity at Addlestone when it had just made plans for the survival of its Birmingham workforce which depended on the closure of Weymann's. Purchase by MCCW duly took place in 1964 and closure followed in 1966.

Although Weymann's then ceased to exist the MCW Company remained in existence, becoming the reconstructed arm of the MCCW combine which then became responsible for bus manufacture. When bus production in Birmingham ceased the Company was sold on, and its name changed to Vanefield Ltd, though with no connection to the former coachbuilding activities.

APPENDIX 2 : THE JOINT COMPANY

Metropolitan-Cammell-Weymann Motor Bodies Ltd.
Company No. 266744, Registered 5th July 1932

The new sales organisation, the background to which is explained in Chapter 2, was registered as Company number 266744 on 5th July 1932, and at a meeting on 30th July the five shares in the company were allocated to the five Directors. The Share capital was £6,000, with ownership being divided 60:40 between Birmingham and Addlestone. Accordingly the Directors were Tom Lancelot Taylor (Chairman) who was currently Chairman of MCCW; Archibold John Boyd and Arthur Stanley Bailey, Directors of MCCW; Baden Rhys Aubrey Homfray-Davies and Edwin Gilbert Izod, Directors of Weymann's Motor Bodies (1925) Ltd.

TL Taylor, the new Chairman, lived in Chapel Allerton, Leeds, AJ Boyd lived in Woking, whilst AS Bailey lived in Worcestershire. BRA Homfray-Davies and EG Izod both lived in Ham, Surrey. The Chairman would be appointed annually, rotating between the two companies. The Registered Office was at Vickers House, Broadway, Westminster, London SW, and the Sales Office was duly set up in that building.

A Joint Agreement was prepared covering aspects of responsibility and, importantly, the ratio of division of orders and their placement in the two factories; the 60:40 ratio would apply throughout. For legal reasons orders were placed on the Sales Organisation – MCW – and subcontracted as appropriate.

The Official Share Holding Return for Metropolitan-Cammell-Weymann Motor Bodies Ltd, here dated 22nd March 1933, but prepared on 30th June 1932, and showing that the 2,500 Shares were held one each by the five Directors, with a further 1497 held by MCCW in Birmingham and the remaining 998 held by Weymann's. Thus was the 60:40 ratio established which formed the basis of the division of orders between the two companies until MCCW bought out Weymann's and closed the Addlestone plant in 1966.

APPENDIX 3 : WHO WAS WHO and WHEN

WEYMANN'S MOTOR BODY LTD
(In existence from 1923 - 1925)

DIRECTORS

Eugen Aron   [Chairman]
Hermann Aron
Charles Terres Weymann
Maurice Tabuteau

WEYMANN'S MOTOR BODIES
(1925) LTD

CHAIRMEN 1925 - 1946

CT Weymann	to 01/1932
AW Rogers	1932-1937
RA MacQueen	1932-1937
EG Izod	to 10/1946

WEYMANN'S MOTOR BODIES
(1925) LTD

DIRECTORS 1925 - 1946

Charles Terres Weymann	Resigned 05/01/1932	
EG Izod	Died in office 10/1946	#
Col. Llewellyn Evans		*
Louis Coatalan	Voted off 02/1932	
Jesse Frank		*
Maurice Dollfus	Voted off 02/1932	*
Lord Montagu of Beaulieu	For two days in 1926	
BRA Homfray-Davies	From 1931	
Sir Joseph Napier	From 1932	
AW Rogers	From 1932 - 1937	#
RA MacQueen	From 1932 - 1937	#
AT Froggatt	From 1934	
FC Webb	From 1937	
DJA Davies	From 1938/9	
James Don	From 19/01/1943	**
Capt FH Formby	From 10/1946	**

* =	Bernhard Scholle Director or other BS connection
# =	Central Mining Company connection
** =	United Molasses appointee

APPENDIX 4 : IDENTIFICATION - BODY MAKER'S PLATES AND TRANSFERS

The new company was intended to be non-profit making, and in addition to promoting and gaining sales would also provide the means of exchanging technical know-how and enable the two existing companies to work together on future developments. Although each factory remained autonomous their futures were now firmly tied together in the new organisation.

Initially, identification of Addlestone-built vehicles was simple. A small metal plate incorporating the Weymann Trade Mark was fixed to each vehicle and, where appropriate, it also carried the licence number as shown in the adjacent illustration. Later a coloured transfer was produced, in the manner then common to most bodymakers, and this was placed on the body panelling behind the front nearside wheel. The same transfer was also placed on the lower deck bulkhead and examples in both positions can be discerned throughout the illustrations used in this book. It has not so far been possible to recreate an example of this transfer but research continues. A larger metal

Reproduction of the body plate fitted to cars and early buses.

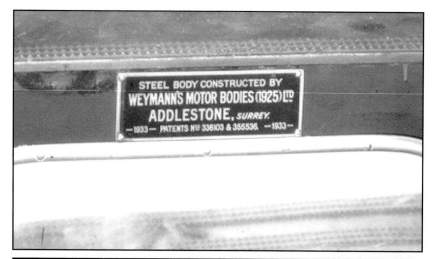

Weymann's body plate as fitted to pre-war vehicles and attached to the staircase riser.

Wartime Weymann's and then postwar vehicles from both Addlestone and Birmingham carried plates of this style, making it difficult to determine which factory had actually built the vehicle in question. Plates of this style can often be seen at flea markets, but examples of the prewar style seem to be elusive.

plate was next produced and fixed to the staircase or step riser. An example is shown and this plate was accompanied by the transfers as previously described.

Birmingham-built vehicles carried their own identification as will be described and illustrated in the forthcoming volumes on the history of Metro-Cammell.

During the war, when all output came from Addlestone, a new style of plate was introduced, two versions being shown. There were others which quoted the patent numbers involved. Body plates fitted to completed vehicles gave the clue as to whether the completed vehicle was metal framed – in which case the Birmingham Patents were involved – or not. The situation is a complex one and is part of the reason for the lack of understanding by many as to the relationship between the organisations.

The issue was further complicated by the fact that Weymann's bodies built to Weymann's own Patents (the 'W' Series), or of Composite construction ('Coachbuilt' in Addlestone nomenclature) were not built to MCW or MCCW Patents, neither were any examples built in Birmingham.

A completely different plate was produced for the London Transport RT buses and will be shown in Volume 2 with the details of the huge contract to build those vehicles.

Separately, and in addition to the above, Weymann's applied their body number plates to their products. These consisted of a circular brass disc, stamped out and carrying the Company name, together with the vehicle's body and chassis numbers. It was fixed in the driver's cab and examples have been found on old bodies dating back at least to 1932. An example from the Devon General Leyland Lion mentioned on page 35 is shown below and some at least of the postwar preserved vehicles still carry these plates. Others have a small oval white plastic plate with the body number stamped on in black, but when the changeover from brass to plastic took place is not yet known.

Example of the circular brass stamped body number plate as photographed on 1932 flexible body W953, on chassis number 2605, by Nick Taylor of the Oxford Bus Museum.
Courtesy Nick Taylor

The twin-staircase Bournemouth Corporation Leylands of 1939 (page 159) carried a plate of the type shown below, recording the fact the front staircase was a registered London Transport Chiswick design, for the use of which Weymann's presumably paid a royalty.

APPENDIX 5 : SOME PRE-WAR SURVIVORS FROM THE ADDLESTONE FACTORY

Mention has been made of surviving or preserved vehicles throughout the text; the oldest known survivor is the Gilford saloon illustrated below, and in original condition at the foot of page 96. It is now resident in the Science Museum's collection at Wroughton near Chippenham. The photographs show its sorry state, though the engine has been restored and is displayed separately. The body has been considerably rebuilt over the years, largely in the thirties from the appearance of the work, which clearly involved modification of the original roof structure and framework and replacement by a fixed (non-opening) one. The body alone would need a huge amount of work and it is difficult to imagine anything short of a very substantial lottery grant being sufficient to see it restored to original condition. An equally deserving but perhaps even less likely option exists with a former Devon General vehicle, also a flexible example. A surviving Austin motor car is shown on page 22.

This flexible-framed half-and-half panelled coach, like many other items in store, is not normally available for viewing at Wroughton but researchers may make special arrangements to inspect some of these items. The Gilford, body number W810, GW713, was originally supplied to Direct of Ealing and was purchased for preservation by the late PJ Marshall, an early and far-sighted preservationist. An interesting letter concerning a sister vehicle has recently come to light from the pages of the contemporary trade press and is reproduced alongside.

Photographs Courtesy John Banks (both)

FLEXIBLE COACHWORK
Experience of a User.

Sir, We notice in your December issue that Mr Thomas makes mention of the Weymann body, and gives the impression that the Weymann company are now building orthodox coachwork instead of their flexible system. Being users of Weymann bodies, we got in touch with the makers, who inform us that nothing is farther from their thoughts.

We have had one all-fabric body and others with metal-panelling to the waist-line on flexible framework, and we find that the latter construction is most satisfactory and adequately flexible to withstand all road shocks. We are convinced from our own experience that this construction is far in advance of any other form of coachwork in its ability to withstand the stresses imposed in present-day coach service operation. We have, of course, no interest in Weymann Motor Bodies, Ltd., but feel our experience of their product may be of interest to you.

Southsea.   OLYMPIC MOTOR
                SERVICES, LTD.

This letter appeared in *Bus & Coach* in January 1932 in response to journalist Thomas's comments which gave rise to fears that Coachbuilt construction, which he had recently been invited to examine at Addlestone, was to replace Flexible. Olympic's letter was accompanied by one from Weymann's, (also printed) confirming the true situation as stated by Olympic.

It is particularly interesting to see the comments confirming that the metal-panelled body was indeed still capable of flexing.

MORE SURVIVORS

Two splendid examples from the Brighton fleet have survived, examples being shown on page 65, and the motor bus, FUF 63 was put back into full working order during 2001 and can be seen at rallies and running days. It is in as-withdrawn condition and represents the best chance to see a true pre-war Weymann's bus in all its glory. Miracles do sometimes happen, however, as the two photographs on this page demonstrate. The former South Shields trolleybus in the upper view, withdrawn from service prior to the system's closure in 1964, spent some time in storage in southern England before moving to the Sandtoft trolleybus museum near Doncaster. Seen as photographed in the summer of 2001 it is due to be fully rebuilt, with work starting in 2002, and can be expected to be completed to a very high standard when other exhibits at that museum are examined. It will be restored to working order and will operate on open days alongside another excellent restoration piece, the former Derby Utility vehicle seen below.

South Shields No. 204, a Karrier E4 model, was new to the operator in 1937 and carries body number C5083. Seen at Sandtoft in July 2001 its restoration will represent a real challenge to the dedicated team who are to tackle it but when complete it will represent the oldest known surviving Addlestone vehicle in operation.

Derby Corporation was allocated two Sunbeam W4 trolleybuses, which were delivered in 1944. Number 172, RC8472, carrying body C8014 had been saved for preservation when the system closed in 1967. After a period of years in storage it also ended up at the Sandtoft Museum where it eventually received a full overhaul – back to running order in near original wartime condition. It is seen here in service on a hot day in July 2001.

John A Senior (both)

MORE SURVIVORS

Another example of the Weymann's wartime Utility buses has been preserved and this also resides in the Science Museum's overspill site at Wroughton. It came to fame in 2001 when the Royal Mail included it amongst their collection of bus stamps, recognising its place in the history of the development of the bus. The photographs show its angular lines and wooden slatted seats. Kept in full running order it too can be seen at rallies and running days. A list of all known surviving Weymann's psvs will be included in Volume 2.

Swindon Corporation received this single Weymann-bodied Guy Arab II in July 1943 and it has been preserved in near original condition. Like the Derby trolleybus it is of highbridge type, but retains its drop windows – one per side per deck – in addition to the opening vents at the front of the upper deck. The varnished wooden slatted seats will being back memories to those old enough to have ridden on such vehicles – the writer confesses to remembering riding on Utilities when they first entered service with Lancashire United Transport in 1943 and noticing the smell of the varnish on one on what must have been the vehicle's first day in service – it soon succumbed to the less-pleasant thick twist favoured by the smokers.
Courtesy John Banks (both)

Section Two

An Illustrated Survey of Weymann's Design Development to 1945

Alan Townsin and John Banks

(Illustrations from the Senior Transport Archive unless otherwise stated)

We have seen the growth of the Company recorded in Part 1, and now we turn our attention to the design of the vehicles themselves. As with any bodybuilder, design was influenced by customer preferences, method of manufacture, and changing legislation where it affected matters such as weights and dimensions.

Weymann's had a further complication in that, as explained in Part 1, it built its vehicles using three different methods of framing. How these were suited or adapted to customers' needs will become apparent in this second section.

The "patented flexible" construction of the cars was adapted to a form of cellular construction when metal panelling was introduced, first on cars and then on buses. The metal panels allowed high-gloss paintwork and by 1931 Weymann flexible bodies had fabric covering only for the roof.

Large bus operators as well as customers requiring lorry cabs tended to prefer the simpler conventional composite construction, with wood framing using orthodox joints and metal panelling, simpler to make and repair, which Weymann's began offering in 1930. Composite construction, always called "coachbuilt" at Addlestone, was at that stage the only option for double-deck bodies, first built in 1931 and for which substantial orders began to be obtained from 1932.

The setting-up of Metropolitan-Cammell-Weymann gave access to the very successful design of metal framing developed by Metropolitan-Cammell, introduced to Addlestone in 1932. This, using specially designed and patented steel sections, was anything but "flexible". A feature owing its origins to the railway companies where the designers had previously worked was the use of hot rivets for the joints, the principle being that the joint tightens as the rivet cools. The result was a very strong and durable structure, long life being aided by effective rust-proofing. Such bodies often required little beyond routine attention over operating lives of 15 years or more - the surviving 1939 Brighton Regent, FUF 63, had never had a major rebuild when withdrawn as late as 1965.

It also became evident that the body was capable of contributing much of the rigidity of the complete vehicle, a concept explored in some trolleybuses built for London Transport in 1938-40. Weymann's unit construction system eliminated the body underframe, an idea to be pursued in various much later designs.

With hindsight, one wonders why Weymann's continued to offer the choice of flexible (with W-series body numbers), alongside coachbuilt (C) and metal-framed (M) bodywork right up to 1940. There was a steady output averaging some 35 such vehicles per year between 1933 and 1939, then dropping to just five in 1940. This was 23% of the total in 1933, dropping steadily to less than 1% in 1940. The continuing presence at the Motor Shows of a flexible example was probably to recognise the importance of those operators who were flexible users and who were satisfied with this type of construction as well suited to their uneven roads.

Meanwhile, alongside this work, the orthodox coachbuilt body could be built in minimum-cost form, the British Electrical Federation single-decker contracts being the subject of severe cost competition as well as being built for an intended life of a mere eight years, even though elegant and well finished from the passengers' viewpoint. On the other hand, bodybuilding being still very much a bespoke trade, Weymann's could produce composite bodies capable of long life if desired, some double-deckers built for Hull, for example, being found worthy of transfer to later chassis.

At that date, no one knew how long metal-framed bodies would last, even Homfray-Davies making no specific claim as advocate of the metal body in a famous debate with Charles H. Roe, who supported composite construction, held in 1937. What was also unknown at that time was that a major war would cause many thousands of buses to be kept in use far beyond their normal lifespan, despite unavoidable neglect in matters such as overhaul and repainting. Weymann's products were to acquit themselves particularly well when so tested.

Having considered matters 'under the skin', let us now look at the visual development of the designs which, certainly so far as double-deckers were concerned, progressed from the rather ugly ducklings of the early thirties to the elegant swans of 1940 and paved the way for the vehicles which so many people still remember from the halcyon days of the fifties and which will feature in the next volume of this history.

Above: Weymann's second PSV was a coach-bodied Leyland Tiger TS2 delivered to the Irish operator H M S Catherwood in March 1929. The fabric-bodied vehicle, on patent flexible frames, is illustrated on page 23. Ongoing research into Irish transport matters by Geoff Lumb has recently revealed that Catherwood opened their own bodybuilding facility at Donegal Road, Belfast in that same month and began producing bodies of the type illustrated here. It appears most likely that these bodies used Weymann's frames or, alternatively but less likely, were built under licence from Weymann's to the latter's design. Wycombe Motor Bodies were similarly involved in building flexible bodies to be mounted on Gilford chassis and again it appears that these may have been of Weymann's manufacture. Any information on this aspect of the Addlestone factory's activities, which links with Don Dixon's recollections of the manufacture of Riley car frames *(see page 42),* would be welcomed and detailed in *Weymann's Volume Two. (Geoff Lumb Collection)*

Below: The first multiple order for coach bodywork was for five coaches (body numbers 600-4) on AEC Reliance chassis for Motorways (1930) Ltd, of London, SW1. They were for use on Continental tours and were luxuriously appointed, with seats for only 18 passengers. The design was in the style of a sedanca de ville car body, with the driver in the open and the passenger compartment enclosed. The full-fronted cab was having a brief run of popularity and a noteworthy feature was the domed front dash panel, fitted almost flush to the radiator front, the latter a concept that was to be taken up by Weymann's for its bus bodies a decade or so later. Note also the wheel discs, also a luxury car item. Four of the coaches passed to Varsity Express and then, in 1933, to the Eastern Counties fleet. In 1935 they received slightly older but more conventional Dodson coach bodies transferred from Leyland Tiger chassis.

Above: This three-quarter-rear view of 26-seat body number 609, based on a Thornycroft BC normal-control chassis, shows the somewhat square-cut style of rear dome panel often found on bodies using the Weymann flexible construction with fabric covering, both cars and coaches. Horsehair packing was used to obtain the smooth curvature required. It is thought to have been built in 1929 but was registered in Hampshire in 1931 as OU 8820 for use as a Thornycroft demonstrator, eventually being sold to James Geddes, of Brixton, Devon, in January 1933.

Below: Like the other chassis types on this pair of pages, the Daimler CF6 was another of the generation of six-cylinder models much in favour as a basis for coach bodywork at the end of the 1920s. Body 652 was sold in December 1929 to Bangham, of Margate, trading as Thanet Express; the body style incorporated two hinged doors in a manner then common, but the spare wheel location was unusual. It was registered as KR 62. See page 25 for a framed but unfinished example of this type of body.

Above: As self-confidence grew, standardisation followed, and here we have a pair of basically identical bodies using the new aluminium-panelled form of construction. Both were on the Gilford 168OT chassis then very popular with independent coach operators. At that date it used Lycoming six-cylinder engines imported from the United States, and reputedly giving up to 60mph in these relatively light vehicles, making the 20mph quoted on the side as the legal limit seem ridiculous. Orange Bros, of Bedlington, Northumberland, was the first of many operators to place repeat orders for Weymann's coach or bus bodies. This example was from its first order, for 26-seat coaches for the operator's services linking London with Newcastle and Scotland, comprising three on Gilford 168OT and four on AEC Regal chassis with newly-introduced more powerful engine and with similar speed capability, placed in service in spring 1930. Gilford No. 21 (TY 7077) had body W768. Further Weymann's bodies were purchased annually until 1933, when the Orange business was acquired by Tilling. It was put under the wing of United Automobile Services and taken over by the latter in 1934, although continuing as a separate subsidiary until 1950.

Below: Olympic, of Southsea, took two very similar Gilford 168OT models, registered TP 9181/2 with bodies W797/8 in June/July 1930. Another originally basically similar coach, though later substantially rebuilt, GW 713, with body W801, delivered new to Valliant Direct, of Ealing, W5, is in the Science Museum collection at Wroughton.

>> *Opposite page:* In December 1930, this advertisement appeared announcing the availability of what was called orthodox coachbuilt construction. Subsequently, separate body number series distinguished the two types - the Weymann's patented type continuing in the existing series but with W prefix, while coachbuilt bodies were numbered from C1 upwards. The AEC Regal demonstrator shown is thought to have body W825, becoming Osborne, of Tollesbury, EV 428 in March 1931.

REPEAT ORDERS PROVE WEYMANN CLAIMS !

No claim is made for Weymann Metal Panelled Coachwork unless it can be proved in the acid test of gruelling service. Above is a typical Weymann luxury type coach of 28-seater capacity.   It is but part of a repeat order just given us by a well-known Operator.   A large number of Weymann vehicles of similar type were installed upon this service last year, and we congratulate our friends upon the increased business that has resulted.   Ourselves we congratulate upon the verdict passed on the coachwork—"The Last Word in Silence and Comfort."

GIVE <u>YOUR</u> PASSENGERS

WEYMANN

COMFORT — *IT PAYS BOTH WAYS*

Weymann's Motor Bodies
(1925) LTD.

Head Office & Works : ADDLESTONE, SURREY
Telephone: WEYBRIDGE 1051.

Above: The first order for "coachbuilt" passenger bodies (C60-84) was for 25 saloons built in January/February 1931 on AEC Regal chassis for Green Line Coaches Ltd, the LGOC offshoot running limited-stop services linking London with surrounding towns. The first 59 body numbers in the 'C' series had been given to lorry cabs built for AEC but this order came from LGOC, using its own body design, and formed part of a batch of 100 identical 30-seat vehicles, the others being built by Duple at Hendon (50) and Ransomes at Ipswich (25). The contemporary fondness for low build was not followed, these being quite lofty vehicles with crisp styling having clear links to LGOC buses of the time. This view shows Body No. C65 on T231 (GH 3805), smartly turned out in the first Green Line livery of green and black with silver roof, before entering service from Ware garage in January 1931. The coachbuilder's association with this fleet also took another form - for many years there was a Green Line garage in a former timber store on Weymann's site.

Below: A small batch of six 20-seat coaches on Commer Invader 6TK chassis was supplied for the Green Line fleet in June 1931. That shown was the first, GN 4790, with body C161.

<< *Opposite page:* This July 1931 advertisement shows one of five Weymann's bodies (W849/50 and W869-71) on Leyland Tiger TS2 chassis supplied to James Watkinson, trading as Scout Motors, of Preston, in April and July 1931. The wording refers to "Weymann vehicles" the previous year but none were supplied by the Company, so it seems likely that six Tigers bodied by Spicer in 1930 used the patented construction under licence. It is also known that Duple built at least one such coach in 1929 on a Dennis G chassis.

Above and left: Resplendent in gleaming paintwork, Weymann's first venture into double-deck body construction, completed in May 1931, was a bold one, with the complexities of being for a trolleybus and a six-wheeler at that. Although in Wolverhampton livery, Body No. C144 was built as a protoype for Sunbeam, whose first trolleybus, of type MS1, it also was and whose works were in that town. Registered JW 526, it was exhibited at the Commercial Motor Show in November 1931. Wolverhampton purchased three of a slightly improved version, type MS2, with similar Weymann's bodywork though seating 59, in 1932, the prototype then being modified to MS2 specification and this was also purchased. *(Dave Hurley, courtesy Geoff Lumb Collection)*

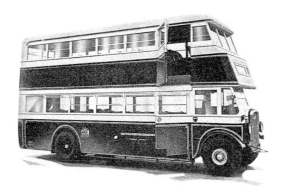

Left: Weymann's first double-deck body on a motor-bus chassis (Body No. C145) was this 48-seat AEC Regent, one of the first with 16ft 3ins wheelbase to suit the new 26ft overall length. It was completed in July 1931 as an AEC demonstrator, painted in Sheffield livery and registered MV 105. It appeared at the Commercial Motor Show at Olympia that November and was purchased by Sheffield a year later. It was of low-height layout, with two side gangways on the upper deck, which seated only 22, this layout partly accounting for the profile, of a style not repeated. Upper-deck emergency exits were under review at the time, this vehicle having a door near the front on the offside of both decks.

Above: It seems clear that Weymann's designers were at first searching for a distinctive double-deck style. The Daimler CP6 demonstrator (Body No. C169), built for the 1931 Show and registered KV 64, broadly conformed to trends of the time though the concave profile was not to prove popular. Another intriguing feature was the pronounced "vee" effect at the front of the upper deck - it did not recur at Addlestone but a similar feature applied with a straight profile was adopted by Leyland for its first-generation metal-framed body in 1933, producing the same problem of how to house the destination box. After its spell with Ashton-under-Lyne *(see page 32)*, the bus returned to Daimler and in 1934 was fitted with a very early example of the AEC 7.7-litre diesel engine, thus acting as a prototype for later COA6 models. This photograph is thought to date from about December of that year, when it returned to Weymann's for repainting in Coventry livery before joining that city's fleet. It was purchased in 1936 by Coventry and retained until 1949, still with the fleet number 6 it had carried when with Ashton.

Below: Just ahead of the above Daimler in Weymann's C series of body numbers were C167/8, a pair of Leyland Titan TD1 models on which 48-seat bodies were built to Leyland's "Hybridge" design, possibly subcontracted from that concern, for Redcar Services, Tunbridge Wells, registered KJ 2577/8 - a similar pair of buses had Leyland-built bodies. They passed briefly to Maidstone & District in February 1935, before becoming London Transport TD192/3 in July of that year, then passing with many other TD-class buses after their withdrawal from LPTB service to Liverpool Corporation in 1940. It seems possible that the treatment of the upper-deck waistline at the rear, peculiar to the Leyland Hybridge design, was copied for the above Daimler demonstrator.

Marlow & District Motor Services Limited had been founded in 1925 and had a fleet of twelve buses when the business was acquired by the Thames Valley Traction Company Limited in 1929. All but one were of Karrier make, the business having been owned by the Clayton family, who lived in the area. Father, K F Clayton, and son, R F Clayton, were then in charge of Karrier Motors Limited, in those days based in Huddersfield, Yorkshire. Until 1933, Marlow & District continued as a subsidiary of Thames Valley, of which Clayton became a Director. Two new Karrier Coaster buses with Weymann's 24-seat bodies (Nos W904/5), dating from April 1932, were the only new additions to the Marlow & District fleet during that time. The Coaster was basically the CL4 model as introduced in 1926, looking somewhat dated even when new. Few full- or near-full-sized bonneted single-deckers were bodied by Weymann's. *(Geoff Lumb Collection)*

The Devon General Omnibus & Touring Company Limited belonged to the National Electric Construction Company Limited, a subsidiary of BET, having tramway origins and of which all the bus-operating constituents that were Weymann's customers in the thirties ordered flexible bodies. Devon General's first examples, however, were Leyland Lion LT5 models with coachbuilt 31-seat saloons dating from 1932 to a style of Weymann's own which was to become familiar in this and other fleets for several years. The first of all was the vehicle shown at the top of the page, No. 32 (OD 1827), with body No. C313, delivered in March and one of those with various forms of opening roof. The second picture *(G H F Atkins)* shows 36 (OD 1831) with body No. C315, having a slightly shallower fixed roof. In addition to the characteristic frontal appearance, these buses were noteworthy for the moulded style of waistband, a feature that was later taken up by other operators though less usually on Weymann's bodywork. Devon General also had a need for limited numbers of smaller vehicles and three Leyland Cub KP3 models received Weymann's 20-seat coach bodies Nos C432-4, that shown being the first of these, fleet number 100 (OD 2836). The centre section of the body had a folding canvas roof, this continuing in favour for local touring work in the area. The Cub, introduced as a light six-cylinder model in 1931, was quite popular for a time.

Above: The Great Northern Railway (Ireland) chose Weymann's to build 28 rear-entrance 30-seat bus bodies in March/April 1932. Of these, 24 were on Albion Valkyrie PT65 chassis, all but one having coachbuilt bodies (Nos C381-403), of which GNR 258 (AZ 9556) with body C396 is seen above. The Model 65 was the initial series of Valkyrie, the successor to the 30/60hp models of the late twenties and inheriting their dated-looking front end; the more common variant in Britain was the PW65 long-wheelbase version. The PT65 and the even shorter PX65 chassis, respectively of 16ft 8ins and 15ft 8ins wheelbase, were necessary to comply with Northern Ireland Construction & Use Regulations, which enforced a 26ft maximum length. These regulations predated U.K. mainland legislation but were the model on which the latter was based. The last of the GNR order for PT65 chassis had a flexible body, W906. *(Geoff Lumb Collection)*

Below: The remaining four coachbuilt bodies for the GNR fleet (Nos C377-80) were on the recently introduced Dennis Lancet chassis, with a bold new style of front end, although like the early Valkyrie in having a simple four-cylinder side-valve petrol engine, much as used in the earlier E-type. The bodywork was basically similar though the chassis design gave a quite different overall look, and it seems that the rear overhang had been reduced from the usual standard on the Lancet to arrive at the required length. *(Geoff Lumb Collection)*

The largest order for double-deck bodies yet received, and one of the first orders handled through the new MCW organisation, came from the Mansfield District Traction Company Limited for its tramway conversion in September/October 1932 and called for 30 normal-height 54-seaters (Body Nos C493-522) on the AEC Regent chassis, for which Weymann's by then standard double-deck body outline was adopted. This had a sloping profile with protruding cab front, but treated in a more conservative way than the original AEC-designed version first seen at the 1931 Show in prototype bodies built by Park Royal and Brush, and then followed in one batch of buses built by Weymann's for Morecambe. The profile was more upright although the cab front was prominent and well-rounded in a way typical of many Weymann's double-deckers until the late thirties. There were six bays to the main structure instead of the five of the original and the skirt line was higher. Four of the buses, led by No. 55 (VO 8555) with body C494 are seen posed in the drive at AEC's Southall works before delivery, while another is seen soon after entering service with Mansfield District. Note that only a half cab-door was provided.

Above: Leeds City Tramways Department received six AEC Regal 32-seat single-deckers with Weymann's bodies C435-40 in August 1932. Then recently appointed as General Manager there was W Vane Morland, one of the newer generation of appearance-conscious managers; he brought an attractive turquoise and cream livery used previously by him at Walsall Corporation, replacing the princess blue and cream until then in use in Leeds. This view of No. 29 (UG 1023) with Body No. C437 dates from wartime, with more sombre matt grey paintwork and with the original destination box, which had been neatly built into the body, replaced by a later type. These buses were also noteworthy in having fluid flywheel transmission. *Below:* Swindon Corporation chose the shorter Cub KP2 model for a single 20-seat bus with Weymann's "patented" body No. W956 supplied in June 1933 as No. 39 (WV 3236).

Above: The Leyland Cub was also growing in popularity as an export model. This example with body No. W965 was one of a pair completed in July for Misr-Airwork, Cairo. The "streamlined" body style and customer's title confirms that it was intended as an airport coach. That same year, Imperial Airways, then the most prestigious British airline, took a Commer Centurion with Weymann's coachbuilt body No. C598 for service in Cairo, then an important staging point for early air routes to India and beyond.

Below: Interior comfort levels were improving rapidly in the early 1930s. Save perhaps for the cushion in the foreground, over the rear bogie wheels, those in this Sunbeam MS2 trolleybus could almost be described as sumptuous, although the rearward-facing front row and high waistline visible in the cab beyond would have prevented passengers seeing where they were going. This was the first of Wolverhampton's delivery of three such buses of June 1932, No. 92 (JW 992), with body No. C333. The quite generous curvature of the ceiling cove panels, very probably unchanged from that in Weymann's first double-deck body, was to remain a Weymann's characteristic right through to the post-1945 styles.

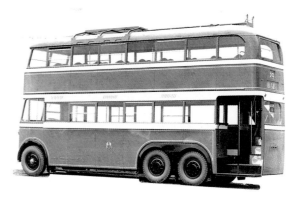

Above: Walsall Corporation took fifteen Sunbeam MS2 trolleybuses in August-October 1933, the first large order for the model. Five 60-seat bodies each were built by Beadle, Short Bros and Weymann's, possibly based on a Sunbeam outline drawing; No. 165 (ADH 11) with body No. C540, was numerically the first of the batch. *(Dave Hurley, courtesy Geoff Lumb Collection)*

Left and below: Bournemouth was also involved in a major trolleybus conversion. After demonstration of Sunbeam No. 92 from Wolverhampton's 1933 batch whose interior is shown overleaf, one of the four vehicles obtained on hire from manufacturers was this further Sunbeam MS2, for which Weymann built a 60-seat body (C560), delivered in May 1933, to much the same outline as its contemporary standard motor bus design, save for being full-fronted, with prominent and well-rounded projecting cab front. Although this vehicle, like all the initial four, was purchased and Sunbeam was successful in securing orders for a total of 102 further MS2 chassis from Bournemouth supplied in 1934-6, the body orders for all but five went to Park Royal, who used a modern-looking design with a smoothly curved profile, which soon made this vehicle look dated. *(Both: Geoff Lumb Collection)*

Above: Bristol had been an independent manufacturer, originally a department of the local tramways company which had begun running bus services, and although the Tilling group of bus operating companies acquired an interest in 1931, in mid-1933 its outside customers were still largely non-associated concerns such as the Norwich Electric Tramways Company, to whom eight G.JW models were supplied in June of that year. They had bodies to Weymann's standard double-deck pattern of the time, though the proportions of the chassis meant that the cab front protrusion was unusually large. The final vehicle, No. 47 (VG 5545) with body C568, is shown. The Norwich company came under Eastern Counties control from December 1933 and the original six-cylinder petrol engines were replaced by Gardner 5LW engines in 1937/8 but the original bodies were retained until withdrawal in 1952/3, two having latterly been converted to open-top.

Below: This historic bus was the first production Daimler COG5 single-decker, that firm's model having the Gardner 5LW five-cylinder diesel engine as well as fluid flywheel transmission. It was registered FS 7036 for demonstration to Edinburgh and built in time for display on Daimler's stand at the Commercial Motor Show in November 1933. The 34-seat body was to the characteristic Weymann's style of the period, numbered C602. It was purchased by Edinburgh in March 1934; COG5 single-deckers with Weymann's bodywork were to become standard in that city in 1935-39 though with rear-entrance metal-framed bodies of different style.

Construction of metal-framed bodies at Weymann's began early in 1933, and although using the same form of framing as Metro-Cammell, these soon established their own identity. The first body, M1, was a double-decker on an AEC Regent chassis for City of Oxford, already a customer for both Weymann's flexible and coachbuilt bodies. The second metal-framed body, (Body No. M2) delivered in April 1933, was that seen here, built as a replacement for Green Line AEC Regal T232,

one of the original Weymann-bodied batch of 1931, the original body having been damaged beyond economic repair. The new body was to a unique design, one of the first coaches having the stepped-waist style fashionable for a time, and perhaps intended to demonstrate that metal bodies need not be of austere appearance. Three months later, Green Line became part of London Transport. When a larger-scale single-deck rebodying programme was decided upon early in 1935, 43 further Weymann's metal-framed bodies were supplied, though these were to London Transport's own bus outline. Of these, 31 were originally fitted to AEC Reliance chassis mostly dating from 1929, and twelve on further Regals. The rather flamboyant body may not have been to the undertaking's taste for in 1938, when it was decided to move the 1935 bodies on Reliance chassis to further Regals, T232 received its third different Weymann-built body, the 1933 body somewhat surprisingly being sold off on the Reliance chassis. *(The Omnibus Society)*

Above: Another example of quite advanced styling ideas applied to early Weymann's metal-framed bodies was this comparatively rare half-cab, half-canopy 32-seat coach with body No. M23, the first of a pair on AEC Regal chassis dating from December 1933 for Keith & Boyle (London) Limited. This firm, which used the fleetname Orange Luxury Coaches, had a branch in Bournemouth at the premises of subsidiary Shamrock & Rambler Limited and these vehicles were registered in that town as LJ 8798/9. In the habit of these fleets, they had individual names, "Alpha" and "Beta". The chassis had 8.8-litre oil engines, this being the only six-cylinder diesel offered for front-engined AEC models at the time; it required the protuding radiator shown.

Below: There was interest in centre-entrance double-deckers among Yorkshire company fleets at that time. Yorkshire Woollen District chose this layout, which required royalty payments to English Electric, Roe and J C Whiteley, the patent holders, for nine Leyland Titan TD3 oil-engined buses of late 1933. They had bodies M27-35; the first of these, No. 269 in the fleet (HD 5041), being shown. They were based on the standard metal-framed outline, but used a three-window style at the front of the upper deck, as used on some double-deck British Electrical Federation bodies built around this time. The Clayton destination boxes were another feature often found on Federation bodies and it seems clear that there was some common body design work between these buses and the TD3 demonstrator, body No. M22, later registered TJ 4511, shown on page 37.

Twelve AEC Regent lowbrige buses with Weymann's metal-framed bodies (Nos M36-47) entered service in April/May 1934, early enough to receive "General" fleetnames, before the new regime had decided upon "London Transport" as its new identity. They were for the hilly route 410 between Bromley and Reigate, which passed under a low railway bridge. This was operated by Godstone garage and the buses became known as the "Godstone STLs" although not given the numbers STL1044-55 until the country bus fleet came under direct Chiswick control in 1935. Front-entrance double-deckers had been rare until Short Bros introduced what it described as its "dustless double-decker" on an AEC Regent demonstrator in late 1932, and these Weymann's bodies incorporated the same form of angled dash-panel with a sliding door in their lowbridge 48-seat bodywork. The bulky 8.8-litre AEC oil engine, not found in any other London STL, caused the projecting radiator. If hardly handsome, their chunky "Weymann-look" styling was borne out by their durability: when new RLH-class lowbridge Weymann-bodied AECs became available in 1950, the Godstones' bodies were in such good order that the buses were kept until 1952/3. *(Both: The Omnibus Society)*

This AEC Q (Body No. M49) was one of only two bodied by Weymann's for London Transport, for use in the country area fleet and dating from August 1934. The Q, with engine mounted behind the offside front wheel, was John Rackham's most innovative model. Introduced in 1932, the double-deck version was intended to have the entrance ahead of the front axle, as nowadays usual but very rare at the time, and Metro-Cammell bodied most of the earlier examples to this layout using a stylish AEC-registered body design, including two supplied to the LPTB central area fleet in June 1934, numbered Q2 and 3. The country pair were Q4 and 5, the vehicle shown, BPJ 224, being Q5, though at that stage the country bus department did not display fleet numbers. It had chosen centre-entrance layout with double power-operated doors for these 56-seat buses, resulting in uneven pillar spacing and the need for a fresh design for the metal-framed body, carried out in the Weymann's drawing office. The comprehensive destination display included a screen above the centre entrance. They were petrol-engined and ran on the Reigate-Kingston service until 1938 and then briefly from Hertford but were stored in 1940 and sold in 1946. Note the two fleetname transfers: it is not thought that these Qs were ever used on Green Line services. The emergency window on these and the Godstones was to LPTB specification. *(Alan Townsin Collection)*

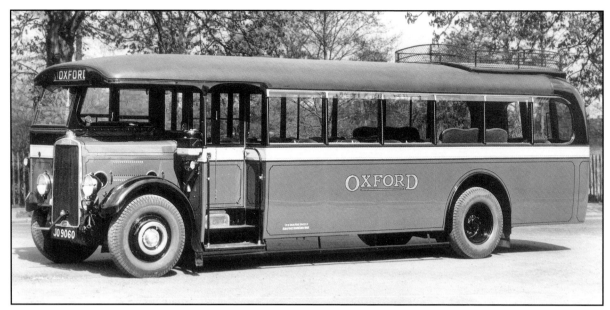

Above: City of Oxford Motor Services Limited, at that time a constituent of the National Electric Construction Company Limited, had begun to give Weymann's part of its bodywork orders from 1932. As often the case among concerns under BET control, it evolved its own policies on vehicles, being one of those which did not elect to use the British Electrical Federation's body designs even when, as in this case, ordering vehicles through the BEF acting as central purchasing agency for associated companies. Oxford had standardised on AECs since 1930, and the eight petrol-engined Leyland Lions supplied in 1934 were the only new full-sized exceptions to that in peacetime until 1961. This model had moved on to the LT5A, with more compact front-end than the LT5, but Oxford continued to favour its usual 32-seat capacity. Weymann's supplied five bodies (Nos W988-92), the example shown being No. 51 (JO 9060) with body No. W990, dating from May 1934.

Below: The Rhondda Tramways Company Limited was another NEC and then BET company, replacing its trams by buses, notably by 30 AEC Regents with 8.8-litre oil engines and Weymann's metal-framed bodies (M51-80) in December 1933 and January 1934. For single-deckers, however, timber-framed bodies were chosen, and the AEC Regal shown was one of four with Weymann's patented bodies (Nos W997-1000) delivered in August 1934. These too had the 8.8 engine and, with up to 130bhp available with a relatively light 34-seat body, would have been lively performers well suited to the hilly terrain. The affinity of the two body designs shown on this page, despite the differences of chassis dimensions and entrance layout, is perhaps most obvious in the gentle curves of the rear dome, probably the product of the same drawing board at Addlestone. Times were hard in those days in the Rhondda Valley and a follow-up order for a further ten similar buses which were to have had bodies W1002-11 was cancelled.

Above: Weymann's were still promoting their flexible bodies as having many characteristics that made them eminently suitable for long-distance work, "smooth-riding" and "rattle-free" for instance, and it is noteworthy that all the AEC Q chassis that they bodied, most of which were for coach operation, were fitted with W-series bodywork, though the outline was to the registered design of AEC's J G Rackham. This vehicle was one of a pair for J Bullock & Sons, of Featherstone, Yorkshire, a substantial independent operator trading as "B&S", No. 161 (HL 6268) being the first, with body No. W994, supplied in June 1934, the second following in August. Duple, Harrington and Weymann's had built bodies to very similar outline in time for the 1933 Show - the last-mentioned of these, a demonstrator with body W967, was registered AMV 124 and sold to Sharp, of Manchester.

Below: AEC, like other chassis makers in those very competitive days, made extensive use of demonstrators, and Weymann's body No. W1001 was built on the oil-engined version of the chassis by then available, in August 1934, the first application of AEC's new 7.7-litre engine. It was registered in Middlesex in usual AEC demonstrator fashion, for use by the South Wales Transport Company Limited, another important part of BET's strong representation in that area. A simplified body style was used, lacking the sloping pillars and some of the more elaborate shapes, though the front retained the gently curved profile and Weymann's styling was evident at the rear. The seating capacity was 39, almost the maximum practical on a two-axle single-decker of the 27ft 6ins length then in force. It was purchased by SWT in 1935, further Q models being purchased, though the body order went to Brush.

Above: Bodies for chassis manufacturers' demonstrators were a significant part of Weymann's business in the 1930s. Daimler COG5 and COG6 double-deckers were selling well, largely among municipalities and several received Weymann's metal-framed bodies to the standard sloping-front style. One of the first was this COG5 with body No. M204, registered in Coventry as ADU 470 in the autumn of 1934 and delivered to the Isle of Thanet Electric Supply Company Limited. It was purchased and four similar buses were supplied in 1936 but the firm was taken over by East Kent, in whose livery it is seen here, in 1937.

Below: AEC was by far the largest user of Weymann-bodied demonstrators in that period, even though such work was shared with other firms, most notably Park Royal. This Regent also dating from late 1934 and with body M232 was put into the Sheffield Corporation dark blue livery of the day, almost certainly to introduce its 7.7-litre oil engine, a unit then newly available in front-engined chassis and fitting into the same bonnet length as the petrol engine. It was purchased in 1935 but Sheffield continued to specify the 8.8-litre engine as better suited to its hilly routes. Its livery had changed to cream with three blue bands by mid-1935.

Above: The fleet of City Tramways Company Limited, Cape Town, also known as Cape Electric Tramways, was a natural user of Weymann's bodywork in view of the financial connection explained in the earlier pages of this volume. A fleet of 50 two-axle trolleybuses was exported in 1935, all on chassis built by Ransomes, Sims and Jefferies Limited with Weymann's metal-framed bodywork; of these, 20 were single-deck, receiving bodies M351-70, and 30 were double-deck, with bodies M371-400. The single-deckers were of rear-entrance layout with rather more front overhang than then usual and seated 39 passengers. One is seen above in the primer paintwork in which they were delivered, ready for finishing in Cape Town. They were of up-to-date style, both single- and double-deck types having the curved profile by then accepted as the contemporary norm by most trolleybus operators in Britain and overseas territories under British influence.

Below: Two of the Ransomes double-deckers in service in Cape Town in a street scene looking much the same as to be expected in British cities, save for the co-ordinated all-over advertising on the vehicles, a practice then unknown in Britain. However, it retained the standard livery colours and style and thus conveyed the operator's identity. The vehicles were of typical Weymann's outline apart from the deep louvres over the windows, designed to provide shade from the sun while providing ventilation. The emergency exit window at the rear of the upper-deck, divided and with well-radiused top outer corners, was a characteristic Weymann's feature. *(Rural History Section, University of Reading)*

117

Above: **This line-up of some of the 1935 fleet of Ransomes trolleybuses supplied to the Cape Town company was posed outside the depot.** *(Rural History Section, University of Reading)*

Below: **The interior of one of the single-deckers. Note that the longitudinal seat over the nearside front wheel-arch extended forward opposite the driver, accommodating three passengers as compared to the two in the equivalent seat just behind the driver's cab. Note the paper stickers, visible in the saloon windows, carrying in this instance the number 33. This was to assist identification on delivery since the vehicles were delivered in grey primer but was even more important where double-deckers were involved since they were shipped and delivered in two halves - upper deck, and lower deck on the chassis - and the pairs had to be matched when the vehicles were completed locally.**

Above: Six AEC Regent petrol-engined chassis with Weymann's bodies M213-8 were supplied to the Cheltenham District Traction Company in the late summer of 1934. Although metal-framed and of five-bay build, there were resemblances to the Mansfield District coachbuilt batch of 1932 in the high skirt-line and use of a half-door for the cab - at that date the Cheltenham company was also a member of the Balfour Beatty group. This view shows Nos 2/4 (DG 9819/21) amid the genteel atmosphere of that town. *(Alan Townsin Collection)*

Below: Bradford Corporation's first direct order for Weymann bodywork, after two examples on demonstrators, was for 20 AEC Regents placed in service in February-April 1935. Number 396 (KY9101) had body M314. Most of the batch ran until 1950-2. They had the 8.8-litre engine and thus the projecting radiator, unlike the 1936 bus with 7.7-litre engine for this fleet *(see page 55)* - such changes affected body length. After a spell during which some Weymann metal-framed double-deckers had the more upright front as seen on the Cheltenham buses shown above, the more strongly inclined style seen here was used on most examples built from 1935 until 1937 and in some other cases later. *(Alan Townsin Collection)*

Above: The Northern General Transport Company Limited was a BET subsidiary which had previously tended to favour Short Brothers for most of its body requirements but in 1935 five AEC Regal buses with 7.7-litre oil engines had Weymann bodies of the flexible type. Number 677 (CN 6690) with body W1052 is shown when new in July of that year. They were rebodied by Pickering in 1946. *(Alan Townsin Collection)*

Below: Although similar to the vehicle shown above in frontal styling, ten Leyland Tiger TS7 oil-engined buses for the Yorkshire Traction Company Limited going through Weymann's works at the same time were of metal-framed construction. Earlier BET orders for Yorkshire Traction had tended to favour composite bodies of British Electrical Federation design (which the rest of this body resembled) but it appears that the BET was experimenting with metal-framed bodies. Number 479 (HE 6749) with body M343 is seen in Barnsley in June 1936. Most of the batch were withdrawn in 1950. *(G H F Atkins)*

Above: Sheffield, having tried the AEC 7.7-litre engine, decided to stay with the 8.8-litre unit for its Regent buses, and No. 103 (BWA 203) with body M348, dating from June 1935, was one of seven for the B fleet managed by the Corporation on behalf of the Joint Committee, which also involved the LMS and LNE railways. The individual vehicles were owned by the partners, in this case the LMS railway. These were basically much as built for Bradford earlier in the year but seated 54 and were in the new cream and blue livery subsequently to become the standard for the Sheffield fleet. *(Alan Townsin Collection)*

Below: In addition to the trolleybuses, Cape Town Tramways began building up a substantial fleet of Daimler buses with Weymann's metal-framed bodywork. They were on COG6 chassis and the first batch of 56-seat double-deckers had bodies M551-60 supplied in September 1935; No. 95, with body M557, is the nearest in this line-up. Further deliveries followed, including four single-deckers, also on COG6 double-deck-type chassis, in 1937 - three are visible in the foreground. A total of 85 Weymann-bodied COG6 buses was supplied to the Cape Town and associated Port Elizabeth company fleets. *(Alan Townsin Collection)*

<< *Opposite page*: The only order for new bodies for existing chassis placed by London Transport in the 1930s called for 43 single-deckers built in September-November 1935 to LPTB design but using Weymann's metal-framed construction. They were also the LPTB's only new half-cab single-deck bus bodies of the period. The unbroken curved profile was like that of the then new standard STL double-decker but there were some features akin to contemporary Q-class single-deckers. R1 (GF 495) *(top)*, with new body M233, was the first of 30 AEC Reliance coaches of 1929/30 so treated; there was also one 416-type rebuilt to Reliance specification which had run as an open-topped double-decker. These 31 new bodies had 30 seats of the standard London style of the time, as shown *(bottom)* in the interior view of R2, with body M236. The other twelve bodies were built on ex-independent AEC Regals of 1930/31 and these, though outwardly similar, had 26 aluminium-framed seats, being intended for Green Line duty and coded 5T4, as shown by T355 (GN 8240), an ex-Queen Line vehicle, *(centre)* with body M273. *(Alan Townsin Collection)*

This page top: The rear end of the new bodies had quite a stylish look - this is Reliance R29 (UU 6603) with body M256 on Country Area service 436A to Staines. In November 1938 this body would be transferred to Regal T266 (GK 3187).

Centre: The rebodied Regals were used on Green Line duty, as with T351 (GJ 8073) ex-Blue Belle, seen at Eccleston Bridge, but were sold to the War Department in 1945 for use in Germany.

Right: In 1938 the 31 bodies built for Reliance chassis in 1935 and hitherto all in green livery were used to rebody Regals, newly fitted with AEC 7.7-litre oil engines, the vehicles being recoded 11T11. From 1939, 22 of them were painted red for Central Area duty, as in the case of T208 (GH 8096) with body M242 seen here. Note that the ex-Reliance bodies differed in cab profile and windscreen shape. *(John Banks Collection)*

<< *Opposite page:* Although this MCW advertisement in the *AEC Gazette*, AEC's house magazine, for November 1935 made reference to both "Weybridge and Birmingham factories", the Commercial Motor Show exhibits mentioned both came from Weymann's at Addlestone. The double-decker, for Leeds City Transport, No. 201 (CNW 902) with body M466 was to a new fully fronted "streamline" design. Regent 7.7-litre chassis with various bodies having these features were a theme of that Show. An almost identical body, M581, was built for Sheffield Corporation but was almost immediately converted to half-cab form, entering service as No. 208 (BWE 526). Weymann's built no further bodies to this pattern but several of its features were adopted for Manchester Corporation's "streamline" design of the following year, many of which were based on Metro-Cammell body shells. *(Alan Townsin Collection)*

Above: The Rhondda vehicle also displayed on the AEC stand at the 1935 Show was the first example of the Regal Mark II model, beginning a new chassis number series at O862001. This was intended as a lighter-weight version of the Regal, using a new six-cylinder oil engine of 6.6-litre nominal size. It differed slightly from the standard Regal in frontal appearance, which may account for the picture in the advertisement not showing the complete bus, which uses a retouched photograph of an earlier vehicle - the correct one may not have been ready in time. The actual 34-seat body was No. W1066.

A Note on Weymann's Body-Numbering series

The numbering series for Weymann's flexible and coachbuilt bodies were altered in 1936. Although the C series (coachbuilt) and M series numbers started at 1, the W series is believed to have been applied retrospectively from around 1932, shortly after Norman Froggatt joined the Company, probably as a reaction to confusion when the serial numbers of the W, C and M series were quite close, giving rise to ambiguity if they were quoted without the appropriate prefix. Accordingly, the original C series for "coachbuilt" bodies ceased at C763, a 1935 Leyland TS7 for Caledonian. A new series began at C5000, a Leyland Lion LT7 for Devon General delivered in June 1936; vehicles were not completed in precise numerical order, so the time gap was a little less than suggested by this. This series continued to C9460, a Bristol L5G for North Western, in August 1950, and the last coachbuilt body produced. The original W series used for the Weymann's patented flexible bodies ceased at W1095, a Daimler COG5/40 for Potteries, in September 1936. A new series began at W7500, a Leyland TS7 also for Potteries, in December 1936, running to C7623, an AEC Regal for Oxford in March 1940, after which flexible construction ceased.

Above: In the mid 1930s, Daimler standardised on Weymann's metal-framed bodies for its double-deck demonstrators or other single vehicles supplied complete with bodies. This had begun with COG5 models in the autumn of 1934. The following year it was the turn of the COG6, which had the bulkhead set back just over seven inches compared to the COG5 to accommodate the lengthy Gardner 6LW engine - note the gap behind the front mudguard. Weymann's produced a body design adjusted to suit, as used for Cape Town Tramways *(see page 121)*. Two further basically similar COG6 buses were completed slightly later (M512 and M513). The first was demonstrator BDU 236 seen here as built in November 1935; it was purchased by Aberdeen Corporation in February 1936. The second body was sold to Bradford, delivered in December and registered locally as AKU 181. In both cases, further batches of thirteen almost identical COG6 Weymann buses followed in 1936/7. Another similar demonstrator, BWK 860, with body M799, followed in July 1936, supplied to the Stalybridge, Hyde, Mossley and Dukinfield fleet and further COG6 orders again followed but with bodies by SHMD's usual supplier, Northern Counties, which had been in liquidation and refinanced.

Below: Amid the larger orders for bigger buses, Weymann's was still willing to supply small orders for vehicles such as the four Leyland Cub KPZO1 models of 14ft wheelbase with 20-seat bodies of flexible construction built for Swindon Corporation in September 1936. The body numbers were among the last in the original W series, the vehicle shown, No.42 (AHR 648) having body W1085.

The LGOC had chosen Dennis as supplier of its small buses but London Transport turned to the Leyland Cub, the KPO3 oil-engined model with 15ft 6ins wheelbase allowing a spacious layout for the 20-seat bodies built to the Board's distinctive design by Short Brothers, of which 74 were supplied for Country Area use in spring 1935. By 1936, Short Brothers was closing down its bus body plant to concentrate on the manufacture of flying boats for Imperial Airways, thereby eliminating one of Weymann's most important competitors, and the Addlestone factory received orders for 22 bodies of almost identical appearance in red livery for Central Area service supplied in April/May 1936. The Cub chassis had moved on to a new range with 4.7-litre engines and the 15ft 6ins oil-engined model was now KPZO2; the LPTB's 22 were built in two batches, M561-80 and M682/3. The pictures show the first vehicle, C77 (CLE 105) when new *(above)*, and *(below)* after postwar repaint into green livery and transfer to the Country Area. *(John Banks Collection)*

Above: Increasing demand for metal-framed bodies caused the Addlestone factory to be extended, with a degreasing plant, Bonderising bath for rust-proofing treatment and new paint and finishing shops, all operational by March 1936. Among the work going through was a batch of eleven 7.7-litre AEC Regents with 52-seat lowbridge bodies for City of Oxford Motor Services Limited. Seen here ready for delivery is K102 (CFC 793) with body M603.

Below: Standard Weymann's and Park Royal bodies often looked similar in the mid-1930s (Park Royal was by then also offering a metal-framed body); migrations of design staff between the two firms were largely the cause. In this wartime line-up of Oxford Regents of 1935-6, from *left to right* are seen CWL 656 (Park Royal), CFC 793 (Weymann's - the bus also shown above), CWL 658 (Park Royal), CFC 789 (Weymann's) and BFC 46 (Weymann's). At first glance they look identical but the front dome contours differed slightly and the slight rounding of the Weymann's upper-deck front-window top corners gave a characteristic and slightly less severe effect; it was also often the case, as here, for the valance panel over the windscreen to be deeper. *(The Omnibus Society)*

One of Weymann's success stories in the mid-1930s was that of sales to Kingston-upon-Hull Corporation, unusual among its customers for double-deckers by that period in concentrating on composite construction. In 1932/33 there had been a mixed intake of such bodywork by Brush, English Electric and Leyland, though a single AEC Q with Metro-Cammell metal-framed body had been a 1933 Show exhibit.

Top: In July 1934, ten petrol-engined Daimler CP6s with Weymann's 53-seat bodies were added to the fleet; these had the upright outline usual on composite bodies from 1932, though with five-bay layout instead of the six then more usual. Number 139 (RH 8475) with body C615 is seen when new.

Centre: In July-October 1936 a further 20 composite bodies were delivered, this time 56-seaters on Daimler COG5 diesel chassis. The outline was virtually unchanged from that of the 1934 batch, except for rounded window-corners but a new "streamlined" livery altered the appearance substantially. Number 157 (CAT 158) with body C5062 is shown when new. The fleet numbers of this batch, 150-69, were confusingly one out of sequence with the registration numbers CAT 151-70.

Bottom: In this picture No. 156 (CAT 157), with body C5061 of the same batch, is seen almost head-on. The slim upper-deck front corner-pillars are usually a good guide in distinguishing Weymann's composite bodies from the standard metal-framed styles of the time. The rare pre-war traffic scene shows the bus in Queen Victoria Square, having just traversed King Edward Street, in which two of Hull's trams are visible. This scene would soon change; the first trolleybuses were imminent and the topography of the whole area was to alter out of all recognition as a result of wartime German bombing attacks. Six of these buses and one from a similar 1937 batch of fifteen were destroyed in a May 1941 raid. Hull switched to Massey bodywork for its 1939 motor buses but standardised on Weymann's metal-framed bodies on AEC chassis from 1946 to 1960. *(All: Ron Maybray Collection)*

129

Above: Most of Weymann's single-deck output in the mid to late 1930s was to customers' own styles, but those for the Balfour Beatty companies had clear affinities with the contemporary Weymann's standard double-deckers. By 1936, the specialist coach bodybuilders were adopting more exotic styles but many of the major operators chose more restrained designs, even though having comfortable high-backed seats and opening roofs, as applied here. Midland General took ten AEC Regal petrol-engined coaches in May/June 1936, of which No. 161 (CRA 660), had body C5036. The "streamlined" livery was in two shades of blue and cream. This company kept its vehicles in very smart condition and six of the batch, including this one, remained in service until 1959, although converted to diesel in 1949 and reseated for bus duties. The other four were impressed for War Department use in 1939 and did not return. *(Alan Townsin Collection)*

Below: Mansfield District, taking delivery of four oil-engined AEC Regal coaches in June 1936, chose a slightly simpler treatment of its green and cream livery than used on the contemporary and basically very similar Midland General vehicles. This was the last of the batch, No. 100 (CAL 200), with body C5082. *(Alan Townsin Collection)*

Above: Maidstone & District Motor Services Ltd became a major user of Weymann's metal-framed double-deck bodies from 1935; seventeen Leyland Titan TD4 models thus equipped were added to the fleet in 1936. They had 48-seat lowbridge bodies to broadly contemporary standard style. However, in addition to the outswept skirt panels beginning to appear on some Weymann's bodies, this operator favoured a moulded style of waistband on both decks. Also, on this and some later M&D batches, there was an upward curve to this moulding on the front face of the upper deck, echoed at the foot of this panel. The vehicle shown, with body M619, had begun life as M&D's 319 (CKO 997) but is seen after sale to North Western Road Car in 1950, with whom it ran as No. 36 until 1955. *(John A Senior)*

Below: The Caledonian Omnibus Company Limited was the one Scottish outpost of the "English" TBAT group, with headquarters in Dumfries, and in the mid-1930s was under BET-group management. At the time, Dennis chassis were favoured for most of its fleet additions and a batch of fourteen of the new Lancet II model was delivered in June-October 1936. The chassis had Gardner 5LW engines and thus did not have the very short bonnet which was a selling point of the model in standard form with four-cylinder Dennis engine. The 32-seat Weymann's composite bodywork was to the latest version of the British Electrical Federation style and was equipped with a sliding roof and roof-mounted luggage carrier. Number 185 (BSM 831) had body C5052. *(Robert Grieves Collection)*

Above: London Transport chose front-entrance layout for its first 89 new full-height double-deckers for the green Country Area fleet: AEC Regents STL 959-1043/56-9 delivered in spring 1935. They were not fitted with doors, having an entrance layout claimed to reduce draughts, and seated 48. Otherwise their Chiswick-built bodies were similar to the latest Central Area rear-entrance 56-seat equivalents introduced in late 1934, with the new gently curved frontal profile and no step in the line from cab front panel to the roof. When 50 more were needed, bodies were ordered from MCW and built at Weymann's in July-December 1936, becoming STL 1464-513. Almost identical in appearance, they incorporated the maker's metal framing, and were 13 cwts heavier at 7 tons 3 cwts and also dearer than the Chiswick product. Despite the close matching of style, they were readily identifiable by the larger radii at the tops of the upper-deck front windows. The first bus, STL 1464 (CXX 451) with body M622, is seen here. It had been planned to use them on the Green Line service from Brentwood to London but in the event they entered service on normal bus duties.

Below: In 1936 Weymann also built the bodies for 50 new Green Line coaches on AEC Regal chassis, T403-52 having the same combination of 7.7-litre engine, fluid flywheel and preselective gearbox as the new STL double-deckers. The 30-seat bodies, built to Chiswick design but again with MCW's type of framing, were to a stylish new outline. The front-end assembly of mudguards and bonnet were all carried by the body structure though leaving the standard radiator exposed; some of the details of this were perhaps a little fussy. Although these vehicles, classified 9T9 by Chiswick, marked a distinct step forward from the earlier T-class coaches, two years later they were to be outclasssed by the 10T10 vehicles having basically similar-looking bodies, though built at Chiswick. The 10T10s had simpler frontal appearance and a newly-developed version of the 8.8-litre engine giving more relaxed perfomance. The bodybuilder's view of T407 shows the standard AEC type of wheel finish but these vehicles received LPTB-type wheel discs for both axles.

Above: One of the 9T9s in service, passing through North Finchley in 1937 on its way south to Victoria and Leatherhead. CXX 172 was fleet number T449c, and the Body No. was M767. *(John Banks Collection)*

Below: In September 1936, Rochdale Corporation received its first buses with Weymann's bodies, to the standard metal-framed double-deck design of that date. They were based on a pair each of Leyland Titan TD4c and AEC Regent chassis, the latter with the 8.8-litre engine which continued to be favoured by municipalities in hillier parts of the north of England. Number 126 (BDK 353) with body M822 is shown. The undertaking switched to Cravens and then Eastern Coach Works for most of its later prewar orders but there were a further five Weymann-bodied Titans in 1939 and Weymann's became the main supplier in the postwar period. *(Alan Townsin Collection)*

Top: The Isle of Thanet Electric Supply Company Limited followed up the demonstrator Daimler COG5 double-decker *(shown on page 116)* by an order for four almost identical buses, with 56-seat bodies Nos M865-8 dating from May 1936, for operation on the former tram routes linking Margate, Broadstairs and Ramsgate. The third of these, No. 4 (CKP 878), is seen in a photograph evidently taken during its first summer of operation. *(R Marshall Collection)*

Centre: The former Isle of Thanet No. 3 (CKP 877) is seen in East Kent Road Car Company livery after that operator had taken over the company in March 1937. Two of these buses were damaged in air raids and two others were used for a time as offices when the Dover premises were hit by bombs or shells fired from German guns about 20 miles away in France. *(R Marshall Collection)*

Bottom: Maidstone & District continued to specify its own variant of Weymann's styling but took a surprising step for a Tilling & BAT company firmly under BET management, as also did North Western Road Car, in choosing Bristol chassis for some of its double-deckers, beginning with twelve low-bridge 48-seaters having body numbers M895-906 in 1936. These were on GO5G-type chassis and there were also four more buses so mounted but with highbridge bodies, Nos M907-10, of similar style for the Chatham & District Traction Company, a Maidstone & District subsidiary. Even more unusually, in 1938 the bodies were removed and all sixteen GO5G chassis were returned to Bristol to be replaced by new chassis of the K5G type, on which the 1936 bodies were mounted. DL273 (FKL 611) entered service in November 1938 and was subsequently preserved - it is seen in this view with body M904. The GO5G chassis were fitted with new bodies by Bristol and allocated to the Bristol company's Bath subsidiary, remaining in service until 1955-8.

Kingston-upon-Hull's first trolleybuses were 26 Leyland TB4 chassis with composite 54-seat bodies, Nos C5107-32, supplied between June and October 1937. Number 1 (CRH 925) is shown when new. By then, an unbroken curved profile was taken for granted on trolleybuses if not yet for motor buses and differences in style between Weymann's composite and metal versions had become slight. Incorporation of the MCW patented trolley-base framing into the roof structure gave a neat effect. In the picture below No. 20 (CRH 944) is seen on 6th October 1953 as it turned at the Newland Avenue/Cottingham Road terminal point of service 62, one of the two new routes these vehicles had inaugurated in 1937. *(Geoff Lumb Collection: L R Storry)*

Rebodying of chassis whose bodywork was life-expired was a common occurrence in the days of traditional buses, but it would perhaps be true to say that such chassis usually received new bodies or ones newer than those they were losing. Sometimes, however, bodies which were older than the chassis were used. Hull Corporation undertook an extensive programme of rebodying or rebuilding its wartime unfrozen and utility buses, in which still sound prewar bodies were reused. The 1937 Weymann's composites, which had been fitted to DKH-registered Daimler COG5s, were found to be in better condition than some of the wartime units, and ten of them were used to rebody AEC Regents and Guy Arabs dating from 1942-4. In the picture above, AEC Regent No. 198 (GKH 379), originally fitted with a Northern Counties body, is seen carrying Weymann's Body No. C5204, which had come from Daimler No. 13 (DKH 13). Below we see No. 216 (GRH 131), a 1944 Guy Arab originally bodied by Massey, with Weymann's No. C5199 ex-Daimler No. 12 (DKH 12). *(Photobus)*

Above: The Trent Motor Traction Company Limited first turned to Weymann's in February-May 1937, when 30 AEC Regent 7.7-litre buses with front-entrance 54-seat bodies, Nos C5133-62, were added to the fleet. They were of composite construction to a new style with slightly curved though rather upright profile: the latter was necessary to allow room for seats in front of the stairs. Previously Trent had favoured SOS chassis, built by Midland Red, for most of its buses, an SOS IM4 being visible in this Derby street scene behind Regent No. 1021 (RC 4627), with body C5139, soon after the latter's entry into service. The magnificent Assembly Rooms frontage behind the AEC has been preserved and is now a feature of the Crich Tramway Museum.

Below: Deliveries of bodies to British Electrical Federation style were interspersed between other products from Weymann's. This example on the then recently introduced Leyland Tiger TS8 chassis was one of 20 for Western Welsh (Body Nos C5232-51) dating from November/December 1937. All are recorded as 32-seat buses, but the sliding roof and livery of No. 294 (AKG 338) with body C5239 indicate that it was intended for express service use.

The Midland General Omnibus Company Limited, based at Langley Mill in Nottinghamshire and the largest of the Balfour Beatty bus concerns, undertook a major fleet renewal programme in 1936-9, entirely of vehicles with Weymann's bodywork. Examples of the 25 front-entrance AEC Regents with metal-framed bodies M989-1013 dating from 1937 are seen here. Number 10 (DNU 957) with body M993 is seen *(above)* in almost as new condition. In the later street scene *(below)*, the continuity of Weymann's standard styling at the rear of the upper deck is conveyed by comparing the rear view of No. 18 (DNU 961) with the postwar rear-entrance Regent, KRB 78, partially visible beyond it on the opposite side of the street. On the right, the view of No. 58 (DNU 971) shows the characteristic style of cab, with windscreen quite markedly angled to the side, of most Weymann's double-deckers of this period. *(Both: G H F Atkins)*

Above: Most London Transport trolleybuses were of standardised external and internal appearance set down by the customer, itself quite different from London motor bus standards. The trolleybuses were bodied by several concerns, using their own structural design. MCW supplied more bodies than any other concern, the majority built by Metro-Cammell with its bigger production capacity. Weymann's share began modestly with ten in 1935 and then 25 in 1937, in both cases on AEC 664T chassis. Among the latter batch, classified E2 by LPTB, was No. 606 (DLY 606) with body No. M691 seen here before delivery. A detail which was standard Weymann's practice was the horizontal division of the rear dome, not found on other London trolleybuses except for one batch of 25 by Park Royal.

Below: From time to time, bodies for demonstrators continued to be built. This AEC Regal with 7.7-litre engine had the latest chassis specification with deeper radiator and mudguards extended over the front dumb-irons as introduced in the latter months of 1937. Weymann's built a metal-framed 35-seat bus body (M1310) to contemporary style, with outswept skirt but incorporating the usual projecting cab front. It may have been run on trade plates at first, its registration JMC 328 implying a spring 1938 date, probably when required for fare-paying passenger use; it was sold to Peake, of Pontypool.

A new version of the metal-framed double-deck body appeared on a batch of 50 AEC Regent models built as the main replacement fleet for the Swansea trams and dating from March 1937. The effect on appearance was quite marked though in itself the change slight - the previous standard sloping profile was replaced by a gently convex curve, though at that stage retaining the projecting cab front. The following sets of illustrations show Regents with 7.7-litre engine, crash gearbox and bodies to the same basic design built in June/July 1937 for three BET companies. A pair for Devon General had bodies M1127/8, this one, M1128, being No. 234 (DTT 47) - in 1938 this became DR234. The chassis had the then standard Ricardo-head engine, type A171. It was doubtless felt that the "English Riviera" climate of the Torbay area justified the generous provision of

opening windows in every main bay on both decks except at the rear of the lower deck - there were also hinged vents at the top of the upper-deck front windows. The destination display used Clayton indicator boxes, a departure from previous standard for this operator, the rear box being over the entrance rather than facing to the rear. Within, the seating, for 54 passengers, with 28 upstairs, and finish were quite simple, though the use of patterned moquette facings and the polished woodwork gave a "quality" effect not fully conveyed in photographs. A further three Regents with similar bodies followed in 1938 but they reverted to the 8.8-litre A165 engines used on earlier examples in this fleet.

The Rhondda Transport Company Limited received three Regents with bodies M1140-2 in June 1937, No. 148 (BTX 579) with body M1141 being shown. These also had the A171 engine though two small chassis differences are evident: the taller filler cap was an option on some AECs of the time, and the nearside sidelamp was on the mudguard, where there was also a width indicator. Here, alternate opening windows were judged adequate, and the continuous louvre over them was slightly deeper. Note that the side and roof

ventilators were also different. Here the destination boxes, though of similar size, were of a different type, fitted flush into the front and rear panels. Perhaps the most striking difference from the Devon General version was evident within, for here the seating capacity was a more modest 50, with 26 above and 24 below, using comfortable-looking quite high-backed seats. The Rhondda coal-mining area was far from wealthy but clearly the company thought attention to comfort and finish was important - note also the superior-looking light fittings and the semi-matt finish to the lower-deck ceiling, though that upstairs was gloss-painted, doubtless for ease of cleaning, important when smoking passengers would probably discolour the finish within a couple of years.

The twelve South Wales buses placed in service on 1st July 1937 were closer to the Devon General specification; the resemblance was actually the other way round, for these were added to the original 50 of March 1937, and like them had the then new direct-injection A173 version of the 7.7-litre engine. All 62 were

supplied to the Swansea Improvements & Tramways Company formerly operating trams in that area, also a BET company and by then a subsidiary of the South Wales Transport Company Limited but continuing to run the replacement services. They had "South Wales" fleetnames, omitting the "Transport Co Ltd" formerly included. The external specification was as shared by the Devon General buses except for the fewer opening side windows. The 56-seat capacity interior was rather more basic than Rhondda's version; the polished metal seat frames and ribbed-aluminium bulkhead facing being practical features felt suitable for urban use. In this case, only the lower-deck seats were upholstered in moquette, with leather or leathercloth upstairs, also quite a common idea on town buses. Note the single-skin upper-deck ceiling, with full-length panels on each side to carry the lighting, a typical Weymann arrangement of the time.

At that stage the front-entrance version of the metal-framed double-deck body retained the relatively upright version of the sloping front with projecting cab cowl. In some details, the three AEC Regent examples with bodies M1223-5 supplied to the Tynemouth & District Transport Company Limited fleet in mid 1937 were quite similar to the rear-entrance buses built for other BET group concerns seen on previous pages. Here there were Clayton indicators at front and rear, though the former was mounted flush with the front panel. The interior views show that the 52-seat capacity was divided 28 up and 24 down, and not 26/26 as quoted in some

reports. The upper-deck view shows how the twin ventilator intakes in the front dome, characteristic of many Weymann's bodies of this period, fed air into a box from which it was distributed along the ceiling. These bodies were replaced by Pickering rear-entrance units after twelve years, the vehicles then continuing in service until 1957.

At the 1937 Commercial Motor Show were two Weymann's patented flexible bodies. Potteries Motor Traction No. 113 (FEH 833), seen here, was a Daimler COG5/40 with 35-seat body No. W7553. This was to quite a stylish design also used for bodies by other makers for this BET company and, although called simply an "omnibus", had several coach-like features. The other was an AEC Regal for Rhondda. In reality, by this stage, little was left of the original flexible concept beyond the use of metal parts to link the wooden frame members; bodies such as that illustrated were completely panelled in aluminium and the shaping on such a design as the Potteries vehicle would give considerable rigidity. From 1935, the main customers were the Oxford, Potteries, Rhondda and South Wales companies, though there were occasional orders from elsewhere, notably Newport Corporation with nineteen Leyland TS8 buses in 1937/8. Even so, output was modest, running at about 40 per year latterly, less than the conventional composite and much less than the metal-framed types. The appearance of exhibits of this type at every Show in the 1930s suggests that there may have been some obligation to continue doing so, perhaps laid down in the early days by Charles Weymann himself.

Above: Composite body No. C5277, delivered to Rhondda in February 1938 as No. 80 (TG 2120), was the only prewar instance of a new Weymann's double-deck body on other than a new chassis. The new 50-seat body on Rhondda's only Titan, a TD1, had an overall resemblance of style to the new metal-framed Regents supplied the previous summer. The different proportions of the chassis made the step in the cab front less pronounced, giving an effect closer to new designs to appear later that year. The vehicle had originally had a Leyland lowbridge body; a Leyland oil engine had also been fitted and TG 2120 remained in service until 1946 when it was converted to a lorry.

Right: Weymann's, like other bodybuilders in the London area, had to send vehicles for tilt-testing at the Chiswick Works of London Transport. Here South Shields Corporation No. 232 (CU 3974), a Karrier E4 with

composite body C5294, passes the requirement before delivery in August 1938, witnessed by A T Froggatt of Weymann's *(far right)*. The South Shields undertaking had been a modest customer since 1934, beginning with Daimler COG5 single-deck buses, but decided on the E4 with Weymann's body for all its prewar trolleybus fleet of 34 vehicles, numbered 200-33, from 1936, the vehicle shown being one of the final two. There were also six COG5 double-deckers with front-entrance composite bodies and one metal-framed one in 1938/9.

A repeat order for single-deckers to British Electrical Federation design on Leyland Tiger TS8 chassis came from Western Welsh, this time for 30 vehicles. The BEF outline had become more rounded at the rear, though still with the characteristic square-cut lower corners of the rear and rearmost side window, as seen in the view of No. 11 (BBO 313) with body C5296, the first of the batch, dating from October 1938. The three-quarter front view shows the last of the series, dating from December and registered BBO 342, with body C5325 - this was the last of ten with luggage carriers on the roof, numbered 326-35. The interior was typical of BEF bodies in having comfortable seats for 32, with singles alongside the rear wheel arches.

>> *Opposite page upper:* In 1938 Weymann's built a further batch of 47 trolleybus bodies on AEC 664T chassis, classified J1 by London Transport, numbered 905-51 with matching ELB registrations (body numbers M1079-125 but not in sequence). In most respects they were similar to the previous year's E2 class, though the widened pillars previously found under the trolley base were replaced by a single one each side, at the front bulkhead and directly above, this housing the feeder cables. One further J1 class vehicle, No. 952, had a Metro-Cammell body.

Below: London Transport, MCW and AEC were involved in developing new forms of construction for trolleybuses in 1937/8. One experimental vehicle using AEC running gear was built in 1937 at LPTB's Charlton works, followed by two more developed jointly by AEC and MCW. Of these, No. 953 (ELB 953), seen here, was built at Weymann's (Body No. M1126) and delivered in February 1938. It used what was called unit construction. There was an almost conventional-looking chassis but the crossmembers were so positioned and extended by outriggers to attach directly to the body pillars. The normal body underframe was eliminated, the lower saloon floor being built directly on to the "chassis" frame. The opportunity was taken to give this vehicle a strikingly new appearance. By extending the front dome panel to merge smoothly into the corner pillars and reshaping the windows at this point a distinctive "streamlined" style was created, soon to become familiar on Weymann's bodies for other operators. Entering into the spirit, AEC fitted the front wheels with a new style of large-diameter chromium-plated hub cap. The result was classified M1 by LPTB and 25 similar vehicles, also of class M1, were built in November 1939-January 1940 (fleet numbers 1530-54; body numbers M1772-95). Metro-Cammell's parallel development of what were called chassisless vehicles, in which the conventional chassis frame was eliminated, began with No. 954, which appeared the month after 953 but, significantly, did not have the new styling, strong evidence that this latter was a purely Weymann's innovation. Similar styling was, however, applied to later London trolleybuses, including 175 more of the chassisless type from Metro-Cammell between March 1939 and June 1940. The war prevented further progress but the foundations had been laid for important future developments in bus structural design by MCW and others.

Above, below and >> opposite page: The South Wales concern turned to the Leyland Titan TD5 in 53-seat lowbridge form for its double-deck needs in 1938/9, Weymann applying the slightly curved profile introduced on highbridge bodies for Regent chassis the previous year, though the effect on appearance was less marked. The first twelve were for the Swansea Improvements & Tramways Company, thus having the sans serif form of fleetname lettering shown on No. 82 (BCY 582), with body M1343. This was one of the initial order for 36 with bodies M1336-71 delivered in February-May 1938. A further 25 followed in June/July, and in March 1939 the last delivery, again of 25 similar buses, was made, again on TD5 chassis, not TD7 as quoted in some

records: the latter model did not go into production until the autumn of that year. Note the small route number box at the rear. The interior views show the effect of the sunken side gangway on the layout of both decks. A passenger sitting by the nearside windows on the upper deck who wished to get off might well have to disturb three other passengers on the same row of seats in order to do so, a process which inevitably took time and needed to be done well in advance so as to avoid the risk of missing the desired stop. Downstairs, passengers sitting by the offside windows were very apt to bump their heads as they rose, despite the warning notice on each seat.

Above: Northern General and its subsidiaries also turned to Leyland for much of their 1938 requirements, Tynemouth taking eight Titan TD5s with bodies very like those on the previous year's Regents. Number 96 (FT 4496) was the first, with body No. M1372. These bodies had quite short lives by Weymann's metal standards, being replaced by new Eastern Coach Works rear-entrance units in 1948.

Below: In the 1936-8 period Edinburgh standardised on Daimler buses with MCW metal-framed bodies but, unusually, the double-deck bodies all came from Metro-Cammell whilst all the single-deckers came from Weymann. Representative of the latter was No. A79 (BWS 213), seen in later years, which had been new in October 1938 as one of a batch of 20 (Body Nos M1627-46). There were 65 such buses, all on the COG5/40 chassis and seating 36, with the cutaway style of rear entrance much favoured in Scotland. *(Omnibus Society Midland Branch/Cull Collection)*

Above: Midland General continued with its policy of running what could best be described as "saloons" of high enough standard for leisure travel as well as bus duty. The 22 supplied in 1938 (Body Nos M1421-42) differed from the 1936 batch (*see page 130*) in being metal-framed and having wider window bays but were of similar outline. The last seven, on AEC Regal chassis, had seats for 32 and luggage lockers for use on summer express services and were in a reversed, mainly cream, livery, as shown by No. 151 (ERA 921) with body No. M1436, seen before delivery. By that date, oil-engined AEC bus chassis had plain bonnet sides without louvres and the new style of chromium front hub cap was standard for a time. *(Alan Townsin Collection)*

Below: The first fifteen of this batch of bodies were in Midland General's standard single-deck livery of two shades of blue and cream. This is one of the ten Regals with 35 seats and no luggage lockers, the balance of five being on Leyland Tiger TS8 chassis. This company's vehicles were always kept in smart condition, even in wartime when many operators' standards were adversely affected by the difficulties brought about by shortages of staff and materials. The vehicle in this picture, photographed in 1940, has the full wartime regalia of masked lamps and white markings. *(G H F Atkins)*

Above: Sheffield switched to the curved-profile body of the style with projecting cab front for later prewar AEC Regent buses but continued in its preference for the 8.8-litre engine with its projecting and slightly higher mounted radiator. Number 358 (EWJ 458) with body No. M1567 was the first of a batch of ten 54-seat examples for the Corporation's own fleet dating from spring 1938.

Below: Plymouth Corporation standardised on Leyland Titan chassis with "Gearless" transmission and Weymann's lowbridge 48-seat metal-framed bodies from an initial batch of fourteen of the TD3c version in

1934 to the final 25 TD5c models in 1939, including No. 216 (BDR 253) with body M1989 seen here - a total of 150 buses of almost identical style, the only significant outward change being to the livery. Some were supplied by Weymann's as frames and completed by Mumford, a local bodybuilder. Similar bus BDR 254 (Weymann's Body No. M1990) was reported in the trade press in November 1940 as having fallen down a 12ft bank onto a paved road surface, ending up on its side but suffering minimal damage. Mr W C S Chatfield, of Metropolitan-Cammell-Weymann, who placed the report, was quoted as saying that repairs were easily accomplished and that "the most remarkable fact is that not one rivet was broken throughout the construction".

Above: The styling of three 31-seat coach bodies built for Rhondda in February and April 1939 seemed unusual yet many of the features were quite similar to those of various existing Weymann's bodies. They were on AEC Regal chassis, Rhondda having adopted the direct-injection 8.8-litre engine introduced the previous year and in that sense could be considered as a provincial equivalent of the 10T10 Green Line coaches, although with crash gearboxes. They were of Weymann's patented flexible construction, proving to be the last coaches of this type. Seen here when new is 161 (DTG 709) with body No. W7603. A further sixteen 34-seat rear-entrance bus bodies also of the flexible type were supplied to Rhondda that year, twelve on similar Regal chassis and two on Daimler COG5.

Below: Northern General Transport's main intake of single-deckers in 1939 was of 53 AECs to a special design known as the Regal B, based on the standard O662 model but with a more compact front-end and bulkhead set forward by about 6in, the rear of the 7.7-litre engine protuding slightly but covered by a cowl. This allowed space for 38 forward-facing seats on the slightly ramped floor, and by careful design of the seats themselves, the knee room was actually slightly better than that on, for example, neighbouring operator United's 35-seat Bristol L5G buses with ECW bodies of the same length. The body design became NGT's new standard from this batch, Weymann building 20, Brush 18 and English Electric 15. This view of No. 880 (DUP 880), with body No. C5402, conveys the characteristic appearance as well as the short cab. Further similar buses were built in 1940 and a post-war version produced on Guy Arab chassis but the bodies on all these were built by Brush.

Brighton Hove & District Transport was the fleetname adopted for Brighton Corporation's new fleet of 21 buses and 44 trolleybuses which replaced its trams from May 1939 under the terms of an agreement with the local company operator - the red and cream livery was also common. All had AEC chassis and 54-seat Weymann's bodywork of the latest curved profile design, with front dome similar to London trolleybus 953 of February 1938 - it had been introduced on deliveries to a few operators from the previous autumn. The trolleybuses were all metal-framed, No. 2 (FUF 2) with body No. M1918, is seen alongside similar No. 16 at the Old Steine in post-war days. Of the buses, all on 8.8-litre Regent chassis, ten were metal-framed, including No. 61 (FUF 61) with body No. M1908 shown here. It was photographed just after recovery from having overturned in an accident and showing no sign of distortion. Thanks to the Manager's involvement in the design specification, and unusually, the eleven buses with composite bodies were outwardly identical, interchangeability of windows and shaped panels having been specified. *(FUF 61: David Toy Collection)*

Above: Bournemouth Corporation had standardised on a rear-entrance, front-exit layout for its vehicles since 1932, so when Weymann's gained the order for 16 metal-framed bodies for Leyland Titan 48-seat buses built in 1939, they followed suit. It was also decided to adopt a full-fronted cab and sliding roof, special attention being given to finish, with Alhambrinal embossed panels for the ceilings of both decks, this latter also a feature of the Brighton fleet. Their TD5 chassis were in a minority by that date in being petrol-engined; the overall result was an exceptionally distinctive and refined batch of buses. The front staircase on these buses was built to an LPTB Chiswick design and carried a metal plate recording that fact. *(Alan Townsin Collection)*

Below: Inside the works in mid-1939. The Bournemouth Titan in the foreground shows clear evidence of spray painting, not standard practice at Weymann's. In the centre lane, an AEC Regent for Glasgow nears completion, while on the left is a Bristol K5G for Chatham & District, one of 37 being supplied to that subsidiary of Maidstone & District and sharing the latter's distinctive moulded waistbands.

Above: In October 1939 AEC completed a prototype underfloor-engined left-hand-drive chassis, its engine a horizontal version of the new design then in production for the first RT-type double-deckers and with long front overhang to accomodate an entrance ahead of the front axle. It was delivered to Weymann's, where metal-framed single-deck body M2075 was completed, the design being in line with transatlantic ideas on what was then usually called a "transit" bus. It is shown at AEC's Southall works after completion. Despite the outbreak of war, it proved possible to ship it to Montreal in 1940, where it remained in service through the war years, then returning to Southall where it ran as an experimetal vehicle for a further period, effectively becoming the first prototype for the Regal IV model, best known in London Transport RF form.

Below: The interior of "the Canadian prototype", as it was known at AEC. The front entrance is just out of the picture to the left; it and the centre exit had power-operated jack-knife doors. Note the unusual outline of the rear window. *(Both: Alan Townsin Collection)*

Above: Devon General returned to Weymann's for 24 single-deck bodies for standard AEC Regal 7.7-litre chassis, delivered between January and July 1940. Harrington had been the main suppliers of single-deck bus as well as coach bodies to this operator in 1936-8. The 1940 bodies were almost identical to the design, peculiar to Devon General, that had evolved for the 1939 Regals. Here, too, the "bulge-front" cab had given way to a curved profile and other distinctive details included the style of glass louvres over the side windows, the bottom edge of each slightly inclined, and the livery layout. The first two numerically, designated XR454/5, were "express" vehicles with slightly superior seating, for 32 passengers, and a sunshine roof, but were the last completed. XR454 (DOD 454) with body No. C5584 is seen here when completed - someone had forgotten to fit the front wheel nut guard ring. The remainder of the batch, numbered SR457-79, were a 35-seat bus version - the missing number, SR456, was a Harrington-bodied 35-seat Regal of similar style that had been intended for the 1939 Show.

Below: By comparison, the bodywork on Devon General's previous two fleet numbers, M452/3, was less stylish than on the batch illustrated above, even though pleasingly proportioned in a fairly conservative manner appropriate to the Leyland Cub passenger chassis, which had been only slightly updated in appearance since its introduction in 1931. The emergency door at the rear was also of use in providing access to the luggage space behind the rearmost row of seats. Fleet number M452 (DDV 452) was a 20-seat country bus having body No. C5419, new in May 1939. They were to prove the last vehicles of such seating capacity to have Weymann's bodywork.

Above: East Yorkshire Motor Services Limited was a Tilling & BAT company in which the BET influence was dominant, and a major user of Leyland Tigers with Federation-style bodywork, hitherto mainly built by Brush or ECW. The first from Weymann's were three rear-entrance 30-seat buses (C6111-3) on Tiger TS8 chassis, notable in having an oval rear window, a feature more associated with a decade or more earlier, yet then still favoured by East Yorkshire. Seen here is C6113, completed in September 1940, as No. 395 (GKH 40), the others following in November. By then bus production was being more seriously disrupted by wartime priorities and a further 24 similar bodies which were to have been C6114-37 were cancelled, together with the Tiger TS11 chassis on which they would have been mounted.

Below: Cheltenham District Traction had been a Weymann's customer when part of the Balfour Beatty group, reappearing in the order books after becoming part of the Red & White group. Five Albion Venturer CX19G models with Gardner 6LW engines received Weymann's bodies M2173-7, the first of these being seen here as No. 29 (EAD 729) when new in February 1940. Four similar buses with bodies M2178-81 went to United Welsh, also part of the group, and there had been an earlier pair for that fleet in May 1939. The by then standard metal body, complete with the optional outswept skirt panels, suited the chassis well. Number 29 remained in service until 1957, CDT by then being part of the Bristol Omnibus Company Limited.

Lancashire United, then one of the largest non-combine companies, took most of its double-deckers from Leyland Motors. There had been a few buses with Metro-Cammell bodywork up to 1936, but the ten Titan TD7s bought in 1940 were the first for this firm to be bodied by Weymann's, probably as a result of Ministry of War Transport allocations. They had lowbridge bodies M2192-201 and had only 48 seats: usual for earlier Titans but rare by 1940. Number 89 (ETE 891) is seen just after completion, as yet unsullied by wartime white paint or headlamp masks. The interior view at the front of the upper deck was probably taken to show the Clayton heater with thermostat control on the centre pillar but also reveals that the forward-facing window glass was square-cut at the top corners, the impression of a rounded out-line being given by the shaping of the louvre.

Above: Intended for the Commercial Motor Show in November 1939, which was cancelled because of the war, was the only example of an AEC Regent RT-type bus supplied to other than London Transport until after the war. The chassis actually had the first production engine for this model but Weymann's body, No. M2202, was a "special", the main part similar to Glasgow Corporation's normal specification of the time but with front end incorporating a similar cab to the London RT-class buses then entering service, with the upper profile adjusted to suit. It was numbered 723 (DGB 371) and was delivered in 1940.

Below: A batch of 50 standard Regent 7.7-litre buses was ordered by Glasgow in October 1939, the month after war broke out, these having 56-seat bodies M2233-82 to much the same design as built for this fleet from 1937, though the opening windows were now of the sliding type. Number 735 (DGB 383) with body M2244, new in June 1940, was looking well-worn when this view was taken in June 1950. *(R Marshall)*

Glasgow Corporation also ordered 30 AEC Regal single-deckers with 35-seat bodies (Body Nos M2203-32) built to a style not previously used. It had a more modern appearance than that of the by then rather dated design still used for the undertaking's standard double-deck bodies. The waistline was quite low and the front-end had a mildly curved profile. Numbers 705/7 (DGB 353/5) are seen when new in February 1940 and in service. Nine of these buses were requisitioned by the Ministry of Supply and although registered in the sequence, were never operated by Glasgow Corporation and some were later sold to other operators.

Left: Potteries took delivery of a batch of ten Daimler COG5 models with lowbridge metal-framed bodies which entered service in June 1940, except for one latecomer in August. The picture of No. 213 (HVT 278) with body M2295 shows no sign of a drop from peacetime standards, with outswept skirt to set off the classic outline. These vehicles were noteworthy in seating 56, with 30 on the upper deck in eight rather than the more usual seven rows.

Centre: The realities of war hit home the following autumn, London being badly hit in an onslaught of air raids known as the "Blitz". Sixteen trolleybuses of which the bodies were beyond repair were sent to Weymann's for replacements. By that stage of the war, material supplies were under tight Government control and although the external appearance was close to LPTB's latest standard, they were of composite construction, numbered C7143-58, and had sliding vents instead of half-drop windows as well as other non-standard features. Their fleet numbers received an "A" suffix and they returned to service between October 1941 and April 1942. Twelve were on Leyland chassis, among them two of type TTB2 originally short wheelbase for 60-seat bodies but these were rebuilt on standard chassis frames to allow them to accept the same 70-seat bodies as the others. Number 95A (CGF 95), of this type, with body C7153 is seen here. *(F G Reynolds)*

Below left: An interim body style used the 1937-type curved front profile with projecting cab front mostly built as metal-framed but here in composite form and finished to the "utility" specification by then in force, with simplified wood fillet window glazing and the pair of hinged ventilators at the top of the upper-deck front windows that was to become familar on most of the later wartime bodies. The two known examples were body numbers C7458/9, both on "unfrozen" Leyland Titan TD7 chassis and not completed until autumn 1942, by which date output of Guy buses to full utility standard had begun. The vehicle shown, with body C7458, was supplied to Newport Corporation - a regular Weymann's customer since 1937 - in October as No. 96 (DDW 24), and C7459, almost identical, went to Devon General in September. Newport also received three bodies, C7160-2, on other unfrozen TD7 chassis in January/February 1942, but it seems these might have been built in the normal way but held in stock pending the arrival of chassis - there was also a single-decker, C7159, fitted to the only Tiger TS11 chassis bodied by Weymann's. *(R Marshall)*

Above: A further interim step to augment vehicle supplies was the diversion of vehicles or chassis intended for export. Among them were fifteen Sunbeam MF2 trolleybus chassis intended for the Johannesburg municipal fleet. These were 8ft wide, but permission was given to body them to this width and to operate them, despite the general UK limit at that date of 7ft 6ins. However, in other respects the bodies (C7318-32) had to conform to the new 'utility' specification, eliminating beaten panels and with limited numbers of opening windows. Nottingham Corporation No. 447 (GTV 47) was the first of five for that fleet dating from October 1942 - the remainder went to Bradford. *(R Marshall)*

Below: The supply of utility bus chassis began with the initial version of Guy's new wartime Arab model, retrospectively known as the Arab I, most having the Gardner 5LW engine and relatively short bonnet seen on most of the examples in Coventry Corporation's fleet in this late wartime view. The example nearest the camera, No. 309 (EKV 709), with body C7374 new in January 1943 and drawn from Weymann's first run of 57 such bodies (C7337-93) of which all but one were on Arab I chassis. Weymann's conformed more closely than most to the official drawing of "the wartime standard normal-height double-deck bus" issued to bodybuilders via the National Federation of Vehicles Trades. Other bodybuilders differed in their interpretation; from right to left beyond number 309 are two by Park Royal, a Massey, another Weymann and a Park Royal - all on the Arab II chassis; a Brush Arab I, another Park Royal Arab II and two more Brush Arab I models can also be seen. *(R N Hannay Collection)*

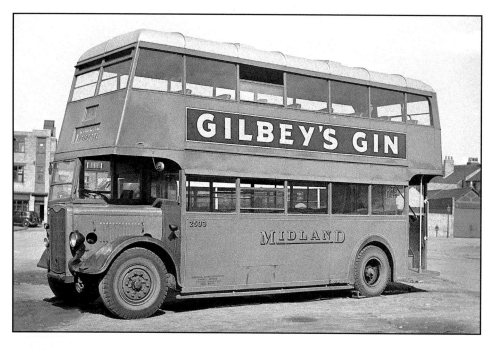

Left: In order to accommodate the minority of cases where the longer Gardner 6LW engine was fitted, the radiator of the Guy Arab was moved forward and, to avoid having to shorten the standard body to keep within the overall length limit of 26ft, after the first 500 had been built special permission was given that such buses could exceed it. Guy then persuaded the authorities that all Arab output should be of the resulting 26ft 4½ins overall length to simplify chassis production and thus was born the Arab II, thereafter standard until shortly after the end of the war, even though most buses still had the 5LW engine, as here. This view of Midland Red No. 2503 (GHA 927) with body No. C7931, new in October 1943 and coming from a run of 95 such bodies (C7899-993) for various fleets, shows the effect on appearance and also how even a simple livery with 'proper' lettering could improve appearance from the drab matt grey in which most utility buses were delivered. The body was largely still in original condition with just one opening window on each deck on each side and retaining the austere outline. *(G H F Atkins)*

Below: An alternative to the Guy Arab appeared when Daimler resumed bus production after a gap caused by severe air raid damage to its factory in 1940. The Weymann's factory provided an initial run of a dozen bodies (Nos C7994-8005) for early examples of the CWA6 model with AEC 7.7-litre engine. They were much as built for the contemporary Arab, and the batch was split among five operators, during September-December 1943.

Merthyr Tydfil Corporation received two, of which No. 17 (HB 5980) with body No. C7999 is seen here in later years. The rounded ends to the lower-deck windows were quite a common means of stiffening up a deteriorating structure - wartime timber quality was often poor. A further eighteen CWA6s were bodied similarly in the period up to April 1944, plus a couple with metal-framed bodies, but Weymann's bus output thereafter concentrated on the Guy chassis. *(R Marshall)*

Above: Among the fifteen body shells to Manchester "streamlined" outline transferred from Metro-Cammell to Weymann for completion, given the latter's body numbers M2630-44 and mounted on Guy Arab chassis, five were allocated in 1943 to Sheffield Corporation. Three of these were on the uncommon Arab I with 6LW engine, including No. 479 (HWA 679) with body M2639 seen here with two others, the second vehicle being a 5LW-engined Arab I and the third another of the 6LW type. The two six-cylinder buses also show a slight variation in the front of the body but this is thought to be related to the bodies having been intended for Crossley chassis. *(R Marshall)*

Below: A further case of bodywork not being fitted to the intended chassis applied to some built for AEC Regents ordered by Liverpool Corporation, which had specified the continuation of the same sloping-front outline as first adopted for that city in 1935, for reasons of standardisation. Of 30 body shells (M2374-403) intended for delivery in 1940, thirteen were completed by the Corporation on the intended chassis as planned but the rest were finished by Weymann's, all but one going to Liverpool but on unfrozen chassis (seven AEC Regents and five Bristol K5Gs) or, in four cases, Guy Arab chassis, in 1942/3. The remaining body from that batch was used as a replacement for a South Wales Regent. A further fifteen bodies (M2645-59) were all fitted to Guy chassis and, again, all but one went to Liverpool. The exception, M2654, was supplied to Midland General as shown, this being on a Guy Arab I chassis with 5LW engine which became No. 190 (HRB 17) in that fleet. The photograph was taken in May 1953. *(R Marshall)*

Above: Known at the time simply as the W model, though later sometimes called the W4, the only trolleybus chassis type available in the later war years was built in the Sunbeam works at Woverhampton, also by then the home of Karrier trolleybus chassis, and badged as either of these makes, usually in line with previous orders. Weymann's built an initial run of fourteen such bodies from mid-1943 to early 1944 (Body Nos C7394-407) and then one of 21 which continued into 1945 (C8006-26), among which Derby Corporation No. 172 (RC 8472), a Sunbeam with body No. C8014 seen here, dated from August 1944. It was one of a pair for that fleet and, happily, still exists in preservation. Weymann's frontal design for the utility trolleybus body was noticeably less austere than the equivalent bus - there was even a little touch of the normal fondness for curves in the cab door window. *(R Marshall)*

Left: Meanwhile, Weymann-bodied Guy buses spread into many unfamiliar fleets. Birkenhead Corporation had largely favoured Massey bodywork and there was a stark contrast from the curvaceous lines of the previous delivery of 40 Leyland Titans supplied in 1939, one of which is seen in the background here, to the austerity of the undertaking's first utility bus, No. 319 (BG 8552) with Weymann body No. C7936. It was one of a pair dating from September 1943. Its appearance was helped a little by the attractive light blue and cream livery. *(R Marshall)*

Above: In late 1944 and early 1945, Weymann was allowed to build a few metal-framed bodies for research purposes, even though generally conforming to the utility specification. A point of interest was how better to overcome problems arising from the greater rigidity of the body structure than that of the chassis on which they were mounted; one answer was the so-called "bearerless body" in which support was confined to special mountings at the bulkheads. There were six highbridge bodies on Guy Arab II chassis, Nottingham Corporation being one of the prominent operators to receive an example in the form of No. 87 (GTV 587) with body No. M2672. It is seen in Parliament Street outside the undertaking's trolleybus depot. *(G H F Atkins)*

Below: Output of lowbridge utility bodies, all on Guy Arab II chassis, began in December 1944, some early examples having numbers among the highbridge type but then a run of 127 (Nos C8701-827) was built in the period up to September 1945. The example shown was Greenock Motor Services Limited's VS 4349, with body No. C8810 of June 1945, one of eighteen for that fleet. By that date, the utility specification had been relaxed but the Weymann's interpretation differed little beyond the more generous provision of opening windows.

Above: Although the war in Europe had just ended, deliveries of Weymann's last batch of 98 utility highbridge bodies on Arab II chassis (Nos C8855-952) extended from June 1945 to March 1946. They looked only slightly different - mainly in a fairly well-rounded rear dome - from those built in the dark days of 1942, though upholstered seats had reappeared. The fuller provison of side windows led to the elimination of the hinged vents above the front upper-deck windows. Edinburgh Corporation was allocated five and, as this undertaking was one of those that had persuaded the authorities that it needed the 6LW rather than 5LW engine, these buses were more "civilised" than they looked. Number G88 (EFS 914) with body No. C8901 dated from November 1945. This is a June 1950 photograph. *(R Marshall)*

Below: Southdown Motor Services was another MoWT recipient from this final batch of Weymann utility bodies, No. 493 (GUF 393), with body C8940 dating from December 1945, being one of 20 supplied, all with 5LW engines. This scene in a sunny Brighton, coupled with Southdown's traditional livery, helps to soften the effect, but this was still quite an austere bus. By the date it was built, Weymann's had begun production of its standard post-war body, with the glamorous looks of 1940 fully restored. *(R N Hannay Collection)*

INDEX

Photograph: G H F Atkins